Economic
Power
Failure

The call to abandon our illusions about our condition is a call to abandon a condition which requires illusions.

—Karl Marx

I sit on a man's back, choking him and making him carry me, and yet assure myself and others that I am very sorry for him and wish to lighten his load by all possible means—except by getting off his back.

—Lev Tolstoi

In the early 1960s, when political dissent was at a nadir, young people organized a new student movement which revived the struggle for social change and gave it new courage, clarity, and gaiety. My generation of social activists owes them a great debt. This book is dedicated to them, in gratitude.

Economic Power Failure:
The Current American Crisis

edited, with an introduction
and commentary by
Sumner M. Rosen

McGraw-Hill Book Company

New York St. Louis San Francisco
Düsseldorf London Mexico Sydney Toronto

Book Design by Marcy J. Katz

2 3 4 5 6 7 8 9 BPBP 7 9 8 7 6 5

Library of Congress Cataloging in Publication Data

Rosen, Sumner M
    Economic power failure.

    Bibliography: p. 287
    Includes index.
    1. United States—Economic conditions—1961-
2. United States—Economic policy—1971-
I. Title.
HC106.6.R67   330.9'73'092   75-1463
ISBN 0-07-053657-0
ISBN 0-07-053658-9 pbk.

Grateful acknowledgment is made for permission to reprint in excerpted or condensed form the following: "Full Employment in the New 'Day of the Dinosaur,'" from "Job Rights under American Capitalism" by Bertram M. Gross, from *Social Policy*, January/February, 1975, published by Social Policy Corporation, New York, N.Y. 10010. Copyright © 1975 by Social Policy Corporation. Reprinted by permission. "Toward Equality Through Employment" by Robert Lekachman, from *Social Policy*, September/October, 1974, published by Social Policy Corporation, New York, N.Y. 10010. Copyright © 1974 by Social Policy Corporation. Reprinted by permission. "Keynesian Chickens Come Home to Roost" by Harry Magdoff and Paul M. Sweezy, from *Monthly Review*, April, 1974. Copyright © 1974 by Monthly Review, Inc. Reprinted by permission of Monthly Review Press. "The U.S. Economic Outlook: Policy Aspects" by Leonall C. Andersen, from The Conference Board *Record*, June, 1974. Copyright © 1974 by the Conference Board. Reprinted by permission. "The New Economics: Handmaiden of Inspired Truth" by Richard B. Duboff and Edward S. Herman, from *The Review of Radical Political Economics*, August, 1972. Copyright © 1972 by the Union for Radical Political Economics, August, 1972. Reprinted by permission. "Petroleum Politics 1951–1974: A Five-Act Drama Reconstructed" by Dankwart A. Rustow, From *Dissent*, Spring, 1974. Copyright © 1974 by *Dissent*. Reprinted by permission.
    "How Economic Policies Provoked the Energy Crisis" by William N. Leonard, from *Challenge*, March/April, 1974. Reprinted by permission of *Challenge: The Magazine of Economic Affairs*. "Energy and the Design of Modern Society" from "The Energy Outlook and Global Interdependence: A Convocation" by Barry Commoner. Copyright © 1974 by Scientists' Institute for Public Information Fund for Peace. Reprinted by permission. "World Trade in the 1970s" by the AFL-CIO Economic Policy Committee, from the AFL-CIO *American Federationist*, April, 1973. Reprinted by permission of the AFL-CIO *American Federationist*, the official monthly publication of the AFL-CIO. "The Eurodollar System" from "The Political Economy of the American Empire December, 1974" by Robert Zevin. Copyright © 1975 by Robert Zevin. Reprinted by permission of the author. "Capital's Last Frontier" by Jules Henry, from *The Nation*, April 25,

Preface

This book is intended to be useful. It is not a polemic or a tract. It is, rather, a map to help guide us through perplexing and troubling times.

I have a point of view and have tried in the introduction to say what I think and why. I hope that the materials included here persuade the reader to agree with me. But I tried to include a variety of viewpoints and information, so that people can make up their own minds. Most economists agree that our economic situation contains new features not experienced before, including worldwide shortages of oil and food, pervasive inflation, drastic changes in international relationships, and new forms of economic organization and management—OPEC and the multinational corporations are two of the most striking. But they differ on whether these new elements mean a new economic era substantially different from the one which began after World War II. Some think that the end of economic prosperity and political freedom is inevitable. Others insist that the old tools of economic management, plus some new ones, will get us out of the difficulties we face without drastically altering our economic structure or changing the quality of life in the United States and other industrial countries. Still others see no alternative to accepting the need for socialism in America, not on ideological but on pragmatic grounds.

I find the last case the most persuasive, though I suspect my version would be more communitarian than most, less hopeful than some about the potential of working-class organizations. I confess that this view accords most closely with long-held preferences as well as with a temperament which refuses to abandon hope. If they must, Americans can accept radical changes and learn to live with them. The shift from a rural to an urban and then to a suburban social structure was such a change. The shift to an industrial and now toward a "postindustrial" or service economy is another. Acceptance of women's rights in economic as well as political and social life has advanced faster than its most ardent advocates would have thought in less than a decade, with a lack of trauma which has surprised many people.

Race is harder; we remain in essence as much the prisoners of racist attitudes and behavior as we were when the racial struggle burst loose in the mid-1960s; important legal and political progress has yet to yield real economic fruit. Our big cities, which should be our glory and national treasure, are shocking evidence of shameful neglect, in which racism has played a role. Our commitment to the weak, the helpless, and the victimized remains parsimonious, grudging, often vindictive. Even if there were no economic crisis these areas of national life would cry out for remedy.

But progressive forces in our society have never given up the struggle. Too often riven by sectarian division, ill-informed, naïve, betrayed by opportunistic leadership, they nevertheless re-form their ranks and resume the battle. Fighters for racial justice, consumer groups, women's groups, advocates of better housing, decent transportation, and humane treatment of the physically and mentally ill, and those who seek to preserve environmental balance—are all involved in economic and social struggle. This book seeks to make their struggle more effective, to help them understand what must be done.

Contents

Introduction

The Challenge

A series of shocks, unprecedented since the Great Depression, hit the U.S. economy beginning with the October 1973 oil embargo. Momentum slowed. The government faltered and fumbled. Economists were confused and contradictory. As we slid from "stagflation" into recession, American self-confidence was badly shaken. Issues of race and war had deep effects on political and social life in the 1960s, but underlying confidence in the ability of the economic system to grow without either depression or runaway inflation had remained. Now that too was in doubt. Was the American era over? Could we find our way back to continued stability and prosperity? In 1975 the answers were far from clear.

I believe that basic changes are not only desirable but necessary if we are to avoid economic catastrophe. Each of our major institutions must learn to understand how the forces of change affect its own power, structure, functions, and relationships to the others. As the impact of economic difficulties strips the veils from our eyes we need to learn about the new economic world waiting to be built from the old, to accept the loss of things no longer possible to keep, and the coming of new ways of working and living. Most important, people must take control of institutions. Business, government, labor, the press, the banks—all had roles in building the economic system which is now under stress. Their faults are many. Each failed to foresee that new forces would require us to change. Among them they share much of the power to control events. On the record they cannot be expected to meet the test. If this democratic society is to survive its people must take command of the dominant institutions. They must make the basic decisions. They must hold accountable those who exercise power. This book seeks to arm people with the knowledge they need to do this.

The Depression of the 1930s was the last time we faced problems of equal magnitude. But war prosperity and the postwar boom arrested our self-scrutiny before it had completed much of the task. There was little reason or encouragement for raising basic questions. Those who did so performed some important work but talked mostly to one another; most people were not listening. Our present troubles are in fact an opportunity to take up those questions and carry them through. We need to seize the occasion, lest another generation find themselves ill-equipped to understand their situation because this generation fails to do what must be done.

Shocks to the System

Escalating Oil Costs. The oil industry utilized the oil embargo to raise oil prices sharply and perhaps permanently. The shock to the economic system was twofold: first, it signaled the end of an era of continued cheap energy in virtually unlimited quantities. Second, it dramatically and abruptly reversed the power of the American economic system to determine the terms of trade and exchange with the nominal owners of major, scarce raw materials. Working together, the Arab oil-owning countries and the international oil companies with whom they are intimately involved imposed a new set of price and output conditions which the United States, Japan and Europe together appeared helpless to alter.

Food. The abundance which had characterized American agriculture ever since the end of World War II appeared to be ending. Beginning with the massive sale of wheat to the Soviet Union in 1972, food surpluses shrank and have now virtually disappeared. In 1973 the United States, fearing shortages, curtailed exports of soybeans and other foods, setting off shortlived panic waves in Japan and other major importing countries. Food prices began to rise rapidly; by late 1974 they showed the highest rate of increase of all major components of the consumer price index, after having lagged well behind other components until mid-1973. Talk of dollar-a-loaf bread matched talk of dollar-a-gallon gasoline.

The symmetry was striking, because in the case of food, as of oil, the problem only a short time earlier had been surpluses not shortages. Since 1969, government policies in the United States, Canada, and Australia—three of the four major wheat producers, along with the USSR—sought to reduce wheat production by reducing acreage; by 1970, wheat acreage in the United States was 80 percent of 1968, in Canada 50 percent, and in Australia 60 percent.[1] Production levels declined as a result. In precisely the same fashion, the oil industry, facing the prospect of massive surpluses in 1968, began to reduce output. In the case of oil, the decisions were made by the companies; the food acreage decisions were governmental.

Monetary Squeeze. The temporary freeze on wages and prices imposed in 1971 was succeeded by a constriction of the money supply by the Federal Reserve which drove interest rates up to all-time highs and kept them there. From an average of 5.9 percent in 1968, the commercial prime rate rose to 8.1 percent in 1973; by July 1974 it had reached 11.7 percent; and in October home mortgage yields reached 10.4 percent. As a result private housing starts dropped to an annual rate below one million for the first time since 1957; unemployment among construction workers had reached 15.0 percent in December 1974. And as automobile output dropped sharply, substantial and spreading layoffs began to affect overall unemployment rates, with particular impact on groups previously less affected—males over 20, and all full-time workers. At no time after January 1974 did payroll employment equal levels reached in late 1973. The only sectors to show any significant gains in employment in 1974 were services and government.

Devaluation and Floating Rates of Exchange. The United States found it necessary to devalue the dollar twice within 14 months, and to abandon its commitment to a fixed dollar value for gold. In effect this action was the beginning of the end of the system of international settlements constructed in 1944 at Bretton Woods. That system was based on the dollar as the world's basic currency. It served as the standard of international value and the medium for the settlement of international debts. Devaluation and the demonetizing of gold marked the end of American economic hegemony in much of the world. Devaluation had important short-run consequences as well. By raising import costs it contributed to the inflationary pressures which were increasingly felt in the early 1970s. But the underlying weakness of U.S. exports was so advanced by then that except briefly in 1973, even two devaluations failed to restore positive trade balances.

The problem of a persistent negative balance of payments also limited the role of monetary policy in the United States for the first

Year	Liquid private capital flows ($ billion)	Balance on current account ($ billion)
1969	8.8	−1.6
1970	−6.0	−0.3
1971	−7.9	−3.8
1972	3.5	−9.8
1973	2.3	0.5

Source: Economic Indicators, November, 1974.

time in the postwar period. Capital flows in and out of the U.S. in the 1970s were large and volatile, as the figures in the table show. Movement of capital into and out of the United States directly affects the balance of payments. When the monetary authorities attempt to correct domestic deviations, they also must take into account these balance of payments effects; one objective may directly contradict the other. Interest rates influence lending and spending. They also trigger international movements of money. In the 1940s, the power of the Federal Reserve to change the money supply was limited by its commitment to stabilize interest rates; in the 1970s, short-run capital flow effects impose a similar limitation. We can no longer manage our monetary affairs as if the rest of the world did not matter.

Recession Remedies. By 1975 the dominant role of inflation in both popular and policy thinking had been displaced by expectations of recession, or worse. Mild inflationary expectations stimulate spending, but once job uncertainties begin to spread, spending falls, particularly on postponable items. That is one reason automobile and other durable goods sales fell in 1974, leading in turn to substantial layoffs in manufacturing. The policy focus shifted from containing inflation to increasing employment. Conventional expansionist policies became the order of the day, as they had been in past recessions, with some new measures added. The Federal Reserve moved toward expansion of the money supply, goaded by a restive Congress and its talk of curbing the independence of the Federal Reserve system itself. The President agreed to seek significant tax relief, accepted a level of federal spending substantially beyond the guidelines of restraint that had been adopted in the preliminary budget for fiscal year 1976, and restored funds cut from social programs.

The President also signed a new program for expanded public service employment going well beyond any previous measures and dropped the posture that such programs could be accepted only for limited periods of high unemployment. Large scale public service employment programs appeared in 1975 to have joined the arsenal of antirecession policies for the first time since the Depression. But with this important exception, the Keynesian policy instruments relied upon to restore prosperity had been conceived in the 1930s and 1940s, developed in the 1950s, and established as bi-partisan orthodoxy in the 1960s.

End of an Era?

Would these measures work? If they did our key institutional leaders could breathe easier. For them the stakes were great. Together they constitute a powerful, indeed overwhelming array of power and command a major share of the nation's intellectual as well as financial resources. The economic system they largely control was once the wonder of the world; the model to be emulated by some and envied by those who could not aspire to emulation. Except for China, there are few places where the American achievement is not the central influence shaping economic aspirations and goals. In 1961, four distinguished American students of economic life[2] argued that the objectives of development—industrialization—"are the same in all societies undergoing transformation." Like others, Americans believed in themselves, their system, and the institutions dominating their economy.

The foundations of this confidence had been laid during World War II. While the 1930s saw a major extension of the role of the state in economic and social life, New Deal measures did not succeed in creating a high enough level of demand to eliminate mass unemployment. Their principal achievement was to alleviate the hardships which had afflicted millions of workers, farmers and small businessmen, but Roosevelt's description, in his 1936 inaugral address, of "one-third of a nation ill-housed, ill-clad, and ill-nourished"—i.e., of mass poverty in America—was still accurate when World War II came. The economic and social transformation wrought during the 1940–1945 period was profound and far-reaching; it set the stage for the era of prosperity that endured until recently. Prosperity buried the nagging questions provoked by the Depression about the basic soundness of the American economy. The "miracle" of massive war production restored the status and confidence of the corporate sector whose spokesmen claimed much of the credit for it. The government was able to manage this enormous war effort without significant inflation, even though unemployment reached low levels never achieved before or since—1.2 percent in 1944.

As they had in World War I, the leaders of the American labor movement found themselves invited to be partners in the war effort and achieved a degree of acceptance by business and government quite different from the marginal, perilous state of unionism prior to the Wagner Act. Agricultural prosperity was unprecedented as American farms were called upon to feed first the armed forces and then the hungry, war-devastated nations in Europe and the Far East. Business activity in the postwar period was fueled, first by the enormous store of domestic savings which consumers had accumulated during the war, and second by the world-wide dearth of productive capacity which made the United States the major source of industrial goods for much of the world. Measured in constant dollars, the gross national product in 1942 exceeded that of 1929, the peak pre-Depression year, by 46 percent; between 1946 and 1965 it almost doubled. Industrial production—again measured in real terms—showed spectacular increases, rising by 80 percent between 1929 and 1942; and by 1965 reaching a level 2.7 times that of 1946. Between 1947 and 1955 productivity increased at an annual rate of 3.2 percent for the nonfarm sector, and 6.6 percent in agriculture! Personal incomes and consumption kept pace, more than doubling in real terms between 1945 and 1965.[3] And the balance of trade showed surpluses which reached a peak of $6.8 billion, on the average, for the 1960–1964 period. In 1958 the United States exported 27.7 percent of all manufacturing exports; in 1960 the United States accounted for 15.9 percent of exports of all kinds in the world. Amid all this expansion, the consumer price index either declined or rose by less than three percentage points in every year except two between 1946 and 1967.

This was the setting for the maturing of American economic hegemony in the world. Long a major economic power, the United States stood virtually alone in the immediate postwar period. It was a time when the British economy had lost its leading role; and the economies of Germany, Japan, and the Soviet Union had been devastated by war destruction. There was clearly little reason to doubt that an era of permanent prosperity—what *Fortune* magazine dubbed "The Permanent Revolution"—had opened for the United States. American goods flooded world markets. The American dollar became the world's preferred currency and the reserve of central banks everywhere, largely replacing sterling. American firms secured access to raw materials on every continent. American capital flowed into Canada, the Arab oil producing countries,

Europe, Latin America, Africa, and Asia. American arms guaranteed the peace; military expenditures overseas have exceeded $2 billion in every year since 1952, $4 billion in every year since 1967. The combination of economic, political and military dominance was massive and overwhelming.

Each of the major institutions of the economy has been shaped by these developments and has found its accommodation with them. Each has prospered. And each grew dependent on the continuation of this state of affairs for its continued survival.

In the meantime, however, the world had begun to change, at first gradually and imperceptibly, then more and more rapidly and visibly. In recent years the accumulated pressure arising out of these changes has been felt with rapidly increasing force. How will the United States accommodate to a new set of economic forces in the world, each of which requires that we change, all together leading us into a new era unlike that which is ending? Many of these changes had been foreshadowed during the 1960s and before.

The prolonged period of prosperity and hegemony which began after World War II functioned as a massive soporific. There were complaints, but who could really argue with success on the scale which we appeared to have achieved? But those who looked more deeply could see trouble coming.

Flaws at Home

The Arms Economy. As early as the 1950s, fear was expressed that our domestic prosperity rested too heavily on the prop of arms spending. In the immediate postwar period military budgets were cut back drastically, though never to prewar levels. But the economic effects of the cold war quickly began to make themselves felt.

"Defense" expenditures reached a low of $11.8 billion in fiscal year 1948. In 1950 the Korean war began; in fiscal 1951 the arms budget rose to $22.5 billion; in 1953 it reached $50.4 billion. From 1953 through 1964, the range was $40.7 billion to $54.2 billion. Atomic energy, largely for weapons related purposes, space expenditures with an undefined military component, and foreign aid, increasingly military, swelled the total. Military purposes dominated the federal budget throughout the 1950s, as they did again during the Vietnam War. A national debate of sorts focused on the question of our ability to sustain prosperity without the arms prop; it reached a mini-peak with the establishment of a Cabinet-level committee in 1963, and Senate hearings on the question held by Senator George McGovern in 1964. Administration spokesmen argued that disarmament or arms cuts would raise no serious adjustment questions which could not be handled using orthodox economic instruments: fiscal and monetary policy, training and relocation allowances. Gardner Ackley, chairman of the Council of Economic Advisors, blandly observed:[4]

> . . . change has been a fundamental characteristic of our system for generations, and . . . by and large our economy has adapted very successfully to profound and sweeping changes . . . the necessary adjustments are no more complex and challenging than the adjustments that, in principle, are required each year to maintain an adequate—but not more than adequate—pressure of total demand on our productive resources . . . the overall problem created by defense reduction is a familiar one.

A few writers disagreed. Seymour Melman and Richard Nelson pointed out how an arms economy monopolizes the use of scarce scientific and technical talent, jeopardizing the long-run technological health of the civilian sector. In a series of articles in *The Washington Post,* Bernard Nossiter documented the inability of major military contractors to find civilian markets for their equipment and skills. Emile Benoit and Kenneth Boulding edited a set of studies on the economic aspects of the arms economy and disarmament.[5] But this literature had little popular or policy impact outside of some studies initiated by the Arms Control and Disarmament Agency. The arms prop continued to play a key role in economic life and serious alternatives to a large arms budget have yet to be developed.

Inequality. The pattern of inequality in the control of wealth and the distribution of income is of long standing. In the 1950s, Simon Kuznets estimated that the income shares of the top 2 percent of income receivers had declined in the postwar period,[6] and many took this to mean that there had been a redistribution of income in the direction of greater equality. It was not until the publication of *The Other America* and the official launching of a "war" against poverty that the question of relative income shares received any serious attention. The enormously influential statement of a progressive, critical viewpoint on the U.S. economy, Galbraith's *The Affluent Society*, virtually overlooked the question of relative shares. Writing in 1958, he relegated the problem of poverty to one of minor dimensions, readily solvable through education, training and other measures.[7]

Inequalities in the distribution of wealth and income have not changed in the United States during the postwar period; some have argued that they are little changed from prewar.[8] Kuznets estimated the share of income received by the top 5 percent and 1 percent of income receivers as follows:

	Top 5%	Top 1%
1920	12	22
1925	14	25
1930	14	26
1940	12	23
1945	9	17

Source: Herman P. Miller, *Rich Man Poor Man.* New York, Crowell, 1971, pp. 47–48.

The data shows this pattern for all classes of income receivers:

Income receivers	Percent of Money Income Received					
	1947	1957	1962	1967	1968	1971
Lowest fifth	4	4	3	4	4	4
Second fifth	11	11	11	11	11	11
Middle fifth	17	18	17	17	17	17
Fourth fifth	24	25	25	24	25	24
Highest fifth	46	43	44	44	44	45
top 5%	19	17	17	16	15	19
top 1%						7

Source: Miller, *op. cit.,* p. 50. Survey of Current Business, October, 1974, p. 23.

The most striking feature of these figures is their stability in a period when the United States experienced an enormous, indeed unprecedented, expansion of total income. Whatever redistribution occurred appears to have shifted income modestly from those at the very top to those just below them, *not* to those in the bottom 40 percent. While median income rose steadily, there was no change toward greater equality. Sustained growth left untested the viability of these patterns of distribution for a period when growth may slow or even cease. The future will subject them to severe testing.

The postwar period has also been celebrated for providing a share of the national wealth in the form of shares of stock, corporate bonds and other assets, to ever larger numbers of people. It is true that if one includes car and home ownership in the definition of wealth, its spread has widened. But if we focus on a more functional view of wealth—as a source of income, a set of assets whose composition can be changed in response to market criteria—then the vast bulk of single family homes are eliminated; they become a store of value to their owners but they may also curb mobility and, given the perverse nature of state and local property taxes, increase both inequities and inequality in wealth and income shares. Looking at "investment assets" (excluding house, car, and life insurance), one 1962 study showed the following:

Family Income	Value of assets (not deducting debts)
$3,000 - 5,000	$4,663
7,500 - 9,999	7,500
10,000 - 14,999	11,202
15,000 - 24,999	39,880
25,000 - 49,999	111,761
50,000 - 99,999	387,573
100,000 plus	1,058,672

Source: "The Distribution of Personal Income," Joint Economic Committee, U.S. Congress, 1965, p. 47.

Note how rapidly assets multiply in proportion to income above the $25,000 level. In 1969, using a different series of figures, the Urban Institute estimated that 4.4 percent of the adult population, with incomes of $60,000 and above, held two-thirds of all privately owned corporate stock. By contrast, they estimated that the half of the population at the lower end of the income scale would realize an average of only $3,000 if they liquidated all assets and paid all debts.[9] A more recent study, done at the Wharton School, has estimated that 30 percent of all stock, in 1971, was owned by the 0.2 percent of the population with incomes of $100,000 or over, and more than 50 percent by the 1 percent with incomes of $50,000 or over.[10] The study is also quoted as having shown "that while there was a decided trend toward more equal distribution of income in the United States from the 1920s through about 1945, the trend toward equality has essentially halted since then."

We can better understand the meaning of these figures by looking at the other side of the income distribution picture and the process which helps to create it. Some argue that because the data show an increase in the share of incomes provided by salaries and wages compared with that provided from property ownership, wage earners benefit more than proportionately from overall increases in national income. This overlooks the fact that stratification within the wage-earning class itself appears to have increased during the postwar period. Several factors help to explain why. An increase in educational requirements for some jobs restricts access and limits those without the requisite skills and education to lower paid jobs; the expansion of educational enrollments in the postwar period led to a growth in what has been termed "credentialism" in the job market.[11] Second, in the urban economy, particularly in older cities, the match between the nature of the labor supply and the jobs available grew more and more unsuitable. The rural exodus which reached its peak in the 1950s did more than change the racial composition of central cities;[12] it drastically increased the low-skilled and poorly educated component of the urban labor force while the levels of skill and education needed to get and keep good jobs in cities were rising and while job growth itself was occurring more and more outside central cities.

The malaise of urban America has been richly documented and need not be repeated here. What does require attention, because it has received less than it needs, is the growth of urban underemployment and the development of what has been called the "secondary labor market."[13] Borrowing from Myrdal's early, neglected model of dual development in backward societies,[14] the dual labor market model postulates a separate, substandard labor force coexisting with the "primary" labor force. Each has its own employers; there is little interchange between the two sectors. Primary workers hold full-time jobs, work for larger, more progressive, more technologically advanced employers and, as a consequence, earn higher wages, progress further up the occupational ladder, keep their jobs longer, and often possess specific skills that have market value. By contrast, members of the secondary labor force are found largely among firms which are small, labor-intensive, capital-poor, and badly managed. They experience frequent unemployment, often interchanging periods of work and welfare, earn low wages, and show little or no upward mobility whether they stay with one employer or change jobs.[15]

This secondary labor market operates both as an independent economic force and as an adjunct to institutionalized racism and sexism, the third factor in this view of income shares. Here again a rich literature exists which needs no elaboration here; our focus is on institutionalized barriers to equality, that present major obstacles to improving the relative distribution of income and wealth and will require serious attention in the future. Institutionalized racism and sexism take several forms. Departmental seniority systems may coincide with patterns of racial and sexual concentration which differ by department; such systems govern both access to higher paying jobs and vulnerability to layoffs, and have—particularly in recent times—exposed those most recently hired, often racial minorities and women, to a higher risk of layoff than those with more seniority in less vulnerable sections of a firm. Civil Service, which now accounts for a major share of all employment, embodies many features which institutionalize preference in favor of, or discrimination against, particular groups in the labor force, and these have seriously hampered access by blacks and other minorities to upper level jobs in state and local government.[16] Informal quotas abound in the private sector, particularly with regard to well-paying, upwardly mobile, or highly visible jobs, and they are found in the public sector as well, although here they are harder to conceal.

Stratification and Unionism. Stratification has also been growing within the wage-earning labor force.[17] This process involves labor unions as instruments of inequality. The explicitly racist and sexist role of certain skilled trade unions in barring or minimizing access to journeyman status in the building, printing, and mechanical trades has been extensively debated over the past decade and is well known. In the industrial labor force where these practices are minimal other things have happened: (1) the gradual erosion of labor's organized stake within the labor force; (2) the ascension within organized labor of the more highly skilled sectors among industrial workers; and (3) a growing gap between the organized and unorganized sectors. Union energies are more and more preoccupied with advancing or defending the status of those it represents, and in particular the interests of the more strategically placed groups within union ranks.

In part these changes in the role and strength of the industrial unions reflect the facts of an aging membership and leadership; in part they are natural consequences of the unions' success over the past 25 years in lifting organized workers from the ranks of the working poor and the exploited into less vulnerable, though still far from privileged, economic and social status.[18] In part they reflect a shifting of the balance in favor of employers, and the erosion of the social impulses which were strong in the 1930s and 1940s, symbolized by George Meany's firm command of the unified AFL-CIO and his firm alliance with the leadership of the United Steelworkers and other former bastions of CIO strength. They help explain the successful effort in 1968 and 1972 to break apart the traditional Democratic coalition which had been formed under Roosevelt during the New Deal.[19]

As the industrial unions weakened and business grew stronger both economically and politically, labor unions could no longer commit their energies fully to the protection or advancement of the unorganized. Increasingly they found themselves locked into specific industrial settings, dependent on the growth and profitability of these industries for the welfare of their own membership.

The growth of fringe benefits after World War II played an important role as well. Historically unions had preferred to negotiate benefits which they could control in direct relationships with employers. When this route was blocked as a result of the wage controls imposed during World War II, fringe benefits—paid vacations, pension plans, health and welfare plans—began to blossom. This trend continued following World War II. One effect was to link unions even more closely to their employers and industries, because that was the source of payments and because administration of these benefits was generally the joint responsibility of employer and union. The growth of fringe benefits also diverted union attention from the effort to legislate social benefits for all workers in favor of a focus on their own plans. In the health and pension areas particularly, a two class system of benefits was created; social security, for example, provides one set of benefits to all eligible retired persons, while negotiated pension plans supplement these, often handsomely. While masses of workers and others lack access to health care, union members often enjoy good benefits with full prepayment.

In this fashion a series of wedges began to divide the organized from the unorganized or poorly organized sectors of the industrial labor force, to confine union energies increasingly to the blue collar sector of the labor force, and to separate union members from blacks, women, young people and others in the labor force. In many respects, the labor movement of the 1970s, though vastly more numerous and influential than it had been prior to the Wagner Act, resembled its pre-1935 predecessor, the AFL, though with one important exception. While unions historically had been independent of the federal government, modern unions have become increasingly dependent on government action and policies. This was seen most dramatically in the process which led up to the Foreign Trade Bill of 1974, but it was also seen in the development of the Pension Reform Act, the Occupational Health and Safety Act, and other recent measures. Labor and employers depend more and more on federal action to solve problems which cannot be solved satisfactorily at the bargaining table, as they once were.

Corporations in Command.   The United States is a business dominated society. We noted the role which World War II played in the rehabilitation of the prestige and influence of the business sector. The post-war boom was immensely profitable to business as a whole. The single most striking feature of the past quarter century has been the stability, dominance, and profitability of the large corporate sector. On the face of it this is a remarkable and implausible outcome of a period of so much change in so many aspects of American life. One might have predicted the rise of important new industrial and economic sectors, the replacement of older by newer firms, successful challenges to dominant firms leading to more intraindustry competition and larger numbers of firms within the major industries, and the growth of whole new sectors of economic activity.

It is true that many changes occurred in the large corporate sector. We saw the growth of the conglomerates in the 1950s, and the multinationals in the 1960s; these were new and important developments. But the continuities with the past are even more striking: the ranks of the *Fortune* 500 are little changed in recent decades. It is also striking how little change has occurred in the patterns of control and dominance which are found in corporate banking circles. This is not to deny that major changes have occurred in products and methods. The rise of Xerox, IBM, and Polaroid bear witness to the power of technological progress as an engine of business success. But it is doubtful that, on balance, this record can be compared with the one industry compiled in the late nineteenth and early twentieth centuries when the automobile, steel, chemical, rubber and other basic industries were being developed. Yet if the technological record in these and other major industries is far from impressive, the dominance of Dupont, General Motors, Exxon, Kodak, General Electric, Alcoa, etc. has continued. The large corporations were able to adapt to, coopt, or control those events which directly affected their self-interest, but they show little of the innovative capability that for Joseph A. Schumpeter constituted the heart of capitalism and the justification for the large corporation.

The basic structure of power and privilege remains fundamentally unchanged; affluence failed to improve the relative standing of the poor and the near poor or to lessen the dominance of the privileged; the labor movement, once the most effective advocate of greater social and economic justice, has lost much of its power to affect the welfare of those outside its own ranks, who are now a shrinking minority of all workers.

The Captive State

What then of the state? Historically, government played a subordinate role in our economic life, though the degree of subordination is exaggerated in much of the popular discussion of our history; government was a key actor in the construction of the railroads, the development of agriculture, and the establishment of access to foreign markets and raw materials for industry. But the modern state is the product of the Depression and the war.

The Depression established legitimate new spheres of action for government. Beyond these areas as well, the involvement of the state in economic life is both pervasive and decisive. Unless that is understood, the significance of political processes in economic outcomes is likely to be greatly underestimated. If workers, tenants, the poor and near poor, small businessmen, and marginal members of the working and middle classes really understood what the central role of government could be in their lives, politics in this country might look very different than it does. It helps, however, to limit ourselves for the moment to three important areas which occupy the foreground of state action, each of which the Depression dramatized. An appraisal of the state's response in each area provides guidelines for appraising government's ability to deal with the problems we now face.

Minimizing Unemployment.   The key problem of the Depression was mass unemployment. Out of that experience, stimulated by the record of failure of New Deal measures significantly to reduce unemployment, and by the fear of a recurrence of depression after the war, Congress passed the Employment Act of 1946. Despite its many compromises and shortcomings,[20] this act mandates the utilization of government power to assure the "maximum" level of employment. By the time of enactment, the postwar resurgence of conservative thinking had already made significant headway, and the sweeping commitment in earlier drafts to full employment was watered down. Nevertheless, the act did symbolize the permanent closing of the fiction that our modern industrial economy could survive and flourish without state intervention. The seriousness of our commitment to the purposes of the Employment Act, the methods we have utilized to carry out its purposes, the debates about its relative importance in relation to other policy goals—even the definition of acceptable standards for measuring our success—provide a useful, if often depressing set of guides to our history as a nation in the period since President Truman signed the law. It is worth recalling his characterization of the act and its significance in his final economic report, issued in January, 1953:

> Under the Employment Act, full employment means more than jobs. It means full utilization of our natural resources, our technology and science, our farms and factories, our business brains, and our labor skills. In the broadest sense, full employment means maximum opportunity under the American system of responsible freedom.
>
> And it is a concept which must grow as our capabilities grow. The growth of opportunity, with a growing population and an expanding technology, requires a constantly expanding economy. This is needed to abolish poverty and to remove insecurity from substantial portions of our population. It offers the prospect of transforming class or group conflict into cooperation and mutual trust, because the achievement of more for all reduces the struggle of some to get more at the expense of others.
>
> Like freedom, it needs to be guarded zealously and translated into action on a continuing basis. Moreover, if we fail in this, our very freedom may be placed in jeopardy.

The measurement of unemployment, and the study of the variables that affect or determine its level, has become a major occupation among economists and statisticians. That the meaning of the term GNP and the level of measured unemployment are perhaps the best known and most widely watched economic measures, testifies to the triumph of these ideas in the popular and political imagination.

In fact we were able, thanks to the expansion of the economy in the postwar period, to absorb a growth of the labor force from 59.4 million in 1947 to 82.7 million in 1970—an increase of 39 percent—with levels of unemployment far below those of the 1920s and 1930s. Economists had done their homework well. They learned from Keynes that the basic error of the classical economists had been to assume that the natural equilibrium of economic life was at or near full-employment levels of output and spending. They learned that private spending decisions might produce an equilibrium above or, more frequently, below the full-employment level of demand, and that deliberate intervention by the state would then be necessary to achieve the required level of demand. From this analysis were developed the policy instruments that are now utilized by every central bank and every government in the industrialized world. The focus of analysis and the criteria for judging monetary policy and tax policy and structures, and the composition, timing and level of government spending shifted to concentrate primarily on the effects they would have on the level of demand and employment. It was in this sense, rather than in adherence to a specific set of policy instruments or goals, that it could be accurately stated that all Presidents in the modern era have been Keynesians.

So long as the basic set of circumstances affecting the American economy were supportive, Keynesian measures to manage the level of demand could be utilized consistently, and with some success, to prevent either excessive unemployment or excessive inflation. Imagine a sailing ship pushed by strong, but not too strong winds; in such a situation, sailors' skills make sure that the ship maintains the right direction and the right amount of sail, but it would be wrong—though it is tempting—to believe that it is the skills which account for the ship's basic momentum. Our economic helmsmen of the past quarter century have claimed a good deal of credit for results which in fact arose from the confluence of basic factors and forces over which they had little or no control, and about which they were often poorly informed. We need to ask whether these methods remain viable or whether the basic situation has so altered that they will prove of as little use as sail and wheel in a windless sea.

But we had at best a hedged mandate to the goals of the employment act, particularly when we look at the record in comparison to the performance of other economies. Since 1962, the Bureau of Labor Statistics has analyzed data on labor force, employment and unemployment in other industrial economies in order to provide comparative data on our performance. For the recent past the results look like this:[21]

Unemployment Rates (adjusted)

	U.S.	Canada	France	Germany	Great Britain	Japan	Italy
1960			2.2	0.8	2.3	1.7	4.3
1965			1.8	0.3	2.3	1.2	4.0
1970	4.9	5.9	2.2	0.5	4.0	1.2	3.4
1973	4.9	5.6	2.4	1.2	2.6	1.3	3.5
1974:							
I	5.2	5.5	3.5	1.5	3.8	1.3	3.0
II	5.1	5.2	3.5	2.1	4.0	1.3	3.1
III	5.5	5.4	3.6	2.6	4.4		3.2

Countries vary in the seriousness of their commitment to keep unemployment low and the skill with which the commitment is honored. Clearly the United States and Canada now lag well behind even poor economic performers like Britain and Italy, and far behind Germany, Japan and France. Phillips curve and other fashionable analytic tools have been called upon in recent years to explain (or rationalize) our apparently declining ability to generate full employment without high rates of inflation, but the data here require more substantive explanations. Inflation rates in the 1963–1970 period were somewhat higher in Japan than the U.S., slightly higher in France, Italy and Britain, lower in Germany; so these societies cannot be said to have purchased lower rates of unemployment at the price of higher rates of inflation, the trade-off which is allegedly required in the Phillips model.[22]

So even in its heyday, the Keynesian record was mixed. We experienced five recessions between 1946 and 1974; in the 1958 recession unemployment averaged 6.8 percent, the highest level recorded for any post-war year through 1974. Eisenhower and his staff were reluctant Keynesians who, foreshadowing their Nixon-Ford successors, feared inflation more than they did unemployment. But Kennedy moved rapidly to accelerate federal spending levels and initiate the federal tax cut of 1964; the results quickly became apparent. It seemed at that time that Keynesian remedies worked—what was at issue was the will to use them.

But things were already changing. First, Kennedy relied almost wholly on military spending to administer the needed stimulus to the economy. Though the backlog of needed social spending was substantial, the drama of urban unrest had yet to be played, and Kennedy did not use the catalogue of public needs for his spending budget. This was not the first time that the military had offered the primary route for Keynesian stimulus; it had happened in the early 1950s as well. Now the pattern became more deeply fixed, moving us still further from the liberal Keynesianism of Alvin Hansen and the first generation of American Keynesians.

Second, the 1964 tax cut, in both concept and structure, symbolized acceptance of two conservative ideas: (1) that the social budget should not grow, and (2) that the best way to stimulate spending was through tax concessions to business to increase investment spending, plus some direct stimulus of consumer spending. Some, who saw Kennedy as the restorer of the type of liberal activism symbolized by the New Deal, were troubled. Others, who viewed the state simply as the instrument and handmaiden of big business, saw the same kind of state action in support of business that Roosevelt had launched in 1933 with the National Recovery Act. But they may have underestimated the potential of progressive state action, as the 1960s were yet to show. Kennedy had also read Michael Harrington's *The Other America* and had begun to develop an anti-poverty program. Had he lived we might have had more than the relative emptiness of the Johnson program. The political forces to support an effective program might well have successfully organized and helped to produce a different outcome. The evidence is inconclusive.

As social pressures ebbed in the late 1960s, the basic patterns of the state's role in economic policy could be seen responding to fundamental power relationships. It emerged clearly in all three dimensions of fiscal policy: the composition of the tax burden, the choice of priorities for public spending, and the short-run devices chosen to adjust the level of aggregate demand.

There have been many analyses of the structure of the federal tax system that demonstrate its arbitrary imposition of taxes on different social groups—homeowners as against tenants, recipients of capital gains as against wage earners, payroll and sales taxes which unduly burden low-income recipients, etc. James O'Connor observed that[23] "every important change in the balance of class

forces has always been registered in the tax structure." In addition
to the inequities between social groups, regressivity or proportion-
ality has almost totally replaced the original progressivity that was
the theoretical principle of the income tax: 85 percent of all income
taxes collected, and two-thirds of all returns, are taxed at the 20
percent rate; taxes on even the highest income groups seldom
exceed 30 percent, and sometimes fall well below.[24] The increasingly regressive and inequitable impact of state and local taxes has
also been well documented.

Unlike the issue of equal access to jobs, which raises far
greater passions, there is widespread agreement that educational
opportunity ought to be equalized as far as possible. There is
equally widespread agreement on education as the strategy of
choice for ultimately reducing inequalities in opportunity that bear
so heavily on blacks and other minority groups. At least since
Galbraith in 1958,[25] this view has had broad, bipartisan concensus.
But efforts to correct inequities in school financing through tax
equalization have made little progress. It is sobering to see how
hard it is to redress this particular imbalance.

Removing or reducing inequities in the federal tax structure
will require a major political struggle. Such a struggle was not
plausible as long as growth appeared to make the system work
even though analysts pointed to inequities. But if the system
cannot be made to work in the future, serious reform may prove
politically feasible.

Priorities for public spending offer an equally discouraging
perspective. Aside from the military, the major sustained program
of public spending over the past twenty years has been for highways. The vast sums expended directly served to support expansion of automobile production and the interests of the automobile,
oil, steel and other industries that provide the materials and fuel, as
well as the producers of highway materials themselves. The secondary effects have been even more profound; the expansion of
the highway system led directly to the suburbanization of American cities and the decentralization of American industry, thus
laying the foundation for the urban crises that surfaced in the mid-
1960s. By absorbing the costs of highways through the tax system,
government vastly lowered the direct costs of home building, auto

and truck driving, and industrial relocation, to those who benefited most from them. By permitting highway expenditures to dominate transportation outlays, government contributed directly to the decline and deterioration of rail, ship, canal, waterway and other modes of transportation, thus furthering the monopoly of road transport for both personal and industrial use.[26] Finally, with a few exceptions like medical, bio-medical and agricultural research, the combined dominance of highway and military related expenditures precluded the development of significant social budgets at the federal level.

The Keynesian apparatus has thus been confined almost totally to purposes that are either directly functional to major corporate interests, or pose little or no threat to either their economic interests or their ideological sway. As the basic conditions of the economy began to show signs of important and permanent change in the 1970s, business spokesmen still argued that further stimulus to profits and investment were needed to meet the deepening recession of 1974–1975,[27] and liberals still sought tax reform, loans to small and medium sized business, tax cuts to stimulate auto sales, easier money for housing construction, more vigorous enforcement of antitrust laws, price and profit controls, and expanded public service employment programs.

In 1975, only the proposal for expanded public service employment is new, though it recalls the idea of a "shelf of public works" as an anti-cyclical instrument which Hansen and others developed in the 1930s and 1940s. Its implications for structural change in the economy are somewhat deeper, however.

The past quarter century has seen the almost total capture of the Keynesian system of demand management by a narrow set of priorities and interests, largely with the acquiescence of liberal economists and political figures, and the organized labor movement. While these groups have consistently sought more aggressive expansionary measures and more equitable taxes, they have seldom dissented in any serious way from either the substance of the fiscal-monetary programs which were adopted, or from the centralized administrative process through which programs were designed and carried out. The decline of legislative control or initiative in the era of massive military, highway and housing support programs met little criticism or opposition as long as the results were reasonably functional for key groups in these ranks. Thus while economists of the AFL-CIO developed some of the best critiques of tax inequities, labor bent little political effort in any Presidential campaign to secure a commitment to serious tax reform and, in fact, conspicuously abstained from the 1972 campaign in which McGovern advocated just such a program. Similarly, there were never more than a handful of Congressmen or Senators who dared to subject the military budget to any serious scrutiny and those who tried received little help from either liberal or labor groups. The Federation of American Scientists and the National Committee for a Sane Nuclear Policy, both with narrow political bases, did more than groups whose constituencies had far greater stakes in a more balanced and open budget-making process.

Protecting the Victims. The second obligation which the Depression placed on the state was to protect the victims of economic troubles. Until the New Deal, relief of suffering in periods of difficulty was the responsibility of private charity or local government. It was an act of charity, not social obligation. Orthodox economic ideology taught that the unfortunate were the victims, not of large social and economic forces, but of their own shortcomings. Social beneficence ratified social Darwinism. In the early 1930s, the AFL distinguished itself by opposing federal programs of unemployment relief. Labor had long been weary of government involvement in economic and social matters; the past had taught them that the state could be expected to put its weight on the side of employers, and they expected that to be the case once again. They feared that benefits which depended on government action would reduce labor's independence; they believed that what government gave, government could take away. These beliefs, like the faith in craft unionism, had been developed from long experience and were functional for that experience. They did not yet understand that the Depression was a watershed which was to change economic and political life drastically and permanently.

Only gradually did the federal government recognize its obligation to help the victims of the Depression. At first the help was seen as temporary. Not until 1935 did the Social Security Act become law, legislating for the first time permanent protection of the aged and the unemployed as a matter of obligation. Not until 1938 did we adopt a federal minimum wage law and a child labor law. But the principle of social security, then and now, was insurance, not public charity. Old-age pensions and unemployment insurance were to be financed by contributions, and benefits were to be related to prior earnings; this preserved the fiction that only those who had "earned" benefits were entitled to receive them. It is still embodied in the law and still evokes debate; we still have not accepted the principle of a universal right to social relief for all victims of economic change.

But, as the 1960s taught us, the aged and the unemployed are not the only victims. The "war on poverty" produced many analyses of poverty in its varied forms; the working poor, working women, blacks and other minorities, the unskilled and poorly educated, the old, the handicapped, all were made a part of our knowledge and our consciousness. Some groups, like welfare recipients, came to visibility through the efforts of advocates and analysts. Others forced their way to the foreground; the urban riots in Watts, Detroit, Washington, Newark and other cities made us recognize that urban blacks, involuntary migrants from southern agriculture, posed a major new problem for which we had no ready solution though the problem had been developing under our noses for two decades.

We have not been successful in developing the mechanisms established during the Depression to meet these greatly augmented needs. The problems are both conceptual and fiscal. The fiscal shortcomings flow inevitably from the preemption of national public funds by other groups and interests. But why could we not augment our public sector in order to meet these needs, if we could not find the political strength to shift our social priorities? Here ideology triumphs. In his neglected book, *Blaming the Victim*,[28] William Ryan surveyed the social policies we use to deal with the problems of unemployment, housing, mental illness, inadequate education, illegitimacy, poverty, and justice. He observes that policies consistently proceed from the assumption that the victim is at fault. Preferred remedies therefore stress measures to correct the fault, whether it is lack of motivation (manpower programs), lack of understanding (health), lack of aspiration (education), or a "culture of poverty" which needs to be rooted out. Proposals to attack social problems through direct grants of money are consistently defeated by the argument that the poor and underprivileged cannot be expected to help themselves, but must be helped by established institutions. Robert Lekachman has observed that the failure of social amelioration programs in the decade of the 1960s "coincides with its service strategy." Little attention was paid to the alternative, redistribution of resources and redistribution of power.

More was involved here than a failure of political organization and the articulation of the needs and demands of the deprived. The United States still does not accept the idea of a social obligation to its victims. We cling to earlier ideas, Calvinist and Darwinian in origin, that men's destinies are at root theirs to control.

As a result we accomplished relatively little in our painful and prolonged encounter with our victimized millions in the 1960s. We still operate two distinct systems of relief and support, one for the non-poor, the other for the poor. One is federally controlled, the other is controlled by states and localities. One defines its recipients as legitimate and treats them that way; the other manipulates and humiliates its recipients, seeks to reduce their numbers, and preserves them in want and dependency, psychological as well as financial.

The efforts of blacks, chicanos, Puerto Ricans and others to deal in militant, organized ways with their plight has produced little real change. Containing these protest efforts proved to be easy. Leaders were enlisted into antipoverty, manpower and other officially sponsored programs. Programs were themselves expanded sufficiently to accommodate many of the victimized groups; the expansion of welfare and manpower training enrollments in the 1960s shows how quickly this could be done. Minority business efforts received enough support to persuade many that serious efforts at amelioration were being made.

These were symbolic more than substantive in their ultimate effects, but they achieved two purposes: to persuade the victimized, or at least their leaders and spokesmen, that government cared and was responding, and to persuade the larger public that the problem was being dealt with. This was important politically; it helped to separate the victims from their supporters, to convert protest in the eyes of the public from a set of just demands to what appeared to be self-indulgent, carping complaints by people who no longer had legitimate grievances to raise. Politically these tactics were highly successful. They made it possible for George Wallace to capitalize on the accumulated resentment and fear which black protest had aroused among working class and lower class whites, and opened the way to Nixon's successful efforts to split apart, at least for the moment, the coalitions which had formed the basis for Democratic majorities since the 1930s.

The substantive record, however, showed no basic change in the plight of the poor and the victimized. Despite strenuous efforts, all white or largely white skilled trade unions preserved their status, keeping the influx of blacks to a trickle. At the other end of the scale, despite a substantial increase in the total number of medical school places, black physicians still constitute only a small percent of the total, and the number of native Indian, Puerto Rican and chicano physicians is very small. The ratio of black unemployment remained double that of white unemployment, after more than a decade of manpower programs focusing largely on the problem of unemployment among blacks. Teenagers continue to experience rates of unemployment which, were they generally prevalent, would exceed Depression levels; it was 18.4 percent in December, 1974.

Comparisons of income show substantial and continuing differentials between blacks and whites, even those with similar education and in comparable jobs. Furthermore, the differences between the races in education, skill and occupational levels have not been significantly reduced in the past decade. As a result, race- and sex-based differences in status and income show only a little change ten years after Johnson proclaimed a war on poverty—and the dollar gap between white and black income has actually widened.[29]

Our approach to the problems of poverty was consistent with the underlying perceptions of the society. The poverty problem was seen from the outset as primarily an urban and black question.

Any program for direct relief of suffering due to poverty was therefore required, first, to survive the difficulties which arise in any effort to help cities. Cities, particularly large ones, are the eunuchs of the American political system. They depend wholly on the states for their rights of self-government and the rural and small town populations that dominate state legislatures characteristically deal with urban problems by seeking to minimize the impact of these problems on their own tax rates and levels.

Because cities were the places where new immigrants congregated, they have always been strange, exotic, threatening places to the noncity groups. As black migration and Puerto Rican immigration succeeded earlier waves, these fears and dislikes were revived, fed by racism. Though the problem of urban poverty, unemployment and underemployment is ultimately the result of the mass migration of rural blacks—first drawn by industrial growth in the north, then pushed out by the rapid mechanization of southern agriculture—the attribution of causation ignored these factors. Instead it focused on the alleged inadequacies of the new urban population, their inability to take advantage of employment opportunities, their lack of basic skills and education. The victims were once again to blame. Urban politicians—John Lindsay became their symbolic embodiment in the 1960s—were seen as opportunistic manipulators, feeding the resentment and anger of the urban masses in order to build their own political careers, challenging the long-established dominance of non-urban groups. Thus every attempt to liberalize benefits and humanize the administration of welfare was resisted. Efforts to federalize the welfare system—to establish uniform minimal benefit levels and federal funding for all or most of the costs—have consistently failed.

By contrast, further decentralization of responsibility in the form of "revenue-sharing" has succeeded, thus reducing even further the future possibility of uniform federal levels of aid and support. Programs to provide employment alternatives to welfare have been tried and, without exception, have proved punitive and discriminatory. One program forced many mothers of small children to enroll in training programs that led to no jobs. Federal welfare rules treated two-thirds of earned income as deductible from benefits so that any incentive to seek employment was virtually destroyed.[30] Small changes in these rules in recent years encountered the problem of rising unemployment and shrinking urban jobs. States like New York engaged in systematic campaigns to force the cities to reduce welfare rolls without regard to the hardship and suffering which this would inflict.

At the outset, manpower training programs appeared to be capable of having some impact on the problem of the unemployed and unskilled. They did not suffer from the stigma of state control since they were federally operated through the 1962 Manpower Development and Training Act (MDTA). Originally this law was intended to help unemployed workers displaced by technological change and unable to meet new skill requirements, a belated aftermath of the automation concerns of the 1950s. But the law quickly became the government's principal instrument for responding to the problem of black unemployment, particularly among the young, when it surfaced in the mid-1960s Watts and later urban disturbances.

The conceptual basis remained unchanged in this law and in the antipoverty legislation that followed it. Again the problem was defined as an inadequately trained and educated labor force. It followed that the solution lay in providing the education and training needed to enable blacks and others to improve their competitive standing in the labor market. Thus the bulk of MDTA and OEO funds, aside from those provided to the community action arm of OEO, were committed to training and educational programs for the disadvantaged. Government funds supported manpower training programs, expansion of two-year colleges and technical schools, and provided subsidies to employers to train and employ the disadvantaged.

In the name of helping the disadvantaged, the federal government undertook a series of actions that directly served the needs of employers, in effect federalizing a set of educational programs that had begun seriously to fail at the local level. These programs had the added advantage, in the short run, of reducing the official measurement of unemployment because trainees were considered to be employed, even though they might never succeed in moving into full-time gainful employment. They conformed to the general concept that, when economic institutions fail to provide adequate employment and income, it is the victims who are ultimately responsible, and government best meets its responsibilities by helping them overcome their difficulties and join the mainstream of the labor force.

In economic terms, these programs all focused on the supply side of the labor market. Later we began to see that there were problems on the demand side as well. Employers had established a set of arrangements which accounted for much of the problem. And it did little good to add marginally to the skills of young urban blacks in a labor market where the number of whites with high school and higher levels of education was increasing as rapidly as was the case in the postwar period.[31] Institutionalized barriers based on race and sex barred even the qualified, and relegated others to lower-level dead-end status. Urban boundaries became walls within which poor people had to live, while job expansion proceeded faster outside cities; lack of transportation made it impossible for more than a handful of poor urban residents to hold jobs outside these central areas.

Manpower programs dealt with none of these factors. They also ignored the problem of the working poor, though without attention to the needs of this group, even good manpower training programs often succeed only in moving the unemployed into their ranks. If those already at the bottom of the hierarchy cannot progress upward, those who join them at the bottom must share that fate. Thus the major social effort that was made to alter the status and potential of those left behind or shunted aside during the postwar expansion was programmed for failure.

Controlling Corporate Power.   The third piece of unfinished business from the Depression was to tame the power of the corporate sector. Big business was seen as a prime factor in the Depression and economists had begun the task of describing and analyzing the phenomenon. Berle, Means, Burns, Hamilton and others came, belatedly but enthusiastically, to the task. Much of that literature is still germane and instructive; it was no accident that in the wake of the new critiques of business that arose in the late 1960s, Berle and Means' classic should have been reissued. The

inquest into the problem of bigness and power reached its peak—
still unmatched—in the inquiries of the Temporary National Economic Committee (TNEC) which was organized by Roosevelt in
1938 and submitted its final report in 1941. By the time its recommendations were formulated we were on the eve of World War II;
in Roosevelt's phrase, "Doctor Win-The-War" had replaced
"Doctor New Deal," and there was neither time for, nor serious
interest in, dealing with Depression-era problems. TNEC's intellectual and legal heritage was greater; it provided a generation of
economists with a framework for thinking about competitive problems in the modern era.

These advances were the last gasp of the reformist energies
sparked by the Depression. As the postwar boom gathered
momentum, the political and intellectual climate was rapidly
changing. Not only did social reform appear outdated and irrelevant; reformers themselves were targets of the know-nothing spirit
which was spawned by the cold war. Reminiscent of the anti-
radicalism which followed World War I, anti-communism in the
1940s and 1950s cut a wide swathe. Purges hit universities, government agencies, and the mass media. The CIO, which had provided
political support to the movements for business reform and social
justice, was deeply affected. Beset by its own purge, facing an
increasingly anti-labor climate of public opinion, and confronting a
larger, more energetic and hostile AFL, the CIO ceased to be the
political expression of reformist energies. Efforts to carry out the
reform measures which had begun in the early New Deal lost
momentum.

It should also be remembered that the response of the New
Deal to business was mixed. While taking measures to invigorate
antitrust prosecutions and strengthen regulatory powers over the
large corporations, the New Deal also worked to keep small and
medium-sized business alive. A host of measures were enacted to
preserve them—regulating chain stores, legalizing retail price
maintenance, outlawing certain forms of price discrimination. Thus
the Depression left a legacy of props and supports for business
along with its efforts to curb concentrated economic power.

The large firms have, not surprisingly, benefited from this set of rules and practices. Their strength and role, however, went unnoticed until, a generation after the Depression, new intellectual energies, stimulated by the problems of war, race, and urban decay, led a revival and further development of the analytic work which had begun in the 1930s. Mills' *The Power Elite* marks the beginning of a new period of analysis of power in America; following Mills, students discovered that William Appleman Williams and a handful of disciples had kept alive this branch of analysis.

The agenda of the 1930s still remains unfinished. The work which was begun in that time of crisis was put aside and was not taken up again. In the mid-1960s Lyndon Johnson announced a program for a "great society" and for a brief period we saw greatly increased funds for education, health, urban renewal, and other social service programs. But these were swamped almost before they got under way by the Vietnam war, and never came close to fulfilling their potential; they were destroyed by the combined effects of extravagant promises, inadequate funding levels, and control by professional bureaucracies that were closely tied to the executive branch and politically dependent on it.

At the same time the Keynesian era is ending because the institutional rigidities that make Keynesian remedies ineffective have become too great. A state subordinate to corporate interests has lost the capacity to look beyond those interests in order to determine what is needed to preserve the system from the blindness and short-sightedness of those who dominate it and benefit the most. The victims are leaderless and powerless. Politicians have mastered the art of dividing the poor from the near-poor, the elite of the labor force from those lower down, black from white, urban from suburban, women from men. Such methods yield tactical success, but they bring with them the likelihood of strategic defeat; by itself the ruling class probably cannot find its way out of the economic dead ends into which they have brought us over the past two decades. Keynes and his disciples depended on the creative energies of capitalism to generate the forces of growth, which the state then would direct in the interests of stability and domestic order. These energies have waned or disappeared; no amount of clever management can substitute for them.

Light at the End of the Tunnel?

There is under way a set of new developments that could lead to an alteration in the relationship of the state to the corporate sector, on the one hand, and the people, on the other. O'Connor, drawing on the work of Fabricant and Goldsmith, contrasts the great size of the public sector as whole—accounting for 25 per cent of GNP and a comparable share of total employment—and the small size of the state's share of productive assets. Directly or indirectly the state finances and maintains the arms industry, the housing stock, the transportation network—particularly highways and airways—and an increasing portion of domestic energy production; but it owns no aircraft or missile plants, no railroads, shipping, or airlines, and very little housing. This degree of subordination is without parallel in major industrial countries, capitalist as well as socialist. Even more striking is the absence of public discussion of this anomaly; even where capitalism is most strongly entrenched elsewhere—in France, Japan, Germany—the issue of ownership, planning, and control is kept in the forefront of political life by left-wing parties, the press and intellectuals. Not so here.

Will this change? There is reason to think so. If we turn from the industrial, energy, transportation, and communication sectors to look at services, the picture begins to look somewhat different. Overall employment in the service sector has grown more rapidly than in the others; within this sector, education and health showed the highest rates of growth over the past decade (though this began to slow in the 1970s). And these are activities in which state support is both substantial and highly visible: most education is now in public institutions; the public share of health costs has increased steadily, and now amounts to one-third of the total. With the prospect of national health insurance, the level of health expenditures will rise and the private share will decline so that, for all practical purposes, we will have a publicly financed health care system in the future.

The dismantling of the myth that education would solve all social problems was painful but decisive; popular confidence in the public education system appears to have been substantially and permanently impaired. Reorganization of urban school systems, new forms of accountability and openness, and more varied standards of achievement, all made headway in the decade following the urban riots. Ivar Berg added fuel to the fire by his findings that educational standards for many jobs had been substantially overstated. The Supreme Court took the process a big step further when it found in the Griggs case[32] that employers could not apply standards of educational attainment or test scores unless they were demonstrably related to job requirements. The wide practical impact of these developments is yet to be felt, but they clearly help remove one of the principal links which, in the past, has placed the educational system so completely under the domination of employers' needs and desires.

Similarly, the past decade saw a rising tide of criticism of the health care system. Once touted as the best anywhere, its standing has fallen with the public as well as with informed observers. The American Medical Association, once all-powerful in influencing national health policy decisions, now represents fewer than half the nation's physicians, is rent by internal dissension, and has lost much of its political clout. The Committee of 100, organized in the 1960s by Walter Reuther, was able, over a decade, to mobilize enough popular, political, and professional support to move a nationally financed health care system to the verge of enactment by 1975. Once a neglected handful, the reformers in academic medicine and in public health now wield significant influence in health policy and health education. Prepayment, group practice, salaried physicians, prevention and health maintenance, and consumer participation, have all moved from the reformist literature into the field of actual policy, challenging the former dominance of conventional private practice.

In both education and health the outcomes are not yet clear. But the chances are growing that the politics of their funding, operation, and control will constitute a departure from the pattern of corporate dominance that has, so far, characterized the role of the state in American economic life. Even a modest degree of explicit public control in one or two key sectors of economic life means something new, at least since the establishment of the Tennessee Valley Authority in 1933. In its share of GNP, health care will shortly exceed that of the military; in its employment effects it already does. Public discussion has not yet begun to come to grips with the implications of such a development. But even at this early stage, we clearly need publicly drawn standards of performance; the first efforts at comprehensive health planning demonstrated that public and community groups were deeply interested in putting such standards into practice. In health, a nascent consumer movement has already begun to seek the right to participate in policy making, the right of patients to know the facts of their medical condition and to make their own decisions, the right to consultants' opinions when surgery or other drastic therapies are recommended, access to comprehensive care, standards of qualification for practitioners, including periodic re-licensing and postgraduate training. In education, the demands have focused more on reduction of scale—replacing large, impersonal, bureaucratic systems with smaller, more responsive ones; enlarged roles for community; and greater accountability. But the direction is the same in both cases—toward more comprehensive public enterprise under public control.

There is also a basic crisis in housing, though it is, so far, hidden, and lacks a constituency as well as a policy and advocates. But the scandalous shortage of decent housing in contrast with other advanced societies is as marked as the shortage of health care. Because it is so much a part of the larger urban crisis, and affects mostly the poor, it does not capture the political imagination of the middle class. But if we need a national energy corporation, we need—at least as much—a national housing authority, with power to build housing on a large scale, at costs that lower income people can afford. It will take time, but inevitably the case for such a national policy will reach our political awareness, and join the areas of health care and education as part of a trinity of public sector commitments which are seen as indispensable requirements for a decent, livable society. And the crisis of employment in the building trades might hasten the day of its arrival as a viable political issue!

The reconstruction of our network of ground transportation, and the reconstitution of viable city-suburb mass transit, cannot be accomplished except through state intervention—on a scale and with a degree of direct control comparable to that required in energy, health, and housing. Having destroyed transit systems in favor of a car-truck-bus monopoly, the private sector has lost its legitimacy as the instrument for carrying out these public purposes; only government itself can do so. The argument for this component of the public sector of the future is compelling.

Toward a Social Sector. These trends would be less persuasive if the society did not find itself increasingly dependent on these sectors to absorb new entrants to the labor force. In the past we were able to conceal many of the defects of traditional labor markets by a variety of devices—increasing the military forces, increasing school enrollments, and enlarged training programs. As these methods lose their absorptive power, the society turns to explicitly public job creation. This was already happening in small ways a few years ago with the enactment of the Emergency Employment Act of 1971 and the Public Service Careers Program of 1969. While these had short-run purposes, their long-run implications soon emerged: the first revision of manpower training legislation since 1962, the Comprehensive Employment and Training Act of 1974 (CETA), contains permanent statutory authority to create public service jobs in periods of unemployment. For the first time since the emergency programs of the Depression, federal legislation requires the federal government to reduce unemployment by direct creation of public service jobs.

These jobs will be most numerous in the areas of public service where the needs are seen to be greatest, and where existing manpower and social capital are most inadequate; health, education, and housing will surely be important. Job creation cannot occur without creating the capital needed to make the jobs productive and meaningful. So the obligations imposed under CETA, and subsequent legislation yet to come, involve the state directly in the creation of social capital, not for the use or benefit of private capital, but for politically determined areas of social need. This opens the way, for the first time, to a social priorities agenda, a social capital budget, and the determination of major national decisions through the open process of political controversy.

In the struggle over health insurance, the various efforts to keep the system under control of the private insurance companies and organized medicine failed, and a national consensus had begun to emerge by 1975 which, while falling short of a national health service on the British model, was far more advanced, more socially controlled and responsive, than had been expected a decade earlier. The reconstitution of education is more problematic: adequate funding levels in the future will depend at least in part on corporate support—which, in turn, depends on how functional the educational system is seen to be. But forces of reform, forces in support of independence, redefinition of purpose, and standards of performance, grew during the 1960s. As for housing, the scenario remains to be written.

If the economy is to function successfully in the decades ahead, a key requirement will be that the state assume the role of planner and setter of priorities, independently of the interests that have so far dominated that process. Growth involves the required magnitude of investment; but it is important that the right choices be made. Our vulnerability to the oil blockade on the one hand, and to "administered price" inflation on the other, was greatly heightened by the fact that the structure of the economy, the shape and composition of our productive and distributive capacity—our stock of capital—had been largely determined by the corporate sector and the military-industrial complex. While economic policies—the failure to raise taxes in 1966, the manipulation of the money supply before the 1972 election—played triggering roles, the propensities and the consequences had been built in over many decades. Economic structure does not wholly control economic performance, but it limits choices, establishes the predispositions of the system, and goes far to determine the flexibility available when response is needed to sudden and substantial changes in the economic situation. World War II was such a time; it was necessary, and it proved possible, wholly to redirect the productive process to meet enormous, unprecedented needs. One of the key factors favoring success was the availability of substantial idle capacity and manpower. Another was the moral force of a

national, indeed world emergency, which was dramatized by
Roosevelt and Churchill. We should thus not be overly complacent
in judging how successfully we will be able to manage the transition from the era now ending to that which was symbolized by the
oil embargo in 1973–1974.

The World We Must Live In

It has been necessary to describe our domestic situation at some
length in order to be able to place our economy in the world setting
that has emerged in the past decade, first gradually, and then at a
rapid clip. Two major factors govern this process, which is still
going forward. First, the United States is no longer the sole
dominant economic system in the industrialized world. From the
devastation of World War II new centers of economic power were
constructed. Many will recall the shock when the Soviet Union
demonstrated its scientific and technological progress by developing nuclear weapons long before American experts thought it
possible, then by beating the United States into orbital space flight.
Japan moved from subordinate to first-class industrial status. Germany showed a similar pattern. The world had become multi-polar.
German growth led the rest of western Europe but the French,
Italian (in part), and other national economies were not far behind.
Following the organization of the European Economic Community, Kennedy envisioned the creation of an integrated industrial
Atlantic economic system, linking an enlarged EEC with the
United States. His assassination, and the divisions exacerbated by
the Vietnam war, frustrated progress in that direction. But the
troop withdrawals, Nixon's removal, and the return to power of
internationalist business groups, may signal the resumption after a
long delay of progress in that direction.

The Kennedy design sought to anticipate the economic effects
of the movement for political independence in the colonial world.
Clearly the example of the OPEC success in controlling oil output
and prices has been a powerful stimulant. Successful organization
by the U.S. of the industrial world would have marked the devel-

opment of a new, cooperative phase in the efforts of the developed world to maintain their hegemony in world markets and their continued access to world supplies of needed raw materials and oil.

The failure to achieve these goals may prove to be the real price of Vietnam. Resurgent nationalism was able to establish sufficient momentum so that the belated efforts organized by the United States after the oil embargo to unify the strategies of the industrial countries were unsuccessful. The result was a scramble for oil, the launching and then abandoning of crash programs to replace oil imports, even the implied threat of military action to secure access to Arab oil fields.

But another route out of the crisis had begun to be explored in the late 1960s, born of the larger dilemma of possible exhaustion of natural resources and the growing fear that pollution of the atmosphere and the oceans might threaten life itself.

Despite the reluctance of economists to take it seriously, the idea of a no-growth economy has begun to take shape. In part it can be interpreted as an admission that it may be impossible to tame and control the international oil companies and other multinational corporations. But some writers are pursuing an alternative vision of the good life to that which has so far dominated the popular imagination both here and in the world. They respond to the rejection of materialism which flamed for a time among American youth, a part of the mosaic of the 1960s.

In the meantime, the vacuum in international economic decision making has been filled by a new phenomenon, the multinational corporation. Superficially it appears to be the modern, international form of the corporation which, for Schumpeter, embodied the purposes and function of capitalism. He argued then that hostility to their predatory practices, their power, and independence of the state, was misconceived, because they were the necessary instruments for the conception and maturation of major innovations in product and process. Certainly today's multinationals—ITT, IBM, GM, Remington Rand, Unilever—display some of the same attributes: great power, independence from attempts at state control, and a single-minded pursuit of profits. But one looks in vain for the creative justification. These are not instruments for the development of new methods of production, or new products.

They are cannibals. Their rationale is the division of labor in conformity with imperfections in world labor and capital markets, differences in tax laws, and the possibility of political influence. They treat sovereign nations the way the robber barons of the nineteenth century treated the individual states. But while this behavior ultimately led to the assumption by the national government of the responsibility to regulate the barons and control their excesses, no international equivalent exists or is likely to be created. Multinational corporations respond to the falling rate of profit in mature capitalist countries by recreating their systems of production and assembly on an international scale.

The device of the multinational corporation has so far proved to be highly effective for transferring even advanced production processes to low wage economies, and for minimizing as well as concealing taxable profits. One of the ironies of the multinational corporation is its perverse realization of an idea of international solidarity—which had originally been put forward by trade union movements prior to World War I. A related irony is their success in establishing markets and trading relationships with the Soviet Union, China, and their respective allied economies, after the long period in which official U.S. doctrine forbade or minimized such trade. Complementary economic goals have largely buried ideological barriers that once polarized the world. Finally, multinationals have begun to stimulate trans-national collaboration among unions in the same industries who must negotiate with the separate components of single corporations, in a way that recalls the development of national unions as a consequence of the establishment of national markets in the United States.[33]

Some see the multinationals as the chosen instruments for stabilizing political relationships between east and west—Soviet Union and United States—by establishing new forms of worldwide collaboration around a new international division of labor.[34] Episodes like the efforts ITT tried to organize to overthrow the Allende regime become in this view the modern replacement of military intervention, but with the tacit agreement of the two superpowers consistent with their division of spheres of influence.

In the case of oil, the future remains unclear. The OPEC countries now control crude supplies and prices, while the division of world markets for oil remains under the control of the companies. The stability of the producers' cartel cannot be predicted; the pressure of excess capacity may well confirm the forecasts of those who expect the cartel to fail and world prices to fall. Effective reduction of consumption levels in industrial countries would clearly contribute to making this outcome more likely. But this requires a quality of leadership and a degree of unity that were conspicuously lacking in the period which followed the 1973 embargo.

The oil crisis administered other major shocks to the established mechanisms for smoothing world trade, which had succeeded for a quarter-century in sustaining rising levels of trade without altering the relative poverty of the less developed countries which contain the majority of the world's population.

The consequences of the oil blockade and its aftermath go further than a redress of the terms of trade, which have had major inflationary consequences for the United States and the other industrialized countries. The 1973–1974 imbalances were so massive that they produced a significant potential transfer of wealth as well, from the industrialized to the OPEC countries. The long-run consequences of this cannot be foreseen. Because the OPEC countries, except for Iran and Venezuela, lack both development and the pressures for it, their options are wide; they can hold their dollar balances or invest them, without taking any steps which cannot be interrupted, suspended or reversed. Much will depend on whether Iran seeks to establish hegemony within the group and to initiate processes of development which make it necessary for others either to follow suit or to fall permanently under Iranian influence. If the dynamics of industrial development begin to exert their effects in this area, the situation of the industrialized countries will improve. They will then become the indispensable sources of technological and managerial knowledge, industrial capital, and organized capital markets. They would also provide important markets for these countries, just as they did when Japan experienced her highest and most sustained growth after World War II. With luck and care, Israel industry and markets would fit into this picture. If Iran moves in the modernizing directions charted by the Shah in the early 1970s, the effects of Arab efforts to isolate and destroy Israel would be weakened.

But there may be serious limits to any large-scale effort by the

Arab and other developing countries to join the industrialized modern world. Western and Soviet industrialization took place in an era when population pressures were largely absent in the world; resources were relatively plentiful, widely distributed, and accessible at low cost; technological progress was fruitful and steady; and belief in modernism powerful and pervasive. The nations now setting out along this path, and those—like Turkey, Taiwan, Brazil—which have already progressed a significant distance in this direction, face worldwide conditions very different from those which prevailed as recently as the mid-1950s. Further conventional industrialization may be obsolete, if not positively dangerous to human survival itself. But nations will nevertheless insist, if they can, that historical inequalities among nations be ended or substantially reduced. As long as competitive industrial development appears to be the only effective method for raising the relative living standards of less developed societies, those governments that have the resources or the power to command them will continue to move in this direction. To them, warnings of global peril or rapid exhaustion of minerals and fuels will sound like self-serving arguments made on behalf of the affluent minority in the interest of preserving their relative affluence. No eloquence of Commoner, Heilbroner, or the Club of Rome will persuade them to listen.

What alternatives are there, then? First, the major industrial countries will have to demonstrate by their own actions in their own societies that the ecological and resource-exhaustion arguments are taken seriously. Only a few steps, more symbolic than substantive, have so far been taken to translate these concerns into policies—legislation to control strip-mining, environmental impact requirements imposed by federal legislation, and such. But these provide a basis on which to build. What they foreshadow—and what must come—are comprehensive economic planning mechanisms which can make explicit the social costs and returns of economic decisions and choices, and can compel the private sector to adhere to socially determined priorities. We saw that the pattern of our economy has shifted decisively in the direction of services; those provided and financed by the state occupy an increasingly important place. In this regard we are fortunate, having begun to create and use a set of mechanisms that make it possible to carry out the necessary exercises and to give them policy form at the national level. But these are so far limited; the general form for priority setting still conforms to O'Connor's description of corporate dominance. The task ahead is to extend the scope of national priority setting and to make and keep it visible and controllable in the public interest. This will be hard and may prove impossible, despite its necessity.

A second requirement is to reduce relative inequalities in present patterns of consumption among nations. We have scarcely begun to think about what this means or how to achieve it. But the rapid and massive transfers of purchasing power which followed the oil embargo showed that such reductions could be imposed. One of the ironies of this experience is that the industrialized countries, which experienced a loss of status, generally show much less internal inequality of income than do the less developed countries with lower average per capita incomes. But internal inequalities in modern societies are great enough and long-lived enough to pose serious, if not fatal obstacles to successful transition to lower average living standards, if that is required in the future as a result of both declining possibilities for sustaining overall industrial growth, and weakened trade strength *vis-à-vis* the raw material countries.

So this second requirement leads to a third: that the degree of internal inequality in the United States, Britain, Germany, Japan and other mature industrial countries be reduced. Without it, Heilbroner's picture of disappearing democracy and freedom becomes plausible, but with it this prospect may prove less likely than he predicts. In essence, as China shows, a society in which there is a general agreement that necessary sacrifice is equally imposed is capable of vast, indeed revolutionary change. By contrast one in which the costs of change are unequally imposed, so that the privileged continue to fare relatively well while those more vulnerable are sacrificed, cannot survive the coming era of change except with the loss of political and individual freedom.

Here again, the United States cannot avoid its role as the leading industrial nation. We must learn to accept the idea that the end of inequality is not only a good thing but a national necessity.

Objective conditions have made acceptance of such a national purpose plausible; we now know that inequalities based on race, sex, age, inherited wealth, social class, or education are spurious and self-serving. We know, too, that the notion that private profit is the best, most reliable guide to economic and social arrangements that serve the public interest, is invalid; the evidence is everywhere. We lack two things, which constitute the urgent business of our best minds: a plausible model of an economy that subordinates private to social necessity (not just interest), and a politics that gives people ways to make the social choices that are involved in such an economy. These changes proceed from necessity; they transcend conventional ideologies, and they are deeply political. This should make them achievable within the framework of American conceptions of civil liberties and democratic process.

Many of the selections that follow are condensed, some drastically. Although I wished I could have included them in their complete form, doing so would have limited this book to fewer articles, fewer authors, and a much narrower range of ideas and points of view. The cost of publishing such a lengthy work would have limited its readers to a very few.

All the selections are valuable and interesting in their full length. I urge the reader to consult the acknowledgments page for information on where each can be found.

The End of the Keynesian Era?

The problems we face in the short run have deep roots and will ultimately require major changes. But the short-run choices we make will help to determine how successfully we are able to come to grips with the underlying features of our economy. As they faced the prospect of rising unemployment and declining output in 1975, Republican and Democratic policymakers alike focused primarily on well-known measures to stimulate employment, limit inflation, and reduce oil imports. The Democratic program placed greater stress on tax cuts to consumers, particularly in middle and lower income groups, easier money, stimulus to housing construction, and expanded public service employment programs. The Republican approach was somewhat more conservative about the amount of stimulus needed, was less redistributive, and continued the traditional reliance on tax incentives to business investment. Democrats' response to the oil issue included rationing and taxes on high-horsepower automobiles to curb oil consumption; the

Administration relied largely on consumption and import taxes. Both sides paid lip service to long-run needs—neither proposed concrete measures that would make significant progress toward solving long-run problems. While there appears to be agreement on the goal of national self-sufficiency in energy supplies, no leading spokesman has proposed measures to reduce energy needs over the long run or to shift the patterns of energy consumption. There were, for example, no serious proposals to reduce national dependence on trucks and automobiles in favor of rail or water transportation. Nothing was said about improving urban settings in order to stimulate more urban-based housing and business activities, though these require far less energy or fuel than suburban settings.

The conflict between high levels of employment and price stability—a "sound dollar"—was fought out but never settled during the first debates on what became the Employment Act of 1946. Bertram M. Gross was a drafter of the original bill in 1944, and has traced the contours of that struggle for us. More recently he worked with members of Congress and the Senate to establish the entitlement to full employment as a national mandate.

The debate continues. When the Director of the Cost of Living Council, John T. Dunlop, testified before the Joint Economic Committee in May, 1974, he predicted that inflation would "remain a nagging persistent problem for our economy for many years" and saw little hope of reducing it to really low rates. At about the same time, Wilfred Lewis, Jr., director of research for the National Planning Association, observed:[1]

> We can no doubt look forward, if not in next year's economic report, then shortly thereafter, to receiving an explanation of why 5.5 per cent, or say even 6 per cent unemployment, rather than this year's 4.9 per cent, is really the definition of "maximum employment."

Writing in 1956, Paul Samuelson had predicted that these differences were bound to recur:

> I should like to put forward the hypothesis that the relatively minor economic differences between the Republicans and Democrats during 1953–1956 has been in the nature of a lucky accident. For

reasons that will not necessarily be relevant in the future, *we have been able since 1951 to have a very high degree of prosperity and also to have stable prices.* The drop in farm and other staple prices made this possible.

In the future the dilemma between very high employment and stable prices is likely to reassert itself with increasing force. Then it will be found that the Republicans do differ from the Democrats in the greater weight that they will give to the goal of maintaining an honest dollar in comparison with the clashing goal of keeping unemployment extremely low.

In this clash of ideologies, social welfare functions and not scientific economic principles must play the decisive role.[2]

But Herbert Stein also pointed out, correctly, that the liberal economists advising the Kennedy Administration saw economic problems primarily in these terms:

The Kennedy economists, like most American economists of 1960, believed that the chief economic problem of the country was to achieve and maintain high and rapidly rising total output. That is, the problem was full employment and economic growth. The keys to the management of that problem were fiscal policy and monetary policy, with fiscal policy being the senior partner in the combination. Full employment, or economic stabilization, and economic growth were the main objectives and guides of fiscal policy; budget-balancing was an irrelevancy. The economy was not in need of any basic structural reform, of the character of the National Recovery Act, French planning, or nationalization of industry. In general, the "free market" worked well and was not to be tampered with, but particular issues of government intervention in the market must be considered on their merits and without prejudice. Steps to make the distribution of income more nearly equal were good but they were not the urgent need and not the main road to improving the economic condition of the mass of the population, and they had to be evaluated with due regard for their effects on economic growth.

Liberal Keynesian economic policy making reached its moment of maximum influence at that time; its monument was the 1964 tax cut, whose consequences are still with us. There were those who had reservations—Charles C. Killingsworth, for instance, believed that direct intervention was needed in order to deal with structural unemployment among particular groups and in geographic areas where unemployment was deeply rooted. But the reservations were in the nature of amendments or emendations to the basic Keynesian approach to economic problems. As Killingsworth said, in an article evaluating the effects of the 1964 tax cut:

> A structuralist is correctly defined as a Keynesian who believes that changes in the structure of the economy can have an independent effect on the levels of employment and unemployment.[3]

The contentions of the structuralists were largely brushed aside in those days. But this debate foreshadowed the larger one we must now confront: whether the arsenal of Keynesian instruments on which a generation of economists and policy makers of both political parties have relied must be consigned, now, to the relic heap of the past, or assigned a far more modest role in economic thinking and policy making. Like the stagnation theorists of the 1930s, and the automation prophets of the 1950s, the structuralists raised the question of whether there was a long-run tendency for unemployment to rise and remain high as a result of deep-seated factors that would not respond to aggregative measures.

In the 1960s, in the same way, the prospect of long-term inflation suggested—strongly—that aggregative measures might no longer do. In rebuttal, one of the founders of modern Keynesian economics insisted that the triumph of Keynesian measures in a full-employment economy need not be accompanied by the contradiction of persistent inflation. He relied on a better, more coordinated combination of fiscal and monetary policy: fiscal policy (taxation, government subsidies, etc.) was predominant, and monetary policy (interest rates and changes in money supply) was controlled by the Administration, with adjustment mechanisms—like cost-of-living clauses—to protect sections of the population against short-run inflationary movements. He summarized his optimistic views this way:

> Improved guideposts, presidential authority to raise or lower taxes within specified limits and, finally, monetary policy working in tandem with fiscal policy, could give us full employment *and* "rea-

sonable price stability." In the meantime, let us not blame our
inflationary pressures on the New Economics.[4]

Some were not satisfied by these reassurances, but few quarreled
with the basic Keynesian approach. John K. Galbraith, at this
time, made persuasively worded proposals for more funds for
public and social needs—and argued that his proposals were sol-
idly Keynesian. His quarrel was with a totally numerical approach
to demand management. He preferred to enlarge the size of the
social budget rather than to cut taxes, as the mainstream had
chosen. For them, "the only test of performance was the potential
increase in gross national product and the potential decrease in
unemployment"; for him, redressing the imbalance between private and public needs was equally important.[5] Other economists
offer other amendments: Wilfred Lewis, Jr., wants policies that
make sure that the stock of productive capital is adequate to
employ fully the labor force using modern technology. For him,
management of demand has to be supplemented by "expansion of
the capital stock relative to the employed labor force,"[6] in order to
permit Keynesian methods to boost employment without imposing
high rates of inflation.

Keynesian policies depend on economic growth; without it,
they probably cannot succeed. This is not always clearly stated by
liberal economists, but it is integral to their thinking. Writing in
1972, the chief economist of the AFL-CIO, Nat Goldfinger, called
for policies "to provide the basis for economic growth and full
employment" though, like Galbraith, he saw them in the sphere of
social need, not private industry. Leon Keyserling, an architect of
the Employment Act of 1946 and Chairman of the Council of
Economic Advisors in the Truman Administration, has consistently argued for sustained economic growth as the precondition
for full employment; in 1973 he wrote:

> We need a real annual rate of economic growth of about 8 percent to
> restore full employment and full production by the end of 1974, and
> about 5 percent thereafter to keep up with advances in productivity
> and technology and the growth of the civilian labor force. In sharp
> contrast, the real annual rate of economic growth, after being
> satisfactorily high but not too high from the fourth quarter of 1972 to

the first quarter of 1973, was only 2.6 percent from the first quarter of 1973 to the second quarter of 1973. Today the real growth rate is probably even lower. We are already in a period of economic stagnation, and our experience during the past two decades indicates clearly that this will lead us into an absolute recession, perhaps before the middle of 1974, unless very vigorous corrective steps are taken. Under current policies, the outlook is certain that unemployment will increase substantially in the process of stagnation and then recession.[7]

While other economists may state the required rates of growth more modestly or with somewhat less stress on full employment, the necessity for growth cannot be escaped in this mode of analysis. It is the paradigm of modern economic thinking.

Without growth, the choice between high employment and price stability becomes inescapable within existing economic and political arrangements, and the given division between state and private decision making. Thomas Balogh has argued that we will be forced to live with unacceptable rates of inflation unless central government powers are greatly expanded and those of both large industry and their unions curbed,[8] a theme not unlike that of Robert Lekachman, in "Toward Equality Through Employment," presented here. Both writers make the case for a new "social contract" explicitly carried out by the state. But this would require a commitment to egalitarian policies which is not a credible likelihood to any but the most optimistic of Americans. Balogh argues that inflation poses such severe difficulties that no society can avoid making the leap, however difficult. From an explicitly radical perspective, Harry Magdoff and Paul Sweezy focus on credit creation as the indispensable support for economic expansion in an economy dominated by monopoly capitalism; for them, the limits imposed on growth in the future show the "Keynesian Chickens Come Home to Roost."

The end of the era of growth has implications for every aspect of our society. Economists, claims Robert Heilbroner in a recent article in *The Public Interest,* are not very helpful in dealing with discontinuities of this kind. One factor in this lack of helpfulness, one he does not discuss, is that economists of most schools have focused much more on the size of the pie than on its distribution. Lacking a satisfactory theory of income distribution—and unwilling to face the political implications of attempting to alter clear-cut, continuing inequality in wealth and income—economics finds a satisfactory refuge in seeking to increase total output. As long as one could argue that growth would continue to be both possible and necessary, economists might differ over whether unemployment or inflation was the greater threat to growth, but the long-term direction would remain accepted. As recently as 1969, most economists agreed with Alan Altshuler's characterization of the economy:

> The American economy is extraordinarily self-sufficient. International trade amounts to little more than 5 percent of our gross national product . . . Increasingly, the major disputes are no longer about the level of aggregate demand to aim at, but the means employed to get there.[9]

By 1974 the economists were much less certain. The summation of the past decade by Leonall C. Andersen, Senior Vice President of the Federal Reserve Bank of St. Louis, is instructive of their views. He argues that an activist fiscal (or government taxation and spending) policy has been shown not to be effective as a stabilizing force—that inflation is the major danger, and that therefore monetary (i.e., banking and investment) restraint has become the necessary instrument of choice.

This theory is based—implicitly—on the idea that more unemployment = less inflation. A major justification for this theory is the evidence—some call it evidence—one gets from using an econometric construct called the Phillips curve. The Phillips curve has serious technical flaws as an instrument for economic analysis. It is always necessary to examine the assumptions built into any instrument used for policy making; one of those built into the Phillips curve is the "tacit belief that no portion of a wage increase can be absorbed by corporations as a reduction of profit and dividends."[10]

Increasing unemployment affects, first and most, the most vulnerable levels of the work force, those at the lower end of the wage and occupational spectrum. The policy of increasing unemployment was justified by the theory that this would lessen inflation—based on the Phillips curve; the social cruelty was evident by late 1974, and clearly it had not been effective in slowing inflation. The cost of these policies is a key reason why Melville J. Ulmer announces "the collapse of Keynesianism."[11]

What remains useful and usable in the Keynesian arsenal? Can we combine efforts to redistribute income, maximize employment, and curb inflation, in an era when conventional economic growth becomes more difficult and may indeed no longer be attainable? This is the domestic policy conundrum of our time. Efforts to mount and sustain large-scale programs of public service employment are best seen in the context of these questions. Public service employment has much to commend it:

(1) Public service employment can reduce the incidence and effects of discrimination in the labor market against the more vulnerable sectors of the labor force, particularly in cities, where public needs are greatest and public employment programs would be concentrated.

(2) Public service employment provides employment-producing offsets to reductions in military spending. Testifying before a Senate subcommittee in 1972, Bennett Harrison provided some data to show these effects:[12]

$10 billion of federal spending will have more or less the same multiplier effect on GNP and will return more or less the same partly offsetting tax payments, regardless of how it is spent. What *will* differ from one form of government spending to another are the employment and income distribution effects.

According to the Bureau of Labor Standards (BLS), $1 billion of private consumption and/or investment spending generates about 79,000 new jobs, nearly all of them in the private sector.

$1 billion of federal defense spending generates 92,000 jobs: 55,000 in the public sector and 37,000 in the private sector.

$1 billion of federal *nondefense* spending generates 83,000 jobs: 43,000 in the private sector.

$1 billion of state and local government spending generates 110,000 jobs: 79,000 in government and 31,000 in the private sector.

There are at least three messages in these numbers, which were derived from the BLS's input-output table. First, federal grants to state and local governments will create (on the average) more jobs than either direct federal spending (whether for defense or for nondefense purposes) or an equivalent tax cut designed to stimulate private consumption.

Second, and contrary to the expectation of almost anyone who has ever thought about the subject, a billion dollars of federal *nondefense* spending actually creates more *private* sector jobs than an equivalent expenditure on defense procurement and military operations: this suggests that a reallocation of defense appropriations to nondefense uses need *not* create net unemployment in the private economy, and may even have a moderately *stimulative* effect— provided, of course, that we make provisions for those demobilized veterans in need of jobs. In other words, [with] a redirection of military-oriented expenditures to health, education, and welfare programs, urban development, mass transit, and environmental restoration—not only would we as consumers be better off, but the private sector, too, might benefit.

Finally BLS believes that nondefense federal purchases generate more jobs per dollar than federal defense purchases because the latter "include a relatively high proportion of manufactured goods purchased from industries with high productivity, that is, with relatively low labor requirements."

Another benefit of the shift toward greater reliance on public employment would be its effect on income distribution. Earnings from public employment are much more evenly distributed than are earnings from private-sector employment.[13]

In short, such programs help us along toward two important goals—full employment, and balance among the sectors of our society. There may be other benefits, too:

(3) Public service employment is likely to be labor-intensive rather than capital-intensive, though this should not be exaggerated. "Make-work" programs of an emergency nature serve primarily as disguised relief for the unemployed rather than to provide productive employment and services because they lack adequate capital, good management, and effective long-run planning and goal-setting. But the capital used for public service is social, rather than private; the decisions about that capital are not based on the

market-profit objectives of the private sector, but based on public and social policy goals which are established through the open process of political debate and decision making.

(4) Public service employment programs are conserving of scarce resources, particularly minerals and fossil fuels. They thus provide economic growth of a different kind than the growth we have experienced in the past.

The rest of the Keynesian arsenal, however, is in serious trouble, and is unlikely to help us. As the contradiction between unemployment and inflation worsens, the temptation in government will increase to persuade the nation to accept higher unemployment rates as necessary and equitable, the lesser evil. For these ends, public service employment could serve as a buffer, replacing on a much larger scale the role played in the past by the armed forces, manpower training programs, expanded education programs below the college level, and other absorbers of surplus labor. DuBoff and Herman's dissection of Keynesian "new economics" makes it clear that remedial measures like public service employment must meet rigorous tests of long-run consistency with the deeper needs of economic reconstruction.

Bertram M. Gross
FULL EMPLOYMENT IN THE NEW "DAY OF THE DINOSAUR"

The proposed "Equal Opportunity and Full Employment Act of 1976" is a measure that is overdue, timely, and ahead of its time. It proposes to help make a reality of the "unalienable rights" declared by the Founding Fathers almost 200 years ago, of the Economic Bill of Rights transmitted to Congress by President Roosevelt 30 years ago, and of the hopes raised by the passage of the Employment Act 28 years ago.

To provide any deep perspective on the proposed legislation, it would be necessary to contrast that simple old world of 1944 with the strange new world of 1974.

Thirty years ago, while war was raging in Europe and Asia, we had genuine full employment in America. Everyone able and willing to work had a range of choices. Even women. Even older people. Even youngsters. And even black people. But we were all members of the Depression generation, and no one thought that full employment could survive the war. We feared a return to breadlines, riots at factory gates, applesellers on street corners, veterans killed in bonus marches, banks closing down, and bankers jumping out of windows. President Franklin Roosevelt responded to this fear. Running for his fourth term in office, he promised jobs for all after the war—60 million civilian jobs.

At that time I was fully employed night and day by a Senate subcommittee[14] headed by two strong-willed members: James E. Murray of Montana and Harry S. Truman of Missouri. On their behalf I had also been working closely for many years with Rep. Wright Patman of Texas, then Chairman of the House Committee on Small Business. A few days after Roosevelt and Truman won the 1944 election, I was asked to prepare a subcommittee report on "Legislation for Reconversion and Full Employment." This report, made public on December 18, 1944, declared that "unless an economic substitute is found for war contracts, mass unemployment will become a serious threat and the number of unemployed men and women in this country could easily surpass anything that was dreamed of during the last depression." Senator Murray and Senator Truman then presented the first draft of "The Full Employment Act of 1945."

The Murray-Truman proposal stirred up huge waves of comment. From then on, events moved rather rapidly. A tangled web of debate swirled through the Congress and executive agencies and across the country. What was really meant by "full employment"? Could or should the "right to a job" be guaranteed? How far should the federal government go in maintaining prosperity? What should be the content of a hundred or so different programs and policies affecting the level of employment and output and the nature of economic relations with other countries?

A Historic Compromise. Congress rejected the right to employment opportunities promised by Roosevelt—on the other hand, the essence of the 1946 legislation was its expression of a new commitment by the federal government never again to allow another mass depression. While this compromise distressed many of the bill's most ardent supporters, there is no doubt that the Employment Act of 1946 represented an historic turning point in American history.

This Act, "although a statute, in its importance may be said to have made constitutional law."[15] But it has been continuously amended by administrative fiat. Six Presidents have given it widely different interpretations (which have been the outcome of fundamental changes in American capitalism and in the conflicting concepts and values of different groups in American society). I see three "real-life amendments": (1) the shift from counter cyclical stabilization to sustained economic growthmanship; (2) the expansion of growthmanship to include the quality of life as well as the quantity of goods and services; (3) the interpretation of "maximum employment" as a rising level of politically tolerable unemployment. The proposed 1976 Act represents the first effort to amend and extend the law even more substantially—but by open decisions openly arrived at in Congress.

When the 1946 Act was first passed, it was generally regarded as a counter-cyclical measure whose main purpose was to see that the Government reacted positively to any threat of depression. Under President Truman this interpretation gradually changed: the emphasis shifted from stabilization to sustained economic growth. This GNP growthmanship was picked up by the Rockefeller Brothers Fund in the late 1950s, used by Richard Nixon in his 1960 campaign, and then discovered and made into almost a household word by the Camelot council under John Kennedy. With Lyndon Johnson, the ante was raised still higher. Johnson called for a Great Society that "rests on abundance and liberty for all" and "demands an end to poverty and racial injustice, to which we are totally committed in our time." The Administration was oriented toward "quality of life" objectives *with* stable growth.

The Eisenhower Administration had initiated a third process of change: the acceptance of increasingly higher levels of officially reported unemployment, higher unemployment as a means of keeping prices down. Under Richard Nixon this was converted into an open policy of promoting increased unemployment as a presumed anti-inflation measure. Apart from the period immediately preceding his re-election in 1972, when economic expansion was accelerated, this policy has been adhered to since.

—1974

Robert Lekachman
TOWARD EQUALITY THROUGH EMPLOYMENT

Full employment without inflation *is* possible, but only in a community substantially different from the United States in 1974. Rearrangements of power, privilege, income, and wealth distribution are necessary. What I shall maintain here is this: the prerequisites of full employment, combined with price stability, relate to equity of sacrifice and equity of reward. These prerequisites are immediately four in number and in the longer run there is probably a fifth as well:

(1) A guarantee by federal, state, and local governments of public employment as a reliable alternative to private jobs in both good and bad economic times. (2) For those unable or unwilling to work (in all probability a very small number) income maintenance at a decent level as a matter of right. (3) An incomes policy, focused upon large corporations, professional societies, and unions, as powerful and permanent as the organizations which necessitate this public response. (4) On grounds of equity and price stability alike, a serious policy of redistributive taxation. (5) In the future a gradually increasing public and diminishing private sphere of activity, a realization of the Keynesian vision of a "somewhat comprehensive socialization of investment."[16]

Public Jobs. "Transitional" positions are likely to be second-class jobs, evaluated suspiciously by civil service associations and unions of public employees as potential infringements upon benefit, job security, and wage standards won over many years by painful negotiation. A far superior design is embodied in legislation introduced in 1974 by Congressmen Augustus Hawkins of California and Henry Reuss of Wisconsin, and in August of the same year by Hubert Humphrey in the Senate: the Equal Opportunity and Full Employment Act of 1976. Their proposal aims "to establish a national policy and nationwide machinery for guaranteeing to all adult Americans able and willing to work the availability of equal opportunities for useful and rewarding employment."

As a serious and sophisticated attempt to grapple with the concrete details involved in the implementation of comprehensive job guarantees, this proposal is notable for its emphasis upon social and economic equity, and the quality of life for citizens in all social stations.

Flat job guarantees promise additional benefits. Public sector expansion is energy and resource thrifty, particularly if the new jobs are located in health care, education, security of persons and property, environmental conservation, and fire protection. Full employment would surely stimulate job redesign, flexible work scheduling, study and recreational sabbaticals, and a greatly to be desired general humanization of work in offices and factories. By no means least important, full employment promotes social cohesion, and the integration into the labor force of that under- and unemployed underclass whose existence Gunnar Myrdal postulates as a mark of an underdeveloped society.

Income Maintenance. In our country, income maintenance programs include old age and survivors' benefits, veterans' pensions, Aid to the Families of Dependent Children, food stamps, and a variety of other measures, including, I suppose, subsidies to Pan Am, the Penn Central, Lockheed, and other needy corporate citizens. Eligibility is premised upon appropriate status: honorable as in the instance of veterans and the elderly, dishonorable as in the notorious case of the welfare population. Neither legislatures nor courts have defined as a general right an entitlement to public aid. Intermittently courts have moved tentatively in the direction of providing due process protections to welfare beneficiaries. Most recently the Nixon Supreme Court has retreated toward an older conception of welfare as gift or gratuity rather than consequence of membership in civilized society.[17]

Some persons, even on liberal employability criteria, cannot work. Others, either because they prefer the care of young children or alternative life-styles, prefer not to work. The numbers in both categories, in all likelihood, are a small percentage of the labor force. Unwilling workers are unlikely to be productive employees. Hence on both efficiency and equity grounds, the argument is compelling for substituting a general measure of income maintenance for existing cash grant programs covering separate groups. The most convenient mechanism is some version of a negative income tax (NIT), preferably one which is explicitly redistributive in its impact. As a device, an NIT is defined by the presence of a basic grant and tax upon earnings which at some breaking point reduces the grant to zero and enrolls the grant recipient into the company of ordinary taxpayers. Thus even at 1974 prices a $1,000 per person basic grant in tandem with a 50 percent tax on earnings would define as potential beneficiaries not only unemployed persons but also substantial numbers of fully employed but moderately remunerated individuals. Until a man or woman reached an income of $12,000[18] as head of a family of four, he or she would gain either in outright cash subventions (at the low end of the income scale) or tax reductions (at the upper end).

The most persuasive of all arguments for an NIT is its association with individual dignity. As currently administered, welfare degrades both those who administer it and those who ostensibly benefit from it. Once welfare is translated into universal income guarantees, it is possible to substitute the neutral, universally and equally detested bureaucracy of the Internal Revenue Service for the disdained, special-interest welfare officials. Possibly the greatest of psychic benefits a humane society confers upon its inhabitants is a secure confidence in personal worth. Such a sense makes life tolerable for those blessed by it. From society's standpoint, decent self-regard encourages the character of individual effort which eventuates in training, active job search, and subsequent productive contribution.

Controls.   Among economists, traditional dislike of price and wage controls is allied to a strong preference for free markets. Like other branches of theology, free-market economics is an idealized version of human arrangements. The case for permanent controls is associated with a shortage of free markets, the affection of most Americans for size in corporations as well as defensive linemen, and the consequent reluctance of Presidents and Congresspeople to apply antitrust statutes effectively to the giant corporations which dominate the American economy.

Market power confers, upon those who possess it, the discretion to choose—within varying but usually wide limits—combinations of high prices and reduced sales, or alternative packages of low prices and larger sales. In general, market leaders opt for an inflationary strategy, a combination of high prices and heavy advertising. So, no doubt, would you and I behave, if we were lucky enough to be oligopolists. Wage and price controls will not improve the behavior of Arab oil producers nor alleviate shortages of food and fertilizer. Wage and price controls do appropriately react to that element of inflation which derives from the exercise of concentrated market power. Since in the absence of unanticipated alterations in the American economy, large economic units will continue to dominate the scene and their managers will continue, without effective public supervision, to engage in private planning, the appropriate response is to make public supervision effective.

For the real public policy choice is not between planning and competition, it is between private planning regulated by the self-interest of autonomous corporate managers and private planning supervised by elected officials and their agents. Wage and price controls, land-use standards, environmental and occupational safety regulations, even rationing and allocation, are not distortions of competitive markets for the adequate reason that such markets are of diminishing consequence. Indeed, a rational set of controls and regulations represents an opportunity to correct the distortions imposed upon the use of resources by the operations of concentrated private economic power.

The minimal characteristics of effective controls feature permanence and equity. Equity, of course, is an evolving concept, and one of the benefits of establishing wage-price control as a permanent government function is the development and the refinement of standards based upon experience.

Controls liberate monetary and fiscal policy, but they are not of course a substitute for such policy. During severe inflation, effective controls facilitate monetary policy by limiting the corporate borrowing required to finance inventories at rising prices. By diverting demand to controlled industries, they diminish demand in the competitive sector and simplify the tasks of fiscal policy. Controls ought be as pervasive as the departures from the economist's ideal of free competition. One should ask no more. It is dangerous to seek less.

Taxes. Since 1961 presidents and congresses have conspired to reduce taxes five times—thrice across the board in 1964, 1969, and 1971, and twice selectively in 1961 and 1965. A shrinking tax base limits funds potentially available for income maintenance, housing, health, humanpower training, and community development.

It follows that during a 1974-style inflation, sharp tax increases are potentially equitable as well as anti-inflationary if they are imposed entirely upon large inheritances and gifts, corporate profits, large private incomes, and the tax shelters which currently protect the unneedy. The $20–25 billion which such taxes might raise ought in the interests of rude justice to finance new public jobs, facilitate reductions of payroll levies upon the first portions of earnings, and finance income maintenance. If $10 billion was devoted to public jobs, an equal amount to tax reliefs for low- and moderate-income individuals and families, there would still be $5 billion remaining as a reduction of excess demand. Because some such package would be and would appear fair, it could serve as a part of an implicit social contract with unions to moderate contract demands. As tax benefits were made available, real take-home pay would rise. Possibly just as important, rank and file outrage at soaring profits and shrinking real wages would be alleviated.

Socialization of Investment: A Long-Run Prospect. My combination of public job creation, income maintenance, limitations upon property as well as labor income, and redistributive taxation is certainly open to the criticism that it promotes consumption and discourages innovation and investment. Sweden, a country whose standard of living by some measures equals the American, has for nearly half a century been administered by social democrats who have pursued far more egalitarian tax, social service, and humanpower policies than the United States. What probably counts more than after-tax income is one's position in the pecking order as measured by pretax salary and bonus. For true competitors, corporate-style, it is winning that counts, not the size of the purse.

I could be wrong. Concede, arguendo, that the present scale of rewards to managers and entrepreneurs is essential to the evocation of their present efforts and talents. Private investment would then shrink. In the absence of government response, the well-known multiplier effects of reduced investment would diminish aggregate demand and employment. I should look upon such effects with equanimity if not positive delight, for the threat of enduring depression would create favorable conditions for the expansion of public investment to fill the gap. If one believes, as I do, that our single greatest national need is an expansion of the communal enterprises which distinguish civilized from uncivilized societies, then the threats of entrepreneurs and rentiers lose their terror.

Although I consider it highly unlikely that another $25 billion extracted from the wealthy and strong will seriously alter the American version of market capitalism, I will happily take the risk.

—1974

Harry Magdoff and Paul M. Sweezy
KEYNESIAN CHICKENS COME HOME TO ROOST

As we have argued many times in these pages, the monopoly capitalist economy is always in danger of sinking into a state of deep stagnation. There have to be counteracting forces, and there are: otherwise the whole system would have gone down the drain long ago. On the one hand there must be massive injections of purchasing power to supplement the restricted consumption generated by the normal workings of the system; and on the other hand there must be continuously maintained incentives, chiefly in the form of a steadily rising price level, for the rich minority to invest their lavish incomes. Like a leaking tire, the economy must be unflaggingly pumped up if it is not to go flat and come to a full stop.

The simple leaking-tire analogy, however, fails in one respect. As long as the economy is pumped up enough to keep going, all the monopolistic forces within it work overtime to increase their share of the take. This means higher prices, higher rates, higher fees, higher costs all along the line. And this perpetual scramble for more on the part of the powerful and the privileged exacerbates the underlying disproportions which are at the root of the system's malfunctioning. To complete our analogy we would have to say that both the tire and the leak grow with the passage of time, thus requiring a continuously larger and more active pump. The three most important pumping mechanisms can be identified under the following headings: (1) the credit system, (2) government finances, and (3) the central bank.

In principle, government finances can operate either to inflate or deflate the economy. In practice, they almost always operate as an inflator. The hallmark of sovereignty, Veblen once remarked, is the right to make war; he might have added a second, the right to create money. The normal bias is toward an expansionary policy. Any sign of financial trouble, as after the Penn Central bankruptcy in 1970, or a threatened increase in the unemployment rate, which as we have seen is never further away than around the next corner, generates pressure on the central bank to shoot more money into the system.

Let us put together a few figures indicating the extent to which the pumping mechanisms have been operating in the latest period. First, selected data on the growth of debt, which reflects the pumping activity of the credit system. In Table 1 we see that the average rate of increase of bank loans during the upswing of 1971–

Table 1: Commercial Bank Loans

End of year	Billions of $	Percent increase
1965	198.2	—
1966	213.9	8.1
1967	231.3	8.1
1968	258.2	11.6
1969	279.1	8.1
		avg. 9.0
1970	291.7	4.5
1971	320.3	9.8
1972	377.8	18.0
1973	444.5	17.7
		avg. 15.2

Source: The Economic Report of the President, February, 1974, p. 31.

1973 was almost 70 percent higher than in the Vietnam war boom years 1965–1969.

Second, take consumer installment credit, always an important factor in the demand for consumer durable goods: Table 2. What is especially noteworthy is the way this series took off during 1972 and 1973; even allowing for inflation (i.e., measuring in constant 1967 dollars), additions to installment credit in 1972–1973 ran at around double the rate of the preceding years.

Finally, mortgage debt, which in the aggregate is much larger than all other types of consumer credit put together. It used to be that most mortgage debt was incurred in order to build new housing, but in recent years more and more people have been mortgaging or re-mortgaging their homes to acquire money for other purposes. Table 3 goes back to 1961 to illustrate this trend more clearly.

Table 2: Net Annual Increases in Consumer Installment Credit

	Billions of current $	Billions of 1967 $
1965	8.2	8.7
1966	5.3	5.5
1967	3.2	3.2
1968	8.3	8.0
1969	9.4	8.6
1970	5.0	4.3
1971	9.2	7.6
1972	16.0	12.8
1973	20.8	15.6

Source: The Economic Report of the President, February, 1974, p. 320.

From our present point of view the most important thing about this table is the sensational jump in the rate of increase in mortgage debt formation since the relatively depressed year 1970 (the additional debt formed in the first half of 1973 was running at an annual rate nearly double that of 1970). No doubt whatever that this part of the credit system was pumping at or near full capacity. The table also shows clearly the trend to greater non-housing uses of mortgage debt.

Table 3: Net New Mortgage Debt and Its Uses (Billions of $)

	Net new mortgage debt (1)	Outlays for new homes (2)	Other uses of mortgage debt (3)
		(Column 3 = 1 minus 2)	
1961	21.0	17.4	3.6
1962	23.8	19.1	4.7
1963	27.1	18.7	8.4
1964	29.4	19.1	10.3
1965	29.8	19.0	9.9
1966	28.5	18.6	9.9
1967	27.5	15.8	11.7
1968	33.2	20.8	12.4
1969	35.6	21.2	14.4
1970	32.1	18.1	14.0
1971	44.8	26.6	18.2
1972	59.8	35.6	24.2
1973 (first half)	62.8	41.1	21.8

Data are for 1–4 family houses, as estimated by the Conference Board. The data in column (1) are estimates of the flow of new mortgage money made available to consumers each year. They therefore differ from the Federal Reserve Board series which measures only mortgage debt outstanding.

Source: The Conference Board Statistical Bulletin, November, 1973.

We turn now to the pumping mechanism labeled "government finances." In the decade 1945–1954 there were five deficit years and five of surplus (including one year of a balanced budget). In the next decade, 1955–1964, there were seven deficit years and three surplus. And in the nine years 1965–1973, there were eight deficits and one surplus. But even more striking is the way the size of the deficits has been growing. Table 4 shows the deficits from 1965 to the present. Taking into account that 1968 was the peak year of U.S. military involvement in Southeast Asia (more than half a million troops in the region that year), one need only glance at the table to see what has been happening; and even including 1968, the cumulative deficit of the first four years of the 1970s was more than 80 percent greater than the cumulative deficit of the last four years of the 1960s. No mistaking the fact that this pumping mechanism too has been very busy these last few years!

Finally, we come to the role of the central bank in expanding the money supply: Table 5. The huge rates of increase attained in

**Table 4: Balance of Federal Receipts
and Outlays (Billions of $)**

(Plus = surplus, minus = deficit)	
Fiscal 1965	−1.6
1966	−3.8
1967	−8.7
1968	−25.2
1969	+3.2
1970	−2.8
1971	−23.0
1972	−23.2
1973	−14.3

Source: The Economic Report of the President,
February, 1974, p. 123.

1971 and 1972 were cut back in 1973, but, even so, only to
approximately the rate which characterized the years of peak
involvement in the Vietnam war. As in the case of the other
pumping mechanisms reviewed, this one seems to have reached an
altogether new and higher level of activity during the 1970s.

With all the pumps going full tilt and prices rising at an
accelerating rate, you might at least expect that this most recent
period would have been one of relatively full utilization of labor
and manufacturing capacity. But if you had this expectation, you
would be mistaken—see Table 6. Here again we observe a phe-

Table 5: Growth of the Money Supply

	Billions of $	Percentage increase
1965	463	—
1966	485	4.8
1967	533	9.9
1968	577	8.3
1969	594	3.0
1970	641	7.9
1971	727	13.4
1972	822	13.1
1973	893	8.6

Source: The Economic Report of the President, February,
1974, p. 310.

Table 6: Unemployment and Manufacturing Capacity Utilization

	Unemployment as percent of civilian labor force	Percent of manufacturing capacity utilized
1965	4.5	89.0
1966	3.8	91.9
1967	3.8	87.9
1968	3.6	87.7
1969	3.5	86.5
1970	4.9	78.3
1971	5.9	75.0
1972	5.6	78.6
1973	4.9	83.0

Source: Economic Report of the President, February, 1974, pp. 279, 291.

nomenon with which we are familiar by now: the apparent establishment of new norms in the 1970s as compared to the second half of the 1960s. The lowest unemployment rate in the later period is substantially higher than the highest in the earlier, and the highest utilization rate in the 1970s is well below the lowest in the second half of the 1960s. Despite all the pumping with its attendant price inflation, the economy has been limping along at far less than its officially rated capacity. Moreover, except in the area of prices, the responsiveness of the system to more and more vigorous pumping seems to be on the decline. Such was the situation which existed as the economy entered one of its regular cyclical downswings, this time aggravated and intensified by the so-called energy crisis and a worldwide shortage of food which has greatly increased the demand for U.S. agricultural exports and sent domestic food prices sky high. What we seem likely to get is both a recession and still more inflation.

Is there any alternative? Yes, of course there is. Let the recession take its natural course and turn into a full-fledged depression. Then let the depression get as bad as necessary to deflate the debt and price structure, which has always been the functional role of panics and depressions in the operation of capitalism. Finally, start all over again in a situation from which the worst distortions and disproportions produced by decades of inflation have been squeezed out.

The trouble of course is that this is roughly what happened after 1929, and the experience was so traumatic for the rulers of capitalism that they vowed never to let it happen again. Fortunately for them, at least so it seemed, John Maynard Keynes came along at about this time with what he claimed to be the solution of the problem. Keynes argued that the capitalist system could be rescued from depression and kept on a more or less stable high-employment plateau by a suitable combination of fiscal and monetary policies (deficit government spending and increasing the money supply, two closely related processes, as we have already seen). Since the Second World War every time a recession looked as though it might get worse and turn into an old-fashioned depression, the reaction of the governing circles was to turn on the deficit-spending and money-and-credit spigots. It was conceded that this would involve a certain amount of inflation—maybe 2 or 3 percent a year—but that has always been considered better for capitalism than price stability, not to speak of price deflation. For a long time all seemed to be for the best in the best of all possible capitalist worlds.

What was ignored—and still seems to be recognized only by Marxists on the left and financial conservatives on the right—is that this strategy necessarily involves a long-term increase in society's debt structure, with a parallel decline in corporate and individual liquidity.[19] Thus the economy became more and more vulnerable to the kind of shocks which in the old days used to touch off panics; and in order to guard against this recurring threat, the need for still more inflation becomes increasingly acute. Thus the near panic triggered by the Penn Central bankruptcy in 1970 was countered by a massive injection of Federal Reserve credit. Price increases, a bloated credit structure, feverish speculation all had to be tolerated and actually spurred on in order to stave off the dreaded deflation which in times gone by was capitalism's "natural" cure for such ills.

The Keynesian chickens, so freely released from the coop these past three decades, are coming home to roost with a vengeance. The gentle, stimulating, 2 to 3 percent inflation which used to be envisaged and welcomed has turned into a raging flood which is wildly out of control and beyond the possibility of measurement by any one of the traditional indexes.

Jacob Morris, writing in the September 1973 issue of *Monthly Review*, put the matter succinctly when he compared inflation with a drug which had turned from being tonic to being toxic.

The irony is that we may be no better able to survive the poison.

—1974

Leonall C. Andersen
THE U.S. ECONOMIC OUTLOOK: POLICY ASPECTS

Four major propositions guided the implementation of economic stabilization policy over most of the last decade: (1) The dominant view was that fiscal actions, that is, changes in government spending and taxing programs, were the most effective means for guiding the course of output along a full employment path. (2) Monetary actions were viewed as being of minor importance. Federal Reserve actions were assigned an accommodative role in the sense that they should be directed toward promoting a level of market interest rates consistent with the overall intent of stabilization policy. In other words, fiscal policy was given the major responsibility for guiding economic activity; and monetary policy was given an accommodative responsibility for assuring that high interest rates did not choke off desired expansion of output. (3) Stabilization actions should be used primarily for short-run management of aggregate demand. (4) Selective income and price policies could be useful in controlling inflation arising in monopolized industries and in industries dominated by powerful unions. Stabilization authorities were very busy over the past decade, attempting to guide the economy along the path of full employment without inflation. Over almost all of the past decade, their actions were based on the premises just outlined.

The major policy tool this past decade was fiscal action. To cite just a few examples of its use: there was the Revenue Act of 1964, which included across-the-board reductions in personal and corporate income taxes; the Revenue and Expenditure Control Act of 1968, which imposed a temporary 10 percent surcharge on personal and corporate income taxes; and the on-again, off-again investment tax credit. At times, such as in 1969, 1971, and 1973, attempts were made to hold down increases in government spending.

The Federal Reserve was also very active in economic stabilization during the past ten years. For example, from 1964 to 1973, the Federal Open Market Committee met 141 times, and at 70 percent of these meetings a policy of restraint was adopted. Only in 1967 and 1970 did the FOMC adopt a policy of ease at virtually every meeting.

Throughout most of the past decade FOMC actions were directed mainly toward promoting an appropriate level of market interest rates. For the most part, these actions can be said to have been accommodative, in the sense that even if interest rates were permitted to rise they were restricted to levels believed to be not so high as to interfere with the achievement of full employment. When more emphasis was given to movements in monetary aggregates late in the decade, open market transactions were still subject to an interest rate constraint.

Finally, when inflation became severe in 1971, price and wage controls were adopted. Since then, these controls have gone through two complete cycles—from freeze to guidelines and thaw, and back to freeze, guidelines and phase-out. For the most part, these controls were administered on a selective basis.

What have been the end results of these activist economic stabilization actions over the past decade? Our economy has experienced a high and accelerating rate of inflation, which still persists. There was a recession in 1970, followed by a period of slow recovery. At the present time our economy is undergoing what some have labeled "stagflation." Market interest rates rose to their highest levels in 50 years. At times severe dislocations occurred in commodity, labor, and financial markets. It is quite apparent that economic stabilization actions have not produced desired results.

Accelerating inflation started when our economy began to operate at capacity levels, in 1966. In 1970 and 1971, when output fell and continued to remain considerably below capacity, inflation accelerated. It is thus apparent that it is a fallacy to base policy actions on the proposition that stabilization policy need be concerned about inflation only when aggregate demand is pushed beyond our economy's productive potential, and that the rate of inflation will quickly subside if aggregate demand is held below productive potential.

An activist policy cannot easily guide aggregate demand in such a manner as to promote a relatively low unemployment rate with little inflation. Since 1961, the beginning of activism in economic stabilization, the unemployment rate has averaged 4.9 percent. This is the same as in the Eisenhower years, a period which most activists would contend was not particularly noted for efforts to promote a substantially lower unemployment rate. The major difference between these two episodes is the rate of inflation. The overall price index rose at a 2 percent average annual rate from 1952 to 1960, and averaged the same from 1960 to 1968; but since then it has risen at about a 5 percent rate.

Experience over the past ten years casts strong doubts regarding the effectiveness of fiscal actions—the cornerstone of stabilization policy. Adoption of the income surtax of 1968 and the imposition of curbs on government spending since 1968 were taken for the purpose of slowing growth of total spending in the economy. With the exception of 1970, a recession year, total spending growth accelerated each year. For the whole period 1968 to 1973, total spending rose at an 8 percent annual rate, compared with a 7 percent rate from 1960 to 1968, and a 5 percent rate from 1952 to 1960.

Monetary Action.   There is evidence consistent with the proposition that inflation is primarily a monetary phenomenon. This proposition holds that an increase in the trend growth of money is followed by an increase in the rate of inflation. This proposition attributes the basic cause of our inflation to the accelerating trend growth of money since the mid-1960s. Money rose at about a 2 percent average annual rate from 1952 to 1962, accelerated to a 4 percent rate to 1966, accelerated further to 6 percent to 1971, and has been about a 7 percent rate since then. Studies present evidence consistent with the proposition that short-run accelerations and decelerations in the rate of money growth are followed by similar movements in growth of real output. It is thus concluded that monetary actions are an important cause of the business cycle.

Another lesson is that government deficits are an important cause of accelerating money growth. The amount of government debt held by the Federal Reserve System has risen at a much faster rate since the early 1960s than debt outstanding. As a result, the System's holdings of government debt rose from 11 percent of the total outstanding in 1961 to 23 percent in 1973. These rapidly growing purchases of government securities provided much of the basis for the accelerating growth of money.

If inflation is to be avoided, actions should be carried out on a long-run basis, not on the short-run basis suggested by the dominant view. Monetary actions during the last ten years have been directed at various times toward achieving such short-run objectives as lower market interest rates, protection of thrift institutions, or a reduction of the unemployment rate. In attempting to achieve these objectives, the trend rate of money growth was ratcheted upward. The end result has been the present high trend rate of monetary expansion and high inflation.

It is my opinion that the economic outlook depends greatly on how stabilization actions are altered in view of these lessons. As I see it, stabilization authorities have three options. The first one is to follow the advice of such economists as Walter Heller to stimulate the economy by a tax cut. The second option is to learn to live with the present inflation, as suggested recently by Milton Friedman. The third option is to set in motion monetary actions to reduce the rate of inflation over the next several years. I personally do not agree with the Heller proposal, which is based on the dominant views of the past decade. I find the Friedman proposal to be just as objectionable. It is an abdication in the fight against inflation.

So, I am left with the last alternative course of action. It is my view that a proper course of monetary actions can successfully reduce the rate of inflation. This course would be for monetary authorities to produce a gradual, but persistent, reduction in the rate of money growth during the balance of the 1970s. I prefer a gradual reduction so as to avoid a severe jolt to output and employment. Such a policy would be facilitated by a balanced government budget, an acceptance of temporarily higher interest rates, an acceptance of slower growth in output for a year or so, and a realization that time will be required to reduce inflation to the level of 1958 to 1964.

—1974

Richard B. DuBoff and Edward S. Herman
THE NEW ECONOMICS: HANDMAIDEN OF INSPIRED TRUTH[20]

New Economists[21] have formulated a dogma admirably suited to the needs of a government openly hostile to liberal reform. The New Economists share the ideology and values of the dominant power groups in American society. They have considerably more rapport with government and business executives than with, say, ghetto residents, union organizers, members of the Union for Radical Political Economics, or socially concerned Third World economists. The primary intellectual weapon that economists have furnished for regressive fiscal and monetary policies is the doctrine of "economic growth." The triumph of the "New Economics" of growth took place during the "New Frontier" of John F. Kennedy. It was celebrated by Paul Samuelson in a valedictory statement in November 1968. "Our economic system," Samuelson exulted,

> in the 1960s has far surpassed the prophecies of even the most optimistic experts. *The New Economics really does work.* Wall Street knows it. Main Street, which has been enjoying 92 months of advancing sales, knows it. The accountants who chalk up record corporate profits know it . . . and so do the school nurses who measure the heights and weights of this generation and remember the bony structure of the last. You can bet that the statisticians of the Kremlin know it—down to the last hundred million of GNP.
>
> Who does not know it? Of course, the exponents of orthodox finance deny the obvious . . . And how could the New Left forget what it has never learned, or wanted to know?[22]

Growth is "the pot of gold *and* the rainbow," in the words of Walter Heller.[23] Growth produces jobs, rising personal consumption, dynamic technology, national power, and, of course, the famous "growth dividend" that supposedly provides an ever-increasing quantity of resources to the public sector for dealing with the problems our society faces without any fundamental changes in political and social institutions.

As Walter Heller contended, "When the cost of fulfilling a people's aspirations can be met out of a growing horn of plenty—instead of robbing Peter to pay Paul—ideological roadblocks melt away, and consensus replaces conflict."[24] And according to Arthur Okun, "Particularly in the early 1960s, far greater gains were to be made by fighting to enlarge the size of the national economic pie than by pressing proposals to increase equity and efficiency in sharing the pie. Improved overall performance of the national economy could be legitimately sold as good for everybody, and thus fitted into the Johnsonian consensus approach."[25] These economists appear to believe that however regressive the means for initiating growth, the resulting "dividend" will somehow become available to provide benefits later. This is a refined "trickle-down" theory. The New Economists give short shrift to E. J. Mishan's thesis that "growth" in advanced capitalist countries, with modern technology and private profit systems, produces "disamenities" faster than amenities. In the world of the new economics, the phenomenon of multiplying negative externalities is a qualification, a correctible deviation of the primrose path to ever higher levels of GNP.

From the very first triumphs of the "new economics," starting in 1961, growth without reform was the order of the day. The New Economists surrendered unconditionally to the growth syndrome and, along with JFK, beat a total retreat from reform. Tax reform in particular was sold down the river. "This [investment tax] credit," Nixon cannily reminded Congress "was advocated by a Democratic President and enacted by a Democratic Congress in the 1960s." The same could have been said for his accelerated depreciation allowances and suggested tax cuts nourishing middle-class private consumption—both cornerstones of New Frontier economics. The major Kennedy-Johnson tax policies were the investment credit of mid-1962[26] and the Revenue Act of February, 1964, proposed by President Kennedy 13 months earlier. The first allowed a 7 percent tax credit for businesses on purchases of machinery and equipment, as well as more favorable depreciation schedules. It reduced corporate taxes by $5 billion through 1966 and by $3 billion per year from 1967 through mid-1969. The second—the "magnificent tax cut"—provided for regressive personal and corporate income tax cuts.[27] These policies left virtually untouched all the notorious tax loopholes. They returned over $12 billion to middle and upper income families, while the Administration scrounged around to find $1 billion for a "war on poverty." In 1962, just after the peak of the debate over "tax cuts versus tax reform," Council of Economic Advisers (CEA) member James Tobin had declared:

> Redistribution of income and wealth by taxation and government transfer payments was in days gone by another rallying point for liberal political movements. The fire has gone out of this one too. The current liberal political movement, the New Frontier, is providing incentives for business investment through new tax legislation and new depreciation guidelines. The Kennedy Administration is, from all indications, about to be the vehicle for a general reduction in corporate and personal income tax rates, and in particular for substantial lowering of top-bracket rates.[28]

Military Money. Typically, the New Economists treat military spending in a negative and altogether trivial manner: they will talk about it only to deny that it is "necessary" for continued prosperity in America. People who hold that it is, or may be, "necessary" in view of the existing structure of political interests are impatiently dismissed as "Marxian critics" (by Paul Samuelson) or "left-wing foreign critics" (by James Tobin). The relationship between brand-name economists and the most expansive years of American militarism and imperialism can be traced back at least to 1958. At that time, the Eisenhower Administration was coming under attack for its efforts to trim the military budget. The major Democratic Presidential aspirants joined the assault against the Eisenhower defense policy. So did a number of their economists.

The economics underlying this developing Democratic strategy was the thesis that the sluggish U.S. economy, and its high propensities to consume, were shackling us in our "race" with

Khrushchev's Russia. Powerful ammunition for these charges was furnished by J. K. Galbraith's *The Affluent Society;* Galbraith's analysis of the "scientific and technical" margin the Soviets held, and "our failure to match this [Sputnik] achievement," concluded that the causes lay in excessive private consumption. "Our economy, and the economic theory that explains and rationalizes its behavior, immobilizes all but a minor fraction of the product in private and, from the standpoint of national security, irrelevant production . . . A society which sets as its highest goal the production of private consumer goods will continue to reflect such attitudes in all its public decisions."[29]

In 1958 James Tobin, later to join John F. Kennedy's first CEA, opened fire on the Eisenhower Administration for not spending enough on defense. Tobin was incredulous: "At a time when the world situation cried out for accelerating and enlarging our defense effort, the Administration *released* money, labor, scientific talent, materials, and plant capacity."[30] Tobin was echoed by Walter Heller. In testimony before the Joint Economic Committee of Congress, Heller accused the Eisenhower Administration of an "obsession" with cutting expenditures and balancing the budget at a time when the country faced "the possibility of annihilation or humiliation," and when "much of our affluence is being frittered away in indulgences, luxuries, and frivolities." The result, he said, was "as great a risk, calculated or otherwise, as this country has ever incurred in peacetime economic policy."[31] This Party line was taken up by another economist soon to join the New Frontier—W. W. Rostow. The solution, for Rostow and other Cold War liberals, was "a high rate of growth in gross national product."[32]

Once Kennedy assumed the Presidency, he sharply stepped up military outlays, despite his discovery that the "missile gap" he had emphasized in his campaign was only fictional.[33] "First," he said in his initial Annual Message on January 30, 1961, "we must strengthen our military tools." The fact of U.S. military superiority notwithstanding, the new President "foresaw the likelihood of international events forcing an increase in defense expenditures and wished to avoid any tag of fiscal irresponsibility."[34] So in 1961 the Administration increased the defense budget 16 percent— doubling the number of combat-ready divisions in the Army's strategic reserve, expanding the Marine Corps, adding 70 vessels to the active fleet, and giving a dozen more wings to the tactical air forces. Overall, military outlays constituted "75 percent of the increases of [total federal] expenditures under Kennedy through fiscal year 1964."[35] Samuelson still views the question of "defense expenditure and prosperity" simply as "an important digression" within a general theme of an endlessly growing GNP, achievable through rationally managed liberal fiscal and monetary policies.[36]

The New Economists and the Vietnam War. As the war pre-empted the resources and attention of the Johnson Administration and swallowed up the "growth dividend," the New Economists effortlessly shifted gears and accommodated to this new set of politico-military "givens." Now "growth" was to be touted as offering the nation "guns *and* butter" during wartime. The CEA *Annual Report* of January 1966 reassured the President that "Since 1953, the country has invested mightily in defense; it has continually rolled over its stock of defense goods and equipment to take advantage of new developments in weapons systems and has maintained general purpose defense capabilities. The Vietnam conflict, therefore, finds us well prepared. The procurement and personnel increases are modest by earlier standards and by comparison with total supply capabilities."[37] "Today," added CEA consultant George L. Perry, "the demands of the Vietnam war are being met with only the mildest restraints on current production for other purposes. Because of the long and sustained surge of business investment that started in 1963, adequate industrial capacity is available."[38] "Objective" economists were again following the Democratic administration's political line and supplying its economic sales pitch. "It's hard to find a time when the economy has been closer to equilibrium than it is today," CEA member Okun stated in late 1965—exactly the opposite of what he knew was happening.[39] The January 1966 *CEA Report* (Okun, Eckstein, and chairman Gardner Ackley) glowed with satisfaction over the performance of the economy through 1965:

> It was the fifth year of uninterrupted economic expansion, and the second year of declining unemployment as output moved closer to

the economy's growing productive potential . . . Living standards have risen at an unprecedented rate, and businessmen have found new and stronger incentives to expand and modernize their productive facilities . . . Today, our vigorous economy is in a strong position to carry the new burdens imposed by expanded national defense requirements. With another large advance in total production ahead, defense needs will be met while living standards again improve strongly and the capital stock is further enlarged.[40]

Walter Heller (by now back at the University of Minnesota), Joseph Pechman of the Brookings Institution, and George L. Bach of Stanford took the lead in LBJ's pro-surtax campaign, which soon gathered the signatures of 320 economists, nearly all liberals. Their "Statement on Tax Policy" contained not a word about Vietnam. The closest it came was in referring to the threat of "a resurgence of inflation . . . given the projected size of military outlays."[41] Pechman presented this "Statement" to the House Ways and Means Committee, accompanied with these remarks: "During the past 6½ years, the Nation has enjoyed the strongest and longest peacetime business expansion in history. The value and importance of maintaining prosperity and a high rate of economic growth is visible everywhere." (This was after nearly three years of savagely escalating warfare in Indochina, and it was a scant two months after the explosions in Newark and Detroit.) Yet the 10 percent surtax was needed, Pechman went on, to deal with "the problems of prosperity [which are] unhappily, also visible to everybody. The record of price stability, which helped to make this expansion so enviable, was broken about 20 months ago." Vietnam was mentioned only in passing:

> Now that we know more definitely how much more the Vietnam war will cost this fiscal year, the economic prospects are clear. The economy has come through a trying period in very good shape . . . After a summer of riots in many of our major cities, it would be foolish to single out the Nation's welfare and poverty programs as targets for budget cuts. The urban crisis demands attention even though we are fighting a war.[42]

The only scintilla of honor the economics profession could claim by 1968 was provided by an anti-surtax petition, first circulated by Robert Eisner (Northwestern), William Nordhaus (Yale), Kenneth Boulding (Colorado), John Gurley (Stanford), R. A. Gordon (Berkeley), Edwin Kuh (MIT), and Wassily Leontief (Harvard). The letter had 320 signatures by January, 1968, when it was released. "To some of us," Eisner commented, "the tax surcharge proposal threatened to become a sort of economic Gulf of Tonkin resolution, offering advance financing of all the additional men and resources the Administration might decide to commit to Vietnam ... it is sobering to think that so many [economists] are ready to make policy decisions without any deeper insights into the underlying economic relations, let alone their broader political context."[43]

Pragmatic Economists. An elementary economic truth provides the best insight into the malaise of conventional economics and its "new" practitioners. It is something every introductory economics student learns but that his teachers seem incapable of digesting: namely, that if private investment is one way to create jobs, public investment is another. Not a single liberal economist of national reputation has pushed vigorously for public investment in recent years, except for Galbraith, viewed by many of his colleagues as a sort of curious maverick, "more like a modern Thorstein Veblen (big on insight, small on science) than a modern Keynes."[44]

The chronic unwillingness to come to grips with the public sector problem reveals once again where most New Economists stand—squarely in favor of the status quo, albeit with occasional discomfort. Their reformism is shriveled, limited by conservative premises. As liberals and humane individuals, many of them desire an eradication of war, poverty, racism, urban decay, pollution, and social disintegration; but mainstream economists do not really care enough about these objectives to press for them in the light of their short-run "impracticality" and obnoxiousness to men of power. Furthermore, even insofar as these economists give any weight to reform or radical change, their own "growth" ideology leaves them being wagged by the dog's tail, constantly chasing after "reforms" that, somehow or another, seem to get put off and subordinated to the needs of one "crisis" or another.

Some years ago, Otto Eckstein expressed the core of this philosophy: "Our economic system has travelled too far down the road of relying on corporations for the accumulation and management of investible funds to change direction now."[45] To this James Tobin later added that for reducing unemployment in our economy, "the major reliance must be on business expenditures for plant and equipment."[46]

Concluding Note. The conservative and accommodationist politics of the New Economists should surprise no one. There was a brief period when Keynesian ideas were novel and were regarded as threatening by important segments of the business community. At the same time there was even a strand of Left Keynesianism, which used the new economics as a method of social analysis and emphasized its radical implications for income distribution and the role of the state; but there was always a larger group of Keynesians who stressed the "tool" aspects of the new doctrine, along with its "policy neutrality"—its serviceability to policymakers for carrying out whatever objectives they might choose to plug in; the New Economists represent the triumph of that "pragmatic" school. In fact, the critical potential of Keynesian economics never was very great, and the extended prosperity following the Second World War led to its swift decline. The long economic boom, buttressed by massive government spending, was considered to be a vindication of applied macroeconomics. The practicality of this brand of Keynesianism, plus the opportunities it provided for technically oriented model-builders and statisticians, assured the growth and success of the pragmatic school. This was largely a case of a rising demand eliciting an appropriate supply response.

For economists who do effectively service the dominant forces of the system, the rewards are substantial—money, influence, power, and ready access to the media. By the same token, economists who seek such benefits can obtain them only through accommodation to the existing power structure, dealing with it on its own terms, and affiliating with its institutionalized elements (the Democratic Party, blue-ribbon panels, "think tanks," government committees, research and consulting firms). Once settled in this camp, economists become part of the economic and social elite itself—they develop natural ties to the dominant elements in society and similar personal interests in the status quo.[47] They are subject to what Malthus called "the insensible bias of situation and interest," so that the inspired truth to which New Economists are dedicated is part of a class interest which they themselves share.

—1972

Oil

To know whether we can extricate ourselves from the grip of oil shortages, inflation and unemployment we must first know what happened and why. Second, we must look at the policy instruments which we have relied upon for the past fifteen years in order to appraise whether they are still usable and useful. Third, we must integrate short-run and long-run perspectives. If we do not, directions which appear as plausible routes out of present difficulties may end up compounding still more the difficulties of making the right basic choices which are discussed in the final section of the book.

Our modern troubles took a giant step when the oil embargo was imposed in October, 1973. The background to that event is provided by Dankwart A. Rustow's history of the U.S. policies in the oil countries of the Middle East. The story begins with our role in the deposition of Mossadegh in Iran and in the consolidation by the big seven international oil companies of a dominant position in the area. As the governments steadily took over control of crude oil supplies and prices, the companies tightened their control over refining and distribution in world markets, including the United States, with the cooperation of our own government. As revenues flowed in huge amounts into OPEC bank accounts, so rose the profits of the oil companies. William Leonard shows how domestic political decisions enhanced the power of the oil companies and increased our vulnerability to boycott, shifting the balance of incentives to the companies to develop oil abroad rather than here while increasing our addiction to oil in every aspect of personal, social and economic life. Press reports showed the oil companies working hard to reduce production immediately before the embargo; Christopher T. Rand revealed[1] that domestic oil stocks were higher at the height of the embargo than a year earlier when oil was in ample supply. Arthur F. Burns, Chairman of the Board of Governors of the Federal Reserve System, spelled out the financial flows resulting from the fourfold price increases of 1973–74. His analysis omits any reference to the oil companies; neither their role in creating the crisis nor their responsibilities for helping to resolve it are mentioned. But the oil companies now control a major share of the total energy industry; their decisions, past and future, have everything to do with the future supply, cost and use of energy.

Barry Commoner fleshes out the case for public decision-making across the whole spectrum of energy-related economic activities, particularly the consumption patterns in agriculture and transportation, and the rich possibilities of developing alternatives to oil and fossil fuels.

Dankwart A. Rustow
PETROLEUM POLITICS 1951–1974

The Arab countries hide beneath their sands most of the world's known petroleum, accounting for one-third of total production and three-fifths of shipments in interregional trade. Seven oil companies, five of them American, are among the 16 leading multinational corporations, their combined sales totaling $63 billion, or more than the gross national product of India and Pakistan.

In the ten weeks from October 17 to December 25, 1973, the Arab and United States governments and the multinational oil companies acted out the climax of a tense drama, with the nation of Israel, the American consumer, and the peoples of Japan and Europe assigned for the moment to the supporting cast. But this climax was only the fourth of five acts, with the finale still in the future.

Act One: Company Control (1951–1955). The drama as a whole begins more than two decades ago as Iran's aging, aristocratic, principled, nationalist, tearful prime minister, Muhammad Mossadegh, proclaims the nationalization of the Iranian assets of the British Petroleum Company, then constituting one of the largest oil-producing complexes in the world. The British Royal Navy briefly appears in the wings but decides against gunboat diplomacy and steams off. Enter instead the multinational oil companies, also known as the Seven Sisters: Exxon, Shell, B.P., Texáco, Standard of California, Gulf, and Mobil.[2] Secure in their control of the Middle East's remaining oil production, of two-thirds of the world's tanker fleet, and more than half of non-Communist refinery capacity, they refuse to load, ship, or sell what little oil Mossadegh's nationalized operation manages to produce. Enter, too, the Arab countries, foremost Kuwait and Saudi Arabia, which under the aegis of the Seven Sisters quickly augment their production by whatever is missing from Iran, and then some.

Mossadegh by now is on the outs with the Shah, the Iranian army, and the Western powers. Unable to sell his oil yet refusing to retreat from nationalization he is reduced to shifting alliances, now with reactionary *mullahs* and then with the Communist Tudeh party. The climax of the First Act comes in 1953, when Mossadegh is overthrown in a military coup secretly encouraged by the U.S. Central Intelligence Agency.

Meanwhile, across the Persian Gulf, the king of Saudi Arabia, following an earlier precedent from Venezuela, signs a "50–50" profit-sharing agreement with Aramco, the joint subsidiary of four of the Seven Sisters. It gives the Saudis a share of oil income three times as large as that previously allowed to Iran, and it is hailed as a farsighted act of American statesmanship, in contrast to the perfidious skinflint ways of the imperialist British. But the increase to 50 percent is payable in "income tax," not "royalty," and as such comes under a special United States Treasury ruling making it deductible as a full credit against U.S. taxes on the foreign operations of American companies, including their joint subsidiaries. The increased payments, therefore, occasion no expense to the companies but are borne instead by the U.S. taxpayer.

In the final scene, the same beneficent 50–50 scheme is extended to Iran, the team of helpful Americans this time being headed by Undersecretary of State Herbert Hoover, Jr. To save pride—the restored Shah is almost as proud as his archrival Mossadegh—Iran retains its "property" title in the oil fields on condition of returning their "operation" to the international oil companies. Just incidentally, B.P. agrees to yield three-fifths of these "operating" rights to other multinationals, five of them American, one British-Dutch, and one French. Of course there is full compensation, computed by sisterly agreement; and of course the British and French taxpayers are assigned a role just as helpful and statesmanlike as that vouchsafed to their American cousins.

As the curtain drops, the seven companies still dominate the stage, their rights confirmed and their profits at customary levels. The oil income of Middle Eastern governments has gone up from $200 million in 1950 to $1 billion in 1955. And the Western taxpayer has made his debut as the dupe of the play.

Act Two: The Stage Expands (1955–1970). After the hectic pace of Act One, Act Two seems all in slow motion. The predominance of the Seven Sisters is challenged by a number of newcomers: American independents (that is, companies with no previous sources of foreign petroleum), and companies from Western Europe, Japan, and even India—all of them bent on grabbing their share of the Middle East action. Luckily for the Seven Sisters, there are few good concessions to be had just then around the oil-rich Persian Gulf.

But after the Suez War of 1956 and the consequent closing of the Canal, the oil search shifts to Arab North Africa. The richest finds are made in Libya, and this time the Seven Sisters must share the bonanza with a dozen others. Libyan governments, too, find that they can drive harder bargains with a score of companies than any Persian Gulf country can with a single consortium.

Enter OPEC, the Organization of Petroleum Exporting Countries, founded in 1960 by Venezuela, Iran, Saudi Arabia, Kuwait, and Iraq, and joined in due course by all other sizable producers of the Third World. At first it tries the monopolist's ploy of reducing production to drive up prices, and hence its members' tax take. But OPEC members cannot impose any prorationing scheme on the companies, or even agree on one among themselves. Next OPEC tries more successful schemes, such as levying the 50 percent tax on top of (rather than including) the royalty, or getting companies to agree to a "posted price" for tax purposes that disregards the customary discounts offered by subsidiaries to their parent companies. As a result the 50–50 division of profits becomes 65–35 by 1965 and 70–30 by 1969—and all this on the basis of larger rather than smaller production.

The combined pressure from independents and OPEC drives the Seven Sisters to seek new markets. In the years from 1955 to 1970, Western Europe and Japan, in a period of unheard-of industrial expansion, perform their long-term switch from coal to oil. For coal is labor intensive and must be brought up from deeper and meagerer seams, whence its price steadily rises; while Middle East oil flows freely and the companies manage to keep its price at around $2 a barrel (f.o.b. Persian Gulf). Thanks to a fivefold jump in volume and a steady production cost of around 10¢ a barrel, the companies can afford to increase their payments to Middle Eastern governments from $1 billion in 1955 to $5 billion in 1969, while still doubling their own income from the Middle East from about $1 to $2 billion.

A notable exception to this spectacular expansion of markets for Middle Eastern oil is the United States. Here the independent companies, which produce oil at a cost of $1.50 or more, induce the federal government to impose rigid import restrictions. Their rhetoric is all national defense: If the domestic producer is allowed to drown in a flood of imports, where are we to get oil in an emergency? This argument is not just (as with watches) self-serving, it is contrary to all sense. Oil is an exhaustible resource, not a manufac-
ᶦred good. By refusing to buy it abroad when cheap and free from

political strings, the United States (as will become clear in Act Three) is condemned to buying it dear and with strings. The import quota system of 1959, in the apt phrase of one critic, amounts to a "drain-America-first policy," designed to hasten—and not to ward off—the evil day.

The dunce of Act Two is the American consumer who, between protectionist prices granted to the independents and windfall profits accruing to the multinationals, is estimated to have spent an additional $3 billion to $5 billion per annum under the quota regime.

Act Three: OPEC Takes Charge (1970–73). The curtain rises over the battlefields of the Third Arab-Israeli War of 1967. The Suez Canal is closed indefinitely, forcing tankers from the Persian Gulf to Europe to go twice as far around the Cape. A bulldozer rams the TAP-line which brings much of Saudi oil to the Mediterranean, and the Syrian government takes its time over allowing repairs. With demand for oil growing at about 10 percent a year in Europe and 17 percent in Japan, the world market is tighter than ever.

OPEC in late 1970 resolves to raise the tax (after royalty) from 50 percent to 55 percent, and companies operating around the Persian Gulf agree, in the vain hope of buying a five-year respite. Instead, there are almost continuous "negotiations" increasingly resembling dictates. When the Gulf countries get their 55 percent, Libya's Colonel Qaddafi demands 60 percent, since his oil is closer to Europe and lower in sulfur. Devaluations of the dollar provide the occasion for new increases in "posted prices." Meanwhile, Algeria, then Iraq, and then Libya proceed to nationalize Western companies one by one.

Contrasting negotiating styles in Tripoli, Tehran, and Riyadh add a touch of farce to the proceedings. Colonel Qaddafi, the Koran-quoting fundamentalist who seized power at the age of twenty-seven, extracts his concessions in hour-long fire-breathing harangues. The Shah, now firmly on his throne but worried about Soviet power to the north, invokes his reasonableness and friendship with the West to obtain equal or greater concessions—which in turn provoke bigger and better tantrums from Qaddafi. Sheikh Ahmad Zaki al-Yamani, the quick-witted, Harvard-trained oil minister of Saudi Arabia, protests his dedication to free enterprise and aversion to nationalization; instead, he proposes a scheme of "participation" whereby Saudi Arabia and neighboring sheikhdoms will take over an immediate 25 percent interest in the concessions, which is to rise year by year to 51 percent in 1981. The Shah celebrates Persian New Year by "nationalizing" foreign oil "operations" (the "properties," remember, had been nationalized by Mossadegh in 1951), but, reasonable as ever, he promises to let the companies have their customary amounts of oil at cost for the remaining years of the concession. The Kuwaiti legislature, not previously noted for its independence of spirit, balks at ratifying the participation deal: why take just 25 percent now, if Iraq already has taken 51 percent?

As Act Three draws to a close, it becomes hard, even for experts, to remember the "arguments" invoked or the successive "agreements" concluded. But amid all the shadow-boxing, the Middle Eastern countries, now firmly in the vanguard of OPEC, have made three points quite clear. They alone, by sovereign power of decree if necessary, will decide how much oil is produced and offered in the world market. They and not the companies, will get the lion's share of the proceeds—about 85 percent by 1973. And they have forced, for the first time in a quarter century, a substantial increase in the world price of crude petroleum. For subsequent increases the only ceiling in sight is a level ($8 or $9 a barrel?) at which industrial countries will substantially decrease their consumption, or a level ($10 or $12?) at which large quantities of new fuels—such as oil from shale or gas from coal—may become available in the uncertain future. Straining to learn what the traffic will bear, the Arabs and Iranians find out that it will bear a great deal. In 1970 their oil income still was under $6 billion; by late 1973 it leapt to an annual rate of about $18 billion.

The seven companies, in the words of the chairman of B.P., are now little more than a "tax-collecting agency" for OPEC. Yet whatever the reversal of their Middle Eastern fortunes, they still control the world's distribution system for oil, they are maintaining (or, as we shall see, increasing) their profits, and they still are among the largest corporate giants in the economies of the Western countries.

Not surprisingly, the final scene of Act Three takes place in the United States where, from about the middle of 1972, the "energy crisis" slowly filters into public consciousness: schools closing for lack of heat, gas stations turning away customers, a major oil company advertising not the virtues or availability of its products but their imminent disappearance, the President's first "Energy Messages," and an article in *Foreign Affairs* urging a crash program for "energy independence" with a price tag of $60 billion.

By mid-1973, the crisis is widely attributed to our growing dependence on petroleum imports, particularly from unfriendly Arab countries. Senator Fulbright warns the Arabs not to be unreasonable lest more impatient Americans think of invading them, either directly or by Israeli or Iranian proxy. President Nixon pointedly asks Arab rulers to ponder the fate of Mossadegh (who could not sell his nationalized oil? Whom the CIA helped overthrow?—the President is too delicate to spell out his analogy). From the cover of *Newsweek* a young man in desert garb leers at the reader, his hand on the nozzle of a gasoline hose, under a headline proclaiming "The Arab Oil Squeeze." The *New York Times Magazine* asks more bluntly: "Can the Arabs Really Blackmail Us?"

The young Arab on the cover turns out to be a Jewish boy from Brooklyn doing some free-lance modeling in a Bedouin costume brought back from Israel. Other parts of the energy hullabaloo are, for the remainder of Act Three, almost equally misleading.

When the talk of energy crisis begins in 1972, the United States imports only about 3 percent of its petroleum from Arab countries, and petroleum itself accounts for only one-half of our primary energy consumption—the remainder being mostly natural gas and coal. Even after the lifting of the quota system in the spring of 1973, Arab oil imports amount to less than 6 percent of petroleum demand. Moreover, except for an insignificant spell in 1967, no Arab country, prior to October 1973, has ever banned *exports* to America; quite the contrary, for 14 years the Americans imposed an almost total ban on Arab and other *imports*.

By the winter of 1972–73 the United States faces two real problems with regard to petroleum: a slight decline in domestic production ever since 1970, and a shortage of port facilities and refinery capacity (particularly on the East Coast) to handle such additional imports as the federal government might allow. The first is a direct effect of the "drain-America-first policy," and the second an indirect one. For the large companies see little incentive for spending hundreds of millions on tanker ports or refineries to handle imports that the government has not yet allowed. In the resulting tight market, a third problem is posed by the same large integrated companies whose refineries give preference to their own retail outlets and thus tend to squeeze out independent competitors. All three circumstances contribute to the sporadic shortages, now of fuel oil and now of gasoline, throughout the last part of Act Three.

But the economics of import quotas, port construction, and refinery runs mean little to the houseowner without fuel, the parent whose children are sent away from unheated schools, or the motorist stranded at night. The sphinxlike Arab at the gas pump, instead, suggests a plausible origin of the riddle. Even before his appearance on the magazine cover, the multinational oil companies win several significant political and economic advantages: the freeing of imports, the reopening of the Alaska pipeline issue, reconsideration of clean-air standards, higher prices with hardly a murmur from the public, profits at all-time highs, and widespread talk of the need for federal subsidies to develop alternative energy sources at home. Their publicity campaigns indicate that they welcome public concern about the energy crisis—particularly while it focuses on such distant targets as Arab governments or worldwide patterns of demand for an exhaustible resource. The dupes of Act Three are those members of the American public who believe all they see or hear about "energy crisis" in the media, and particularly in the companies' own proliferating advertisements.

Act Four: The Arab "Oil Weapon" (1973). The scene once again is war, as Egypt and Syria attack Israel on Yom Kippur, October 6, 1973. The enormous losses of planes and tanks on both sides make it clear that American or Soviet willingness to resupply their protegés with weapons will be decisive. After some scurrying by Kissinger to Moscow and the Middle East and some pointed messages between Brezhnev and Nixon, which, in the latter's

phrase, "leave little to the imagination," it is clear that Washington
and Moscow concur on cessation rather than escalation of the
conflict. The fighting ceases on the 17th day.

On the 12th day, Arab oil ministers meeting in Kuwait
announce a two-pronged application of their "oil weapon": an
outright ban on exports to the United States as Israel's major
supplier of arms and to the Netherlands, and production cuts that
start at 15 percent but will go up by 5 percent a month until Israel
withdraws from the territories occupied in 1967 and 1973 and
grants the "just rights" of Palestinian refugees.

Gone now are Fulbright's scenarios of Israelis marching along
800 miles of pipeline to make Arab oil safe for American consumption. Gone too are Nixon's hints about Mossadegh's comeup-
pance.

Despite the explanations offered by the twinkle-eyed Sheikh
Yamani and other Arab ministers, the new Arab policy—unlike the
messages exchanged by the nuclear powers—does leave a good
deal to the imagination. Indeed, one finally imagines that this is
part of their purpose. Meanwhile only imagination and inference
can provide answers to questions such as these:

• *Why pick on the Netherlands?* The official reasons seem
farfetched. Could the real reason be that a boycott of the Netherlands, whose refinery space far exceeds domestic consumption,
hurts many European countries a little but none too much?

• *How fully do Arabs cooperate?* Not very fully, it soon
becomes clear. Algeria stands aside. Qaddafi, smarting at not even
having been told about the Yom Kippur War, is unenthusiastic.
Iraq increases output on the charming reasoning that the boycott is
too mild, that Iraq has been sending troops to the Syrian front and
now must pay for the expedition by making more money off the
capitalists. That leaves mostly the Arabian peninsula, or only two-
thirds of total Arab production, as going fully along with the
boycott.

• *What of the oil companies?* Officials of such companies as
Aramco obviously cannot defy their hosts by producing too much
or loading tankers bound for the wrong destination. But the multinational parent companies must somehow allocate their shrinking
supplies among all their customers. They retain a good deal of

discretion in supplying this or that American customer from Ecuador or Angola and in cutting back this or that customer in Europe and Japan in view of the emergency. While the multinationals retain control of the worldwide network of transport and refinery, it remains impossible for producing countries to pinpoint their boycotts precisely. Since five of the multinationals are American and the other two have large assets in the U.S., one may assume that their American customers will fare no worse than others.

• *What is the effect on industrial countries?* In the United States, the actual shortfall by mid-December is estimated to be no more than 3 or 4 percent of petroleum consumption, whereas the effects in Europe and especially Japan threaten to be far worse. The crucial fact remains that the United States, partly drained as it is, still is the world's largest oil producer and (aside from Soviet Russia) the most nearly self-sufficient consumer.

Conceivably, therefore, Americans might get by with curtailing their weekend pleasure-driving, forming carpools, reversing the decay of their railroads, and speeding the search for new domestic oil or nonoil substitutes. If Japan and Europe were caught in a massive recession and vast unemployment, moreover, American industry might even make large inroads into their export markets.

• *What of the financial effects?* Amid the general anxiety about fuel shortages, the petroleum-producing governments, also in mid-October, increase the "posted price" by a cool 70 percent. And on December 24 they increase it by an even cooler 128 percent. This time, the initiative comes from the Shah, although they all, including Yamani, the Shah, Qaddafi, and even Venezuelans, Indonesians, and Nigerians concur and are sure to cooperate. The posted price of December implies payments to Middle East producing governments of $7 a barrel, a combined Arab and Iranian oil income of $70 billion or more in 1974, and a world price of petroleum of nearly $8 a barrel f.o.b. Persian Gulf.

The day after the price increase, on Christmas day 1973, the Arab oil ministers make their last headline of the year by calling off their program of progressive cutbacks. Instead they promise to return to the 15 percent cuts of October and to confine their embargo only to the United States and the Netherlands.

Perhaps Sheikh Yamani and his friends are also using their imagination. The partially effective Arab embargo is having less of an impact in the United States than the oil industry's earlier advertisements, alarmist magazine articles, or the Nixon administration's first assessments might suggest. Specifically, in terms of any outcome at Geneva or along Israel's borders, the oil weapon is likely to prove blunt. United States opinion has been turning toward rather than away from Israel, and in any case the possibilities of American pressure on that embattled nation are limited. We can give to Israel the means of waging war or withhold them; we can even bring its representatives to the conference table; but we cannot impose on it terms of peace that it would consider disastrous. Therefore the outcome at Geneva, if any, is likely to be a tortuous compromise.

Above all—considering the comparative impact of the embargo on the United States, Western Europe, and Japan—the competitive position of American industry and of the dollar itself are likely to be strengthened, and the more so the longer the embargo lasts and the more the prices go up. No wonder that the Arab ministers decide to reverse signals while they are ahead— with Israel at the conference table, the U.S. in an even-handed posture in a nonelection year, ahead very specifically by $25 billion or more in extra revenues for 1974, and ahead with their newly won stature as world statesmen unimpaired by overplaying their hand.

Whatever the particular Arab reasoning, others have reason to breathe a temporary sigh of relief as the curtain falls on Act Four.

Act Five: The $64 Billion Question. A few optimists in Washington evidently were hoping that Henry Kissinger's opening address to the conference of oil-importing countries on February 11 would set the stage for the final act of the petroleum drama. Henry, after all, had built up an enviable diplomatic record by flying to Peking and Moscow to achieve normalcy with China and détente with Russia; to Paris and Hanoi to end the war in Vietnam; and to Moscow, Tel Aviv, and various Arab capitals to get the Arab-Israeli dispute off dead center. So much dramatic talent surely presaged a happy ending for the energy crisis. And this time Kissinger could for once abandon his jet-age diplomacy for the time-tested Metternich-Bismarck model of solving the world's problems by assembling all other statesmen back home at congresses in Vienna, Berlin, or Washington, as the case may be.

The optimists' scenario runs something like this: Canada, Western Europe, and Japan yield to Washington's pleas for a common energy policy and gratefully receive American offers of sharing technological know-how and even emergency supplies for the future. In particular, they listen to the warnings that bilateral deals between France and Saudi Arabia or Japan and Iran can only drive up prices further. Instead, they agree to multilateral diplomacy, e.g., between the Organization for Economic Cooperation and Development representing the industrial nations and OPEC— or, better yet, its individual members—representing the producers.

Before taking up these global negotiations, the industrial countries also meet with the non-oil producers of the Third World for whom, as everyone agrees, the current prices may well spell economic ruin. Meanwhile, Iranians, Arabs, and others have taken to heart the competent arithmetic and plausible syllogisms of Energy Administrator William E. Simon, which prove inexorably that the current higher prices and lower production do not really benefit the OPEC countries, since a $10 per barrel profit today invested at 8 percent compound interest will yield $21.59 in 1984— a level to which even the tightest of cartels is unlikely to push prices by then. And of course, once the oil producers step up their production and begin to lower their prices there may even be some cutthroat competition driving prices yet lower.

Alas, the optimistic scenario is unlikely to provide the actual script for Act Five. Simon and other optimists are repeating the naive mistake (made by Western observers of Mossadegh's nationalization and Nasser's seizure of the Canal) of underrating the technical competence of the players across the table. Neither the Shah nor Sheikh Yamani is an active candidate for a Nobel Prize in mathematics; still, they seem quite capable of compound-interest calculations and other exercises in fifth-grade arithmetic. Moreover, even the Washington optimists concede that "energy independence" for the United States will at best come in the 1980s, and for the rest of OECD much later, if ever. If and when the balance should shift, supply and demand (a pair of concepts so dear to American spokesmen on other occasions) will give ample warning that it is in the interest of oil-producing countries to lower their prices.

The solidarity to which Kissinger appealed was far from evident in the actions, or even the rhetoric, of other industrial countries. Instead there was a scramble by France, Japan, and others for the very bilateral deals Kissinger was denouncing. As for sharing oil supplies in an emergency, no one except the United States had offered help to the Netherlands last fall; and even if there should be any future willingness to share, there might be very little to be shared. Officials of the Common Market for years had been urging member countries to store 90 days' or even 120 days' worth of petroleum—yet when the crisis came last October there were actual supplies for around 60 days. The grim fact remained that, solidarity or selfishness aside, the collective situation of oil-consuming countries would never be symmetrical with that of the oil producers—for the simple reason that the storage of oil profits is very lucrative and the storage of oil very costly. Perhaps a program such as Kissinger announced in February might have been timely in 1968 or 1969—when few people were alive to the problem.

Kissinger glossed over a detail that was sure to become crucial. "The United States declares its willingness," he solemnly intoned, "to share available energy in times of emergency or prolonged shortage. We would be prepared to allocate an agreed portion of our petroleum supply provided other consuming countries with indigenous production do likewise." The shift from "available *energy*" in one sentence to "*petroleum* supply" in the next seems disingenuous, and the reference to other indigenous producers (Canada, Norway, and in a few years Britain) leaves a convenient alibi. But assume that the ambiguity were resolved and the escape hatch closed: will the American public, after spending billions of dollars on autarchy, really allow itself to be cajoled into exporting the tangible results of such hard-won "energy independence"? And if not, can we expect Europe or Japan to believe in our sincerity?

The failure of Kissinger's petroleum scenario leaves unanswered some fundamental questions about the future of the world economy. Will the oil-producing countries succeed in their ambitious attempt to revolutionize the distribution of real assets in the world's economy? Will OPEC continue to show more solidarity than OECD? How soon will the present oil shortage turn into a glut, as a result of such trends as energy conservation in the industrial countries, increased production in Iraq, Indonesia, and Ecuador, new supplies from the South China Sea, and synthetic production from shale or coal? When the turning point comes, will prices revert to their pre-1973 or pre-1969 stability or will they fluctuate as wildly as those of some other commodities?

How large will be the income of the oil-producing countries— estimated by some to be running as high as $70 billion for 1974— and how much of it will they manage to spend on development? How much of the remainder will they spend on local arms races between Saudi Arabia and Iran, or (as mostly heretofore) on short-term investments in the Eurodollar market? Will there be adequate "recycling" of these oil incomes from the Middle East via Beirut, Zurich, or London, back to Frankfurt, New York, or Tokyo so as to finance the bloated foreign-exchange bills of the importing countries? Or will curtailed industrial growth and recurrent devaluation lead to Kissinger's nightmare of "a vicious cycle of competition, autarchy, rivalry, and depression such as led to the collapse of world order in the thirties"?

The future international role of the oil companies also poses some perplexing questions. Having lost their hold on production upstream, will they be able to retain control of the midstream operations of transportation and processing? Or will OPEC countries spend enough money on supertankers and refineries to challenge them in that arena as well and gradually reduce them to a role of mere distributors and retailers? In view of the ample precedents for nationalization throughout the Third World, will the oil multinationals continue to engage in the costly process of worldwide exploration, particularly on the continental shelves? Will even their downstream functions come under attack, as producing countries seek to barter higher production or safety of supply against entry of their national oil companies into the refinery, filling station, and heating oil businesses in the United States and elsewhere—a scenario fully sketched by Yamani as early as 1972?

The oil companies themselves seem to be taking no chances on continuing their accustomed international role. Ever since Act Three of the petroleum drama, as we saw, they have begun to shift their attention to the domestic American scene. For the oil companies themselves the much-heralded energy crisis was quite simply a crisis of imminent expropriation upstream and hence a need to recoup themselves downstream. And while you are shifting attention and trying to recoup, why not recoup yourself more than fully? The United States, after all, remains the leading petroleum producer, and shale oil and liquefied coal can only enhance that stature. It remains the world's largest market for petroleum. And its public rhetoric of free enterprise remains just about the best available guarantee against nationalization or even effective regulation of corporate giants.

The focus of the public discussion will for some time be on the problem of imports vs. domestic production. Measures of energy conservation of a comparatively painless sort can banish the specter of energy blackmail from our foreign policy for years ahead. But our growing economy requires the rapid development of domestic nonpetroleum sources of energy—such as coal gasification or liquefaction, oil retorted from shale, atomic power, solar energy, and others. And the exponential rise in world petroleum prices, with its possible disastrous effects on our balance of payments, makes this development of alternative fuels not only imperative but also economic. With oil selling at $8 or $10 a barrel or more, many substitutes will seem attractive that were prohibitive when oil was only $2 or $3 a barrel.

On the need for a major program for "energy independence," therefore, there can be little quarrel between the oil companies and their critics. The key questions are the conditions under which the program is to be pursued and how it is to be financed. Will thoughtless strip-mining be allowed to turn hundreds of square miles of our country into a permanent moonscape? Or will we require the companies (including large oil companies) who own the coalfields to restore topsoil and vegetation as they go along? If large-scale production of shale oil proves feasible, will the public lands that contain most of the shale be kept public or sold at cutrate? Above all, will the federal government assume the full cost of developing alternatives to petroleum and hand their operation over to industry once high profits become certain? Or will the oil companies, perhaps with suitable exemptions from antitrust regulations, be induced to bear the cost of research and development themselves?

Corporations owe their prime allegiance to stockholders, that is, to profits. There is nothing immoral or outlandish, therefore, about oil companies seeking tax credits, depletion allowances, protectionist quotas, exemptions from ecological regulations, or huge government subsidies for the development of new products. Indeed, such are the standard operating procedures in a mixed public-private economy in which the oil companies have long been among the biggest operators. But it is up to the public—that is to Congress, president, and electorate—to decide which if any of these demands are to be granted.

The American taxpayer two decades ago made his debut as the dupe of Act One of the drama of international petroleum politics. In Act Two that role was taken over by the American consumer, and in Act Three by the newspaper-reading and tele-viewing public. In Act Five, will the American taxpayer be trapped once again in his time-honored and generous role? That, all too literally, will be the $64 billion question of 1974 and beyond.

—1974

William N. Leonard
HOW ECONOMIC POLICIES PROVOKED THE ENERGY CRISIS

Amidst the flurry of charges and countercharges and the profusion of facts and figures, one thing stands clear: national policy (or the lack of it) contributed greatly to the energy crisis. It is also clear that neither our national energy policy nor the American-based petroleum industry will ever be the same again.

Central to understanding the energy crisis is the realization that governmental policies have tended to depress the price of energy, especially of oil and natural gas. In the resulting paradise of cheap energy, prodigality has been the order of the day.

Because gasoline has been so inexpensive (half the price of that in Europe and elsewhere), the American motorist has purchased large, gas-thirsty cars and has been induced by the highway lobby to pour billions of dollars into building intercity and interstate highways. The results are by now well known: we have subsidized truck and bus transportation while our railroads and rapid transit systems have decayed.

Other aspects of the American life-style have also revolved around cheap energy. Buildings have been designed to take minimum advantage of sun and wind. Homes have been inadequately insulated. Shops, stores, and office buildings have often had excessive lighting. Perhaps the greatest waste of all has occurred in industry, the largest user of energy. According to du Pont engineers, inefficient combustion processes, poor heating systems, the wrong equipment, and other defects waste 10–15 percent of the total energy consumed by industry.

Within the overall framework of a cheap energy policy there have been certain mechanisms tending to raise prices above free-trade levels. One of these, the Interstate Oil Compact, was designed to ration the supply of crude oil to eastern markets from the southwestern oil-producing states; but the rationing has not had any real effect since the supply is produced mainly from older fields which for some years have been incapable of producing more than the quantities allowed. A second price-raising strategy, oil import quotas, has had a somewhat greater effect. The quotas were initiated by President Eisenhower in 1959 and remained in effect until President Nixon set them aside in 1973. Industry observers estimate that these quotas resulted in an import price of about $3.90 per barrel compared with a domestic price of $3.00. Nevertheless, the higher price applied to less than a third of consumption, and the domestic price predominated. To the extent that the import quotas did limit supplies of imported oil, they stimulated domestic exploration and production, and additional domestic output was achieved at very low cost. The Interior Department has estimated the cost of these additional supplies at only $1.04 per barrel.

Tax devices and fuel rivalries have more than offset these price-raising strategies, lowering prices of gasoline and other petroleum products to bargain levels. The oil exploration allowance has permitted petroleum companies to expense the costs of drilling, whether successful or not. Even more significant, the oil depletion allowance has afforded companies an opportunity to write off mineral assets in amounts far exceeding costs (acquisition of the asset by drilling has already been written off). This allowance—originally 27.5 percent, reduced to 22 percent in 1969—has been a handsome subsidy to the oil companies. It has lowered income tax payments to the federal government by about $1.5 billion a year.

Curiously, the depletion allowance was adopted as a national security measure to encourage domestic drilling and discovery and hence greater self-sufficiency for the United States. But with time it has had the opposite effect. To the extent that it has stimulated domestic exploration and production since 1918 at a higher rate than would otherwise have been the case, it has accelerated consumption and exhaustion of domestic crude oil reserves, ultimately increasing our dependence on foreign oil supplies.

The depletion allowance has not only encouraged rapid exploration and exploitation of domestic mineral reserves but has also been employed by the multinational oil companies to write off—in reality to subsidize—the costs of overseas operations. And there have been still other lures to foreign oil development: royalties and taxes paid to foreign countries can be taken not simply as a deduction but as a credit against taxes on net income. This makes the profit enjoyed in overseas development by American petroleum companies considerably greater than that realized in domestic operations and draws the multinationals irresistibly into expansion of their overseas exploration and production. We should note that the average increase of 45–60 percent in 1973 earnings of the oil multinationals has resulted largely from overseas activity.

In addition to tax incentives, competition from other fuels has also tended to keep the prices of petroleum products from rising. Natural gas is the leading source of energy for industry, commerce, and homes. As a result of widespread political pressures, natural gas prices have been kept artificially low by the Federal Power Commission. Not only has the low price spurred the consumption of natural gas but it has created gas shortages, particularly since—according to the oil and gas companies—the price has not encouraged exploration for new gas fields.

Obviously, the use of other fuels and the search for alternative sources of energy have been adversely affected by the low price of petroleum and its products. Utility companies have found it advantageous in cost as well as in control of pollution to convert from coal to oil, especially since the expense of developing and transporting western low-sulfur coal has seemed prohibitive. Compared with the low price of energy produced by domestic oil, atomic energy has less commercial attraction. This cost differential has slowed the drive to build atomic plants as much as have the arguments of environmentalists concerned about radioactivity, thermal pollution, and nuclear wastes. As for an alternate source of oil itself, so long as the price of crude oil has stayed between $3.00 and $3.25 per barrel, the production of oil from shale at from $4.00 to $8.00 a barrel has not seemed especially enticing.

Finally, we should note that extreme competition in domestic and international chemicals among chemical, rubber, and petroleum companies has tended to depress prices of petroleum-based chemicals, thus preventing upward pressure on crude oil prices from this source.

New price and tax policies for energy must have high priority. Subsidies and controls that promote unrealistically low prices of domestic crude oil and natural gas should be ended. Prices should be allowed to rise to an unsubsidized level. The depletion allowance has lost whatever utility it ever had, and should be terminated at home and abroad. Further, the right of oil companies to claim taxes and royalties paid foreign nations as credits against taxes on net income is not consistent with the desire of the United States to expand domestic exploration and production of oil. This policy should also be ended.

If out of the present confusion and discomfort a new, realistic, and forward-looking energy policy can be devised, the Arab oil boycott will ultimately appear to have been an unintended blessing.

—*1974*

Arthur F. Burns

STATEMENT BEFORE THE JOINT ECONOMIC COMMITTEE

Roughly speaking, oil revenues of the OPEC nations will amount to something in excess of $100 billion per year, if their current oil exports and prices are maintained. This is four times as large as the figure for 1973. On the import side, some of the OPEC countries—such as Indonesia, Iran, Nigeria, and Venezuela—have large absorptive capacities. But a substantial proportion of the earnings of other oil exporters—notably Saudi Arabia and the states of the Persian Gulf—will not be spent for additional imports in the near future. The two other key factors in the picture—the flow of investment earnings to the OPEC countries and the transfer of resources from the OPEC nations to the less developed countries—are as yet quite small compared to the flow of oil revenues. While the future volume of aid by the OPEC countries is uncertain, their investment earnings promise to grow at a very rapid rate.

All this suggests very large OPEC surpluses—of perhaps 55 to 60 billion dollars in 1975, something like $50 billion in 1976, and continuing large surpluses for at least another five years. The practical counterpart of these surpluses would be the accumulation of a huge mountain of debts by the oil-importing countries—unless the price of oil comes down or unless the consuming nations take major steps to reduce independence on imported oil.

If the price of oil remains at anything like its present level—and there are repeated stirrings in OPEC countries to move it still higher—there will be a massive redistribution of economic and political power among the countries of the world. This of itself carries dangers for our country's future. In addition, the huge and growing financial reserves of OPEC countries may cause very serious problems for some of the countries—both in the industrial and less developed parts of the world—that will simultaneously be piling up, or even just handling, enormous debts.

It is therefore to the interest of the United States and the entire community of industrial nations that we develop institutions to ease the financial strains to which any one of them may be subjected. If the weaker countries are left unprotected to face their oil bills, they may be forced into special arrangements with oil-producing countries. Such arrangements would undercut the bargaining power of the oil-consuming nations, and delay the day when the present exorbitant oil prices are reduced.

The program proposed by the Administration has the objective of bringing the major oil-consuming countries together in a common effort. It has two major aspects: cooperation to reduce dependence on imported oil and financial cooperation. Financial cooperation is important; it can contribute to international economic and political stability in the face of large oil deficits. But financial cooperation alone is not enough. Even with an orderly financing of deficits, the immense burden of carrying and ultimately repaying the debts will still remain. Financial cooperation may ease the transition, but it does not answer the most troublesome question: "A transition to *what*?"

The OPEC cartel will not last forever, and the most promising way of breaking or weakening it is to bring about changes in the demand and supply relationship of the oil market. Already some change in this relationship is taking place. Excess capacity of oil producers is now much larger than it was last year. New oil discoveries have occurred in Bolivia, China, Malaysia, and Mexico, to name a few. The proven oil resources of the North Sea have doubled in the past year. In the United States, the potential of offshore oil fields is enormous. The high price of oil is thus stimulating the search for new oil fields, and also the development of coal, nuclear power, and other alternative sources of energy.

In conclusion, I can only say to this Committee that the problems caused by the recent manipulation of oil prices and supplies are among the gravest with which this nation has had to contend under peacetime conditions. Unless we take stronger measures than we have yet done to conserve oil, to develop alternative sources of energy, and to lead other industrial nations in a common policy to lighten the burdens that OPEC oil actions have imposed on the world, we may endanger our nation's future. The policy that I have advocated this morning is a policy of austerity. I recognize that it must be carried out prudently—if possible, without intensifying the recessionary tendencies that are already developing in our economy. The alternative of drift, I fear, may lead to a permanent decline of our nation's economic and political power in a very troubled world.

—1974

Barry Commoner

ENERGY AND THE DESIGN OF MODERN SOCIETY

When engineers want to understand the strength of a new material they stress it to the breaking point and analyze how it responds. The energy crisis is a kind of "engineering test" of the United States economic system, and it has revealed a number of deep-seated faults.

Although energy is useless until it produces goods or services, and although nearly all the energy that we use is derived from limited, non-renewable sources which will eventually run out (all of which pollute the environment), we have perversely reduced the efficiency with which fuels are converted into goods and services. In the last 30 years, in agriculture, industry and transportation, those productive processes that use energy least efficiently, and stress the environment most heavily, are growing most rapidly, driving their energetically-efficient competitors off the market.

In agriculture the older, energy-sparing methods of maintaining fertility by crop-rotation and manuring have been displaced by the intensive use of nitrogen fertilizers, synthesized from natural gas. In the same way, synthetic fibers, plastics and detergents, made from petroleum, have captured most of the markets once held by wood, cotton, wool, and soap—all made from energy-sparing and renewable resources. In transportation, railroads—by far the most energetically efficient means of moving people and freight—are crumbling, their traffic increasingly taken over by passenger cars, trucks, and airplanes that use far more fuel per passenger- or ton-mile.

Naturally, such energy-wasting enterprises are threatened when the price of energy increases—the only real outcome of the illusory 1973 fuel "shortage." If they were not so serious, some of these economic consequences could only be regarded as absurd: When the multibillion dollar petrochemical industry cheerfully bid up the price of propane—an essential starting material in plastics production—farmers had trouble finding the propane they needed to dry their grain, and then had to pay triple its former price. In order to sustain the surfeit of plastic trivia that glut the modern market, food production was threatened. When, in response to urgent appeals, householders reduced their demand for electricity, the power companies asked for rate increases to make up for the lost business. Automobile manufacturers, having scornfully rejected environmentalists' appeals to produce smaller, more fuel-efficient vehicles, have lost about half their sales, throwing 100,000 auto workers out of work.

What has gone wrong? Why has the post-war transformation of agriculture, industry and transportation set the United States on the suicidal course of consuming, ever more wastefully, capital goods and non-renewable sources of energy, and destroying the very environment in which we must live?

The basic reason is one that every businessman well understands. It paid. Soap companies significantly increased their profit per pound of cleaner sold when they switched from soap to detergents; truck lines are more profitable than railroads; synthetic plastics and fabrics more profitable than leather, cotton, wool or wood; nitrogen fertilizer is the corn farmer's most profit-yielding input; power companies claim that capital-intensive nuclear plants improve their rate of return; and as Henry Ford has said, "mini-cars make miniprofits."

All this is the natural outcome of the terms that govern the entry of new enterprises in the U.S. economic system. Regardless of the initial motivation for a new productive enterprise—the entry of nuclear plants into the power market, of synthetics into the fabric market, of detergents into the cleaner market, or of trucks into the freight market—it will succeed relative to the older competitor only if it is capable of yielding a greater return on the investment. At times this advantage may be expressed as a lower price for the new goods, an advantage that is likely to drive the competing ones off the market. At other times the advantage may be translated into higher profits, enabling the new enterprise to expand faster than the older one, with the same end result.

Some economists believe that private enterprise can adapt to the rising price of energy by turning to energetically efficient productive technologies in order to save costs. Where this can be accomplished by reducing the waste of energy within a given enterprise it may well succeed. But in other cases—for example, the petrochemical industry—the intensive use of energy is built into the very design of the enterprise, in order to eliminate human labor, thereby raising labor productivity and the resultant profits. In these cases improved energetic efficiency can be achieved only by rolling back the rapid growth of such inherently inefficient industries—but, for that very reason, these are precisely the industries that are most profitable. Any attempt to reduce their level of activity would necessarily encroach on the profit yielded by the economic system as a whole.

Another possible adaptation is to pass the extra cost of measures that conserve energy and reduce environmental stress along to the consumer. Thus the energy dependence of agriculture could be reduced by cutting back on the rate of application of nitrogen fertilizer, with the inevitable result that the price of food would rise. This would place an extra burden on the poor, which, in turn, might be rectified *if* the principles of private enterprise could accommodate measures that would remedy the growing gap between the rich and the poor. Once more, this is a challenge to the basic design of the economic system.

In a sense there is nothing new here, only the recognition that in the U.S. economic system decisions about what to produce and how to produce it are governed most powerfully by the expectation of enhanced profit. What *is* new and profoundly unsettling is that the thousands of separate entrepreneurial decisions that have been made during the last 30 years in the U.S. regarding new productive enterprises have, with such alarming uniformity, favored those which are less efficient energetically and more damaging to the environment than their alternatives. This is a serious challenge to the fundamental precept of private enterprise—that decisions made on the basis of the producer's economic self-interest are also the best way to meet social needs. That is why the environmental crisis, the energy crisis, ànd the multitude of social problems to which they are linked, suggest—certainly as an urgently-to-be-discussed hypothesis—that the operative fault, and therefore the locus of the remedy, lies in the design of our profit-oriented economic system.

If we pay heed to the basic facts about the production and use of energy, we can begin to find a rational way out of this tragic and absurd state of affairs.

To begin with, we now know that we can readily squeeze out of the productive process much of the wasted energy that has been devoted, not to the improvement of human welfare, but to the replacement of worthwhile and meaningful labor by the cheaper and more tractable alternative of energy. A number of studies have shown that in the U.S. the nation's energy budget could be reduced by about a third in this way—with no significant reduction in the standard of living. Every unit of energy thus saved is reduced in its environmental impact to zero and relieves the pressure for hasty adventures into dubious and dangerous power technologies such as the breeder and fusion reactors.

In their place we can turn to solar energy, which has none of the faults that promise to cripple the present energy system. Unlike oil, gas, coal or uranium, solar energy is renewable and virtually free of untoward environmental effects. Unlike the non-renewable sources, which become more difficult and costly to acquire as the rate of their use increases, the use of solar energy is readily extendable at no loss in efficiency. The capture of one sunbeam, after all, in no way hinders the capture of the next one. Only solar energy can avoid the capital crunch which promises to paralyze the further development of the present energy system. Finally, solar energy is uniquely adaptable to different scales of economic organization. A conventional power plant now typically requires an investment approaching one billion dollars. In contrast, many solar collectors can be constructed in a range of sizes suitable for everything from a single household to an entire city.

The myth that solar energy is "impractical," or "too expensive," or in the realm of "future technology" is easily dispelled by a series of recent analyses done for the National Science Foundation. For example, a project, based on installing readily constructed solar heat systems in the nation's housing, could readily reduce the U.S. energy budget by 12–15 percent, at a cost that could be recovered, in the form of fuel savings, in 10–12 years.

Consider, now, the implications of these alternatives for international relations. If the industrial countries follow the conventional path, they will have little to offer in the way of useful energy technology to the developing nations, which lack capital, are rich in natural materials and labor, and are usually favored by intense sunlight. In contrast, if the industrialized countries were to develop new productive technologies that emphasized the use of natural materials—synthesized from solar energy through photosynthesis—rather than synthetic ones, and techniques for solar power, they could provide real help in the struggle of the poor countries to develop their economies. This is the kind of help that would enable developing countries to increase both agricultural and industrial production, and to raise living standards to the levels that encourage the motivation for self-limitation of fertility.

If we take this path we can begin to find also new ways to harmonize the needs of industrialized and developing nations and to end the growing trend toward the creation of opposing camps of nations that produce and use natural resources. For example, if for the sake of environmental and energetic sanity, the industrialized countries were to cut back on the production of synthetic substitutes for natural materials such as cotton, their needs could be met, in part, by goods produced from such natural products in developing countries. Thus, Malaysia for example, may wish to supply the industrialized nations not with natural rubber, but with tires; India supply not cotton, but finished fabrics and even clothes; West Africa supply the world not with palm oil, but with soap.

—1974

The Changing World Economy

Long before the oil embargo, the relationships of the U.S. economy to the rest of the world had been undergoing major change, symbolized by the appearance of large continuing negative trade balances, a major historical shift. The readings here trace the changes which have occurred and provide suggested resolutions to some of the dilemmas facing an economy, once all-powerful, which must now find new ways to meet the trading and currency worlds. In the labor movement the deterioration of trade balances and the perceived loss of American jobs had converted even the most ardent free-traders to a protectionist posture. The AFL-CIO Economic Policy Committee states labor's case.

The Eurodollar market has served both as a transmission belt of shifts in relative currency values and as a source of destabilization of short-run capital movements. Robert Zevin explains the role of this market, showing how the instabilities arise from the anarchy of an uncontrolled banking system in Eurodollars.

Economic Policy Committee, AFL-CIO
WORLD TRADE IN THE 1970s

The U.S. position in world trade and the world economy deteriorated in the 1960s and early 1970s with adverse impacts on American workers, communities, and industries. A thorough revision of U.S. government posture and policy is required to meet present realities and prepare for the future.

From 1894 to 1970, the United States government officially reported more merchandise exports each year than merchandise imports. But in 1971, imports were $2 billion higher than exports—the first trade deficit since 1893—despite the fact that the reported volume of merchandise exports includes shipments financed under such government programs as the Agency for International Development and Food for Peace. In 1972, the trade deficit soared to $6.4 billion.

While exports continued to rise during the late 1960s and early 1970s, imports rose much more sharply. Exports are important to many industries. Imports have had an increasing impact on almost all U.S. industries with growing adverse effects on an increasing variety of industries, product-lines, and parts of product-lines.

This deterioration is undermining the industrial base of the U.S. economy. At stake is the American living standard, the nation's productivity advance, and American job opportunities.

The adverse impact of the deteriorating U.S. trade position is particularly harsh on affected workers and their communities. Shutdowns of plants or departments usually result in the loss to workers of their jobs, as well as seniority and seniority-related benefits. Sometimes, the job loss means that the special work skills developed in a specific plant cannot be applied elsewhere. Moreover, workers and their families cannot easily move from one town to another and when they do they incur the expenses of moving, as well as the loss of friends, schools, church, and social relationships that have been developed over many years. An affected community, particularly a small town, can experience a shrinking tax base, losses for merchants and professionals, and the waste of public facilities.

In contrast, investments in a business can be moved around

more easily—from one business to another, to a different part of the country, or to a foreign nation. Equipment can be sold and shipped and tax breaks or other advantages can ease the impact.

Major causes of the deterioration of the U.S. position in world trade and the world economy have been new developments in the post–World War II period that accelerated in the 1960s and early 1970s. Among these developments have been the spread of managed national economies, with direct and indirect government barriers to imports and aid to exports; the internationalization of technology; the skyrocketing rise of investments by U.S. companies in foreign subsidiaries; and the spread of U.S.-based multinational corporations.

Such changes have made old "free trade" concepts and their "protectionist" opposites outdated and increasingly irrelevant. Yet U.S. government policy has failed for the most part to face up to these new developments. As a result, U.S. government policy in the area of foreign trade is more applicable to the world of the late 1940s and 1950s than the 1970s.

Neither changes in dollar valuation nor other piecemeal attempts to attack these problems have worked. The deterioration continues and it may get worse—with an increasing need to import raw materials and fuels—unless a comprehensive U.S. government policy is adopted and pursued vigorously, to meet the realities of the 1970s.

The U.S. ranks first among nations in world trade, but this ranking is essentially based on the huge size of the American economy. In terms of the share of world trade, the U.S. position has been declining throughout the post–World War II period.

Exports from the nations of the world shot up from approximately $61 billion in 1950 to about $238 billion in 1968 and $310 billion in 1970, according to the United Nations. But U.S. exports increased at a slower pace. As a result, the U.S. share of rapidly expanding world exports continued to decline, from 16.5 percent in 1950 and 15.9 percent in 1960 to 14.3 percent in 1968 and 13.7 percent in 1970.

Some decline in the U.S. share of increasing world exports was to be expected in the early postwar years, as the war-ravaged economies of other industrial nations returned to world markets.

But the decline did not end during the 1950s; it continued, became more rapid in the 1960s, and accelerated in the early 1970s.

This decline in the share of world trade was particularly pronounced in the export of manufactured goods. U.S. exports fell from about 27.7 percent of world exports of manufactured goods in 1958 to approximately 23.7 percent in 1968, to 21.3 percent in 1970 and to 19.9 percent in 1971, according to the United States Department of Commerce.

While U.S. exports continued to increase—although at a much slower rate than most other industrial countries—imports rose more rapidly. In the early 1970s, the rise of imports accelerated, despite the recession of 1969–1970, and continued to rise during the economic expansion of 1971–1972.

With imports rising faster than exports, the reported merchandise trade surplus dropped from about $5 billion a year in the early 1960s and $7.1 billion in 1964 to $800 million in 1968, $1.3 billion in 1969 and $2 billion in 1970—and then into the trade deficits of 1971 and 1972.

The worsening of the overall trade balance was concentrated in trade with Canada, Japan, and Germany in the late 1960s. By 1968, the United States was in a deficit trade position of about $1 billion with each of these three countries. By 1972, the U.S. deficit was over $4 billion with Japan, $2.5 billion with Canada, and $1.4 billion with Germany. With Italy, it was $300 million.

The U.S. trade position has been deteriorating in composition as well as in overall volume. The growth of rapidly rising imports has been primarily in manufactured and semimanufactured goods, including sophisticated production—parts and components as well as finished products.

Imports of finished manufactured goods other than food products rose from about 46 percent of all imports in 1960 to 68 percent in 1972.

During the 1960s, the expansion of manufactured exports was strongest in products based on advanced technology, such as computers, jet aircraft control instruments, and some organic chemicals. Even among such products and components, the U.S. trade position deteriorated by the 1970s, with rising imports and a slowing in the expansion of exports. Such industries are generally capital-intensive, with relatively few production and maintenance workers for each dollar of production.

The rapid expansion of manufactured imports in the 1960s was particularly great in several products for which the United States had previously been a world leader—such as steel, autos, machinery, and electrical products (including TVs, radios, and telecommunications apparatus). Imports of these products in the 1960s joined with the continued rise in imports of other products that had previously posed import problems, such as shoes, textiles, clothing, glass, and leather goods—labor-intensive industries with sizable numbers of production and maintenance workers per dollar of output.

Estimates indicate that in 1971 imports were about 18 percent of U.S. steel sales; approximately 24 percent of the U.S. auto market; something like 35 percent of TV sets; over 60 percent of phonographs; about 86 percent of radios; almost 100 percent of tape recorders; nearly 60 percent of sewing machines and calculating machines; 80 percent of electronic microscopes; about 33 percent of shoes. Baseball is an American game, but about 95 percent of baseball mitts sold in the United States in 1971 were imports.

Similarly, large proportions of U.S. production of other industries are being displaced—such as typewriters and shirts, industrial equipment and knit goods, pianos and tires, workclothes and glass.

It's not only finished products; it's also components. If a U.S.-made TV set can be found, many of its components will be imported.

Of course, many imports do not compete with American products. Some imports are obviously essential for U.S. production. Some other imports are important to provide diversity for the American standard of living. But the sharp rise of imports in recent years has been overwhelmingly in goods that are directly comparable to U.S.-made products.

In the 1950s, according to foreign trade experts, only about 30 to 40 percent of imports were considered competitive with U.S.-made products. By 1966, according to a report to the Joint Economic Committee by George Shultz, then Secretary of Labor, about 74 percent of the much greater volume of imports were "nearly competitive with domestic products." About 13 percent of imports in 1966 were products not produced in the United States and another 13 percent were goods "produced in the United States but in short supply," according to Shultz.

By the latter 1950s, the war-shattered economies of Germany, Japan, and other nations were revived, with newly installed plant and equipment and increasing strength in world trade. Some effects of such American-aided revival of war-ravaged economies on the U.S. trade position were to be expected. But these effects did not stabilize during the 1950s.

By the 1960s, the revived economies were greatly expanding their strength in the world economy. The U.S. share of world exports continued to decline.

Japan and Germany became the second and third largest economies in the free world. By 1970, Germany became the world's largest exporter of manufactured goods. In terms of international trade, the United States was no longer the "only big boy on the block," as it had been from the 1930s into the 1950s. Moreover, the United States remained more open to imports than other industrial nations.

Managed nation economies—with varying degrees of government management, regulation, and control—have spread in the past 25 years. The United States is now confronted by complex governmental economic arrangements in other countries to spur exports through direct and indirect subsidies, and to bar or hold down imports, through direct and indirect barriers. Examples include Japanese quotas, required licenses in European countries to import specific products and laws in many nations which require foreign subsidiaries to produce a certain amount of goods for export, as in Mexico, Brazil, and Spain.

Every industrial country gives preference to domestic producers when governments buy products. In the United States, limited "Buy American" laws affect many government purchases, in varying degrees. But in most other countries, more stringent results are achieved by national administrative policies, rather than openly declared legislation.

Developing countries also have extensive trade regulations for a variety of reasons. Many such countries tell firms that they may not sell a variety of U.S.-made products in their countries, but must produce the goods within their borders. The policy of "import substitution" in such countries means imports are licensed and are allowed only when the country itself does not produce the product. Mexico, for example, employs these practices. Brazil recently decreed that foreign-owned factories must produce mostly for export, with quotas on production for the Brazilian market.

The combination of these practices means that imports, which are frequently subsidized or otherwise encouraged by foreign governments, surge into the huge U.S. market, with its high living standards—probably the most open market to imports of all major countries. At the same time, U.S. exports are often retarded by barriers and other practices of foreign governments.

In the 1960s, another factor was the emergence of trading blocs, such as the European Economic Community (Common Market), with its inward-looking, protectionist tendencies. With U.S. encouragement and cooperation, the Common Market of six European nations (Germany, France, Italy, Belgium, the Netherlands, and Luxembourg) was formed to remove tariff barriers and to expand trade among themselves. They have a common tariff for nations outside of their bloc. On January 1, 1973, the United Kingdom, Denmark, and Ireland joined the Common Market—it now includes nine countries. At the same time, the Common Market also extended its common tariff on manufacturers to four additional European countries—Austria, Portugal, Sweden, and Switzerland. The Common Market also has preferential and associated-state relations with countries around the Mediterranean Sea, African countries, as well as other developing countries.

These Common Market countries maintain barriers to U.S. exports and even have nontariff barriers to one another's exports. Thus, for U.S. exports the barriers are double—for the Common Market as a whole and within each of the Common Market's member nations.

The major trading nations have not significantly readjusted their trade arrangements—after achieving great export strength—to provide equitable, two-way arrangements with the United

States. The Common Market and several other industrial countries in fact have made two-way arrangements with developing countries—special lower barriers for their country's exports, in return for special entry rules for developing countries' exports.

The internationalization of technology has been reducing or eliminating the former U.S. productivity lead in many industries. Thus in many industries and products, the American lead in technology and productivity, which enabled high-wage U.S. industries to compete successfully in world markets, even against low-wage competition, has been reduced or eliminated. The worldwide, growing emphasis on science and technology has been only one factor in the internationalization of technology.

U.S. firms have transferred American technology and know-how to their foreign subsidiary plants. And additional technology transfers have been made through patent agreements and licensing arrangements of U.S. firms with foreign companies.

As a result, foreign plants operating with American technology are probably as efficient or nearly as efficient as similar factories in the United States. But with wages and fringe benefits that frequently are 50 to 90 percent lower—and longer working hours—the unit-cost advantage can be substantial. Additional advantages may be available in lower taxes or in operating in markets protected by foreign governments.

One businessman, Nathaniel Brenner of the Welter Corporation, described the export technology in the *Chemical and Engineering News:*

> For many years our advanced products enabled us to compete in international markets despite high prices (and high wage rates).
>
> What has happened in the 1960s and continues is that American corporations, via licensing agreements, foreign plant construction, and other multinational arrangements, have given away for a very small portion of real cost and value, this advanced technology and with it the jobs it created. When a multinational corporation licenses a product abroad, it gives away the technology created by Americans educated at public expense, and the American jobs which produce that product, for the 5 or 10 percent profit represented by the license fee or return on invested capital. Result—the American worker loses a job, the United States loses an export

product and becomes an importer of that product, but the corporation still nets 5 or 10 percent. Result—unemployment plus balance of payments problems. Naturally, the foreign producer can sell for less—he hasn't had to invest in the education, the R&D, or the wages which support the "American system."

High technology is not reserved to sophisticated, capital-intensive industries. Labor-intensive industries—not normally associated with advanced technology—are also affected. For example, the American textile industry is among the leaders in applicants for new patents. The garment industry now includes laser beams to cut garments. The glass industry has new methods of drawing glass. And agricultural production is constantly improved by scientific development. U.S. rice production, for example, has mechanical and chemical technology for planting, washing, and processing rice that depends on scientific advances. Chicken farming became an important issue in the 1960s when America's technological knowhow made it possible to freeze and ship poultry in mass-produced quantities.

Sharply rising investments by U.S. firms in foreign operations are a major factor in the export of American technology and jobs. Direct investments of U.S. firms in foreign subsidiaries, plants, and other facilities soared from $3.8 billion in 1960 to $15.4 billion in 1972 and will rise to a predicted $16.3 billion in 1973—partly financed by outflows of U.S. capital, partly by foreign-raised capital. The book value of such investments in foreign facilities rose from almost $32 billion in 1960 to well over $80 billion in 1972.

These developments have resulted in the export of American jobs as well as technology. Moreover, the outflows of U.S. private capital that have financed part of these soaring investments have been a major factor in U.S. balance-of-payments problems.

Although an estimated 25,000 foreign affiliates are controlled by about 3,500 U.S. corporations, the bulk of these foreign operations is highly concentrated among the corporate giants. Professor Peggy Musgrave of Northeastern University reports that in 1966, "over 80 percent of taxable income which U.S. corporations received from foreign sources . . . went to 430 corporations with asset size in excess of $250 million."

The Chase Manhattan Bank's newsletter reported that "foreign sales of U.S. affiliates in manufacturing alone totaled almost $60 billion in 1968 and are estimated at between $70 and $75 billion in 1970."

The sales of U.S. foreign affiliates in manufacturing, therefore, have been more than twice the volume of exports of manufactured goods from the United States in recent years. Some of these shipments have been to the United States, where the goods and components are sold in direct competition with U.S.-made products. Another portion of these sales is in foreign markets, often in competition with U.S. exports.

Stuart Perkins, president of Volkswagen of America, has stated, "The Americans exported their industry, where other countries exported their products."

This process, which displaces U.S. production and employment, is encouraged and subsidized by the U.S. government. Two tax devices—the deferral of federal income taxes on earnings of foreign subsidiaries until the profits are repatriated and the full crediting of foreign tax payments against the U.S. income tax liability—amount to about $3.3 billion per year, according to Professor Musgrave.

By 1970, intracorporate relations between U.S. companies and their foreign subsidiaries may have accounted for one-quarter or more of what the U.S. government reports as exports and imports. Moreover, that estimate excludes the additional impact on the U.S. trade position of licensing, patent, and similar arrangements of U.S. firms with foreign companies.

The rapid spread of multinational corporations—usually U.S. firms with plants, offices, sales agencies, licensing arrangements, etc., in as many as 40 or more countries—is a factor of growing importance in the deteriorating U.S. position in world trade. These corporations—such as Ford, GM, IBM, Standard Oil of New Jersey, IT&T, International Harvester, Singer, and Pfizer Drug— have substantial portions of their assets in facilities spread through numerous countries. They can manipulate their production and sales internationally with U.S. technology. They can manipulate the location of their operations, depending on labor costs, taxes, and foreign exchange rates. They can juggle exports, imports, prices, dividends, and currencies—from one country to another, within the corporate structure.

The fact that other nations have higher and often prohibitive barriers against U.S. exports, while the U.S. is a relatively open market for industrial goods, means that the multinational companies can have relatively free rein to adjust to rules abroad and avoid rules at home, while U.S. workers' jobs and incomes and U.S. communities pay the price. No wonder that spokesmen for multinational corporations speak of economic freedom and a free-trade policy for the U.S. What they mean is freedom to manipulate operations, prices, sales, profits, and the like and to ship back whatever they wish, for sale in the U.S. market—with a minimum of U.S. government regulation and for the benefit of the managers and stockholders of the corporation.

The deterioration of the U.S. position in foreign trade has significant impacts on jobs, on the collective bargaining strength of unions, on wages and labor standards in adversely affected industries.

In a statement to the Joint Economic Committee of Congress, [Secretary of Labor] Shultz presented a rough estimate of the employment impact of imports. He reported that "about 1.8 million jobs in 1966 would have been required to produce the equivalent value of the 74 percent of imports that were competitive with U.S.-made products." Shultz later updated these estimates, in a statement to the House Ways and Means Committee: "In 1969, if we had attempted to produce domestically goods equivalent in value to such imports, the Bureau of Labor Statistics has estimated that we would have needed 2.5 million additional workers. . . ."

These estimates reveal the loss of about 700,000 job opportunities in the three years, 1966–1969, to the sharp rise of those imports that displace U.S. products. During the same three-year period, the Bureau of Labor Statistics estimates that the number of job opportunities attributable to merchandise exports—including jobs in agriculture, the services and transportation—increased only 200,000.

In combination, these rough estimates indicate the net loss of approximately 500,000 job opportunities in 1966–1969.

The adverse impacts of the deterioration of the U.S. position in foreign trade are much tougher and more direct on workers than on capital, or top-management officials. Capital is mobile—investments can be moved out of an unprofitable business to other industries, companies, and countries. Owners and top management are usually much more mobile than workers. In contrast, workers have great stakes in their jobs and their communities— skills that are related to the job or industry, seniority and seniority-related benefits, investment in a home, a stake in the neighborhood, schools and church.

Most developing countries are confronted by a lack of strong and viable economies, inadequate expansion of per capita gross national product, inequitable distribution of income, and lack of an adequately viable social and political base.

In recent years, the developing countries have placed growing emphasis on increased exports, especially exports of manufactured goods—exports to the industrial countries, particularly the U.S. market—and have been demanding trade preferences from the United States and other industrial countries. This demand by the developing countries, such as those in Latin America, has been joined and supported by some major U.S. banks and multinational companies, as well as some U.S. political leaders. Such preferences would result in substantial benefits for the multinationals which operate subsidiaries in the developing countries. Recently, some developing countries have also demanded an increasing amount of advanced technology and production—mostly to produce for export, rather than for balanced economic expansion.

This emphasis on exports as the sole or major solution to their economic, social, and political problems is unrealistic. It shifts attention away from their need for improved education and manpower training of their populations; improved labor and social standards, including effective minimum-wage measures; increased social-development investments, such as housing; the development of free institutions, such as trade unions and effective collective bargaining; and from their urgent need to effectively curb the large outflows of private capital by wealthy people and business. Its adoption would benefit the multinationals, with only doubtful and minimal benefits—and possibly harmful, distorting effects— on the developing countries, their economies and societies.

Moreover, it diverts attention from the serious need of the developing countries for expanding domestic markets, as the essential foundation for the development of viable economies and societies—domestic markets that obviously must include expanding consumer markets, based on improvements in living standards, with workers and their families sharing in the gains of economic progress.

—1973

Robert Zevin
THE EURODOLLAR SYSTEM

Since the 1940s, the U.S. dollar has been the de facto international reserve currency of the empire. The U.S. has exploited its reserve currency status to export a large and growing stream of dollars to the rest of the world ever since the end of World War II. Until the late 1950s, a sufficient portion of these dollars returned to New York as deposits in banks or for the purchase of treasury bills to effectively disguise what was really happening. Ever since the late 1950s, the United States has had a persistent and growing balance-of-payments deficit. Since the late 1960s, it has had a deficit in current payments for goods and services alone as well. Originally, the primary cause of this deficit was the rapid economic development of Western Europe and Japan to the point where they became effective competitors. Since the formation of the OPEC cartel, the balance of payments of the entire capitalist world has been thrown into severe deficit. This persistent outflow of dollars has been used to pay for the farflung military expenses of empire; to finance a massive diversion of investment from the domestic United States to other capitalist and underdeveloped countries; and increasingly, as well, to pay for massive imbalances in the consumption of raw materials, manufactured goods, and tourism services.

To the extent that these dollars returned to the United States they became, directly or indirectly, deposits in New York banks. To the extent that the Federal Reserve System did not attempt to deliberately neutralize their effect they contributed to a further growth of domestic credit. If they did not return to New York, these dollars found their way to the central banks of other major capitalist countries where they were exchanged for Deutsche marks, francs, pounds, yen, or whatever. In this way they contributed to an unwanted or at least unplanned expansion of the money supply of other major industrial countries in the empire and had the effect of exporting the American inflation to the rest of the empire. To the extent that these inflations reduced the international competitiveness or the domestic real incomes of Germany, France, England, Japan, or any other country they tended as well to export the military and investment costs of empire to these other nations.

The Eurodollar market is a special and quantitatively very important aspect of the international scope of the current inflation. In 1961, there was no such thing as a short-term Eurodollar market. Today, that market has created a supply of purchasing power roughly comparable to the entire domestic money supply of the United States. The proximate motive for the creation of the Eurodollar market on the part of major American banks and multinational corporations was the desire to evade the Interest Equalization Tax, "voluntary" guidelines for direct overseas investment and lending and other regulations of the early Kennedy Administration designed to stem the balance of payments outflow. A closely related result was to create a money-and-banking system that escaped all regulation. Although Eurodollars (or more precisely all expatriate dollars) considered as a distinct currency are the second largest pool of purchasing power in the world, they are the only currency for which there is no central bank to act either as a rescue lender of last resort or a regulator of the growth of deposits and loans within conservative limits.

The Eurodollar system is a classic example of an undercapitalized, unregulated, overexpanded, private, competitive banking system. It is precisely comparable to the American system of state banks in the 1820s and 1830s. The only true reserves of the system are in the form of deposits which various Eurodollar banks in London have with their home offices in New York or, less frequently, London, Frankfurt, Paris, or Tokyo. These total some $5 billion to $10 billion. However, these dollars are hardly "as good as gold," given the precarious positions of the home offices as well as the ambiguous commitment of their respective central banks to rescuing a monetary system which has grown to monstrous proportions outside of their control. As with the American state banking system, these slender reserves are multiplied through a complex round robin of interbank deposits with each bank counting as reserves its gross credit against every other bank. As with the American state bank notes, one Eurodollar is not necessarily equal to another. Banks and private depositors make sharp distinctions among Eurodollar banks. For every participant in this market there exists some group of Eurodollar banks in which it is never acceptable to have a deposit or any other form of credit because of a presumed high degree of risk. This is exactly analogous to the refusal of a New York bank in the 1830s to accept a note issued by a bank in Memphis. Similarly, the bewildering array of conditions and interest rates under which each Eurodollar bank can obtain deposits from every other participant is precisely analogous to the complex schedules of discounts at which the notes of state banks sold depending on the issuer as well as the place of sale.

—1974

The End of Imperialism?

Events may now be settling the long-debated question of whether U.S. capitalism is and must be imperialist. Our ability to dominate other economic systems is surely being undermined by many forces at work in the underdeveloped and developing world. And while multinational corporations may constitute yet another metamorphosis of the urge to dominate, their long-run viability is questionable. We should welcome the end of old-fashioned domination if it is happening, while we work to make sure it happens. The portrait of capitalism rampant in Asia, Latin America, Africa, and the Middle East was a sordid and depressing one. Two brief portraits, from Vietnam and Southeast Asia, remind us why.

Jules Henry
CAPITAL'S LAST FRONTIER

Asia represents one of the last frontiers for investment capital. In this connection, the following quotes from a Saigon dispatch in

The New York Times of May 12, 1965, are important:

> New industry is developing [in South Vietnam] at an encouraging rate. Moreover, American aid officials believe, several companies operating here for a few years with American financial support are plowing back their profits into expansion rather than returning them to the United States.

The article then states that the Vietcong have spared industrial developments in South Vietnam, and goes on to say:

> In one instance, guerrillas made no hostile move against an important dairy products processing plant, backed by American investment, but they attacked a police post only a few hundred yards away.
>
> "When the shooting stops," a United States aide said, "there is every expectation of a lively expansion. . . ."
>
> American investment in South Vietnamese industry is still light, centered chiefly in three plants: a cotton textile mill, a paper mill, and a dairy products plant. Other companies have surveyed the possibilities and expressed interest, but are waiting for the situation to improve.

On December 9, 1965, *The New York Times,* in a dispatch from Saigon, revealed that the Bank of America and the Chase National Bank had opened offices in Saigon. The dispatch continues:

> Their representatives have quietly visited Saigon in recent weeks for conferences with officials of the National Bank of Vietnam.
>
> At least two other big American financial institutions—the First National City Bank of New York and the American Express Company—are also studying the possibility of opening offices in Vietnam.
>
> Their interest has been whetted by the large number of United States servicemen on duty here. But in the opinion of economic specialists at the American Embassy, Vietnamese businessmen are good potential customers.

The United States, however, is not the only country with banking interests in Vietnam. Ten of the fifteen banks now operating in Saigon are owned by foreigners, particularly by British and French interests. The article continues:

> Henry M. Sperry, a First National City Bank vice-president and resident in Hong Kong . . . [said] "We believe we're going to win this war. . . . Afterwards, you'll have a major job of reconstruction on your hands. That will take financing, and financing means banks.
>
> "I think the Government here recognizes the need for American banks. It would be illogical to permit the English and the French to monopolize the banking business, because South Vietnam's economy is becoming more and more United States oriented."

It is clear that investments now being made create a road of no return. Once made, investments must be protected.

The establishment throughout Southeast Asia of industrial complexes backed by American capital is sure to have a salutary effect on the development of our foreign involvements: the vast and cheap labor pool will permit competition with the lower production costs of Chinese and Japanese industry, which have immobilized our trading capabilities in Asia for many years.

The economic stake of the United States in Southeast Asia is presented in a striking way by a full-page ad which Thailand placed in *The New York Times,* obviously to attract American investment. On the same day, the paper carried an article captioned: "Foreign Investors Provide Thailand with Economic Life," and saying:

> The economic progress of the last six years has attracted several large foreign investments, mainly from the United States. Among the larger ones were a $30,000,000 paper mill, a mechanical equipment and machinery plant, and a new luxury hotel. . . .

The economic effect of American armed intervention in Asia can be seen in the fact that in that issue of the *Times* South Korea had three full-page advertisements—more than any other country—promoting the country's economic attractions, and calling for foreign investment.

We are fighting in Asia now for the same reason we fought there in World War II. In 1941, we told *Japan* to get out of China because Japan had monopolized much of the economic capability of that country. Now we think we are fighting to prevent *China* from monopolizing the economic capability of Asia—including China. Thus we have fought an almost uninterrupted series of wars, beginning with World War II, to keep the door in Asia open to American investment. While a military foothold in Southeast Asia will permit the expansion of American capital there, an eventual flow of American capital even into China itself is not entirely a pipe dream for a far-seeing economics statesman.

If China could be made "reasonable" it might accept American investment under some form, just as an occasional country in the Russian orbit has accepted foreign investment. One by one, Socialist countries that have excluded foreign capital have found it impossible to get along without it. The removal of Ben Bella in Algeria was followed instantly by broad agreement with France on the exploitation of Algerian oil; and Egypt, after attempting to struggle along without American capital, has at last initiated talks looking to the expansion of American investment there. The economic surplus pleads, then insists, and may eventually use force to gain an outlet; but it never loses patience, for to lose patience is to dam it up at home, and to dam it up is to suffocate the home economy. We would like to keep underdeveloped countries from going Socialist, but Socialist or not, we want an economic foot in their doors.

I think the issue is clear: our economic stake in Asia is immense and we cannot turn back because, under present conditions, we need a field of play for our economic surplus, and because we already have an investment to protect in Southeast Asia.

Considering the ambiguities and the confusion in Administration statements about Vietnam, and the increasing immensity of our military commitment there, one might conclude that the Administration was mad. But before declaring a man mad, one has to exhaust every clue that bears on his sanity. I think that an examination of our economic situation in Asia makes it clear that the Administration is perfectly sane, as far as sanity goes in such issues, but that it dare not explain its real motives because their revelation would instantly cancel all support for the war. The United States is doing what it has always done: following or attracting the dollar. Our foreign policy has not changed—except in verbiage—since the days of Theodore Roosevelt. In the light of the economic conditions, we are literally at bay with China, not in the sense that China will swallow Southeast Asia physically but in the sense that economic competition with China—and with Japan—is as inevitable as it will be unpleasant. It is clear that we are trying to do in Asia today precisely what we fought Japan for in World War II—we are trying to monopolize a market by force of arms. Therefore, we must look forward to an existence as an armed camp for perhaps the next hundred years; for we must bear in mind that all victories will entail the policing of the areas we have won, and the peoples we have subdued will always rise against us.

A final word is necessary for those who shed tears about the destruction of the Vietnamese countryside and the disintegration of the peasantry. The history of industry shows that it is impossible to create an industrial revolution without a landless proletariat. The uprooting of peasant life in Vietnam therefore is a necessary preliminary to the industrialization of Vietnam. We know that there is more to rice cultivation than seeds and paddies—it is the *social organization* of the peasantry that makes it possible, the close integration of people in a productive system. The uprooting of families, the killing of the young men, the conversion of the daughters into prostitutes or kept women, the killing of the persons who are repositories of the lore and technique of rice culture, the fall in the birth rate, and so on, all make the rehabilitation of the old rice culture impossible and the creation of a landless proletariat inevitable. The uprooted people, however, will find work in the new industrial revolution the war holds miraculously in store for them. There will also be an agricultural revolution, for since the disintegrated peasantry will not be able to farm the land, it will be bought for a song and farmed by "more modern" methods: large enterprises run by managers and worked by hired hands. The destruction of the Vietnamese countryside is the first, and necessary, step to the industrialization of Vietnam and the rationalization of its agriculture.

—1966

Peter F. Bell and Stephen A. Resnick

**THE CONTRADICTIONS OF POST-WAR DEVELOPMENT
IN SOUTHEAST ASIA**

World War II brought to an end the overt colonialism of the West in Southeast Asia. It was thought that the dismantling of the colonial structure would bring with it a new era of "political and social freedom," rapid strides in economic development, and less dependence upon the West. The new regimes were, however, incapable of bringing about social and economic change necessary for development. Political power was still vested in the hands of an elite class whose intellectual if not social origins were based on the previous colonial experience and whose actions were increasingly constrained by Western influence. It is thus not very surprising that the colonial past with its unequal distribution of power and income still dominates the present and will likely continue to do so until social revolution occurs in this part of the world.

What one observes, some 25 years later at the end of the first prolonged attempt to consciously plan development, is that the changes which have occurred have not dramatically altered the standard of life of perhaps 70 percent of the people of Southeast Asia. Population growth robs the region of much of its economic advancement, and the masses of labor, rather than being a factor for progress, have become its most significant problem. The influence of the West is still apparent both in trade and war: the region continues to be dependent on Western goods and technology and Western armies bring new misery to the area, decimating land and people. Furthermore, a new and more subtle form of capitalistic exploitation, that of the multinational corporation, has evolved since 1945. Finally, and perhaps most significant of all, the postcolonial governments have created on a national scale the same uneven development that was the outstanding feature of the previous international colonial structure.

Common Aspects of the Experience of the Philippines, Thailand, Malaya, and Singapore. Although there appears on the surface to be a variety of experiences among these countries in the postwar period, as their individual national plans testify, there is, nevertheless, a striking similarity about their economic pattern. First, as mentioned, all have effectively reproduced an income and class gap within their borders parallel to the gap between Europeans and non-Europeans that existed under colonial rule. This uneven development is exemplified by the persistence of virtual stagnation in the hinterland, in which the majority of the people live, in contrast to the rapid growth of the metropolises: Bangkok, Manila, and Kuala Lumpur. Widening inequality is also visible within the metropolises in the form of industrial dualism: an organized and heavily protected manufacturing sector coexists with a large crafts sector where most of the urban people are employed or where there exists disguised unemployment.

Second, although postwar development always had national independence as one of its primary goals, the result has been increased dependency on the goods and the technology of the West. A new form of dependency, which economists define as the foreign exchange constraint, has been created by the very type of industrialization policies followed. The strategy of much protection for consumer goods and little for intermediate and capital goods has produced an environment where heavy industry was not favored, and in which the countries have had to rely almost completely on foreign sources for many goods which are critical to capital accumulation and modernization. Moreover, many of these consumer-goods industries, established since the early 1950s, are subsidiaries of American and recently Japanese multinational corporations. Along with this foreign investment by multinational corporations, foreign aid and loans provided by the international banking system have tied these countries to the industrial centers and have thus become important instruments of Western imperialism.

Third, all of these countries have pursued broadly similar lines of economic policy, namely they have relied on the forced industrialization, or import-substitution model to foster the development of a national bourgeois class. This strategy has favored the development and rapid growth of manufacturing throughout the area, but its bias toward capital-intensive industries has in turn led to the creation of industrial dualism. Data suggest that in the Philippines and Thailand wages, capital-labor ratios, and profits rates are much higher in the organized sector *vis-à-vis* the crafts sector. Although this may be a result of monopoly power in the factor and/or product markets or biased imported technology, it is the very development strategy that has been pursued which has produced this dualism. What must be emphasized is that this development strategy is a product of political decisions made by ruling elites and dualism is thus a political as much as an economic phenomenon.

One common result of industrial policy has been that the previous export enclaves under colonial capitalist rule have been replaced by industrial enclaves under indigenous bourgeois rule, but in practice dependent on western corporate technology. Similar to the colonial pattern, the concentration of capital formation in these enclaves has resulted in a rising capital-labor ratio, rising productivity and per capita income for a very small group of people. It has created a select group of urban workers in the metropolises at the expense of the mass of unorganized service and/or craft workers. This provides a necessary pool of cheap labor, e.g., servants, retainers, messenger boys, bar girls, and cab drivers, for the middle and upper classes. The consumption habits of these classes are reflected in the misery of the shanty towns that abound in urban Southeast Asia.

While the protection permitted by this import substitution policy favors consumer goods rather than capital-goods industries, the type of consumer goods produced has been for the same small select group of privileged workers, to the neglect of the rural areas and the remainder of the urban population. Thus the very success of expanding manufactures, to which western economists so frequently refer, has been at the cost of meeting the needs of the majority of the people. The very success of manufacturing has been its failure: income distribution is becoming more unequal over time, few jobs have been created by this development pattern, and the overemphasis on manufacturing to the neglect of agriculture has led to rural stagnation and an unlimited supply of labor to the urban centers at low wages. Urban idiocy is now as observable as rural idiocy and, given the mounting population pressure, urban unrest is as likely as rural.

In human terms, the result of the last 25 years has meant

abysmally low levels of consumption, education, health, and welfare for about two-thirds of the people of the region. When one contrasts this with the potential which these countries have had for developing their people and their resources, then poverty, as Fanon said, is not only a tragedy but an absurdity.

The Contradictions of Development and Development Economists. Given the varied precolonial history of these four countries, there emerges, as we have attempted to indicate, a striking similarity in their postwar development pattern. Colonialism from about the middle of the nineteenth century to World War II provided the unifying force which tended to create underdevelopment in Southeast Asia and development in Europe and America. Given this common history of global capitalism, it is not surprising that these four countries have attempted to favor private over public enterprise by the creation of an environment to foster the development of a bourgeois class. Thus the observed biases in the economic structure of these countries are derived from their colonial history and, in the postwar period, from continued attempts to favor one class over another.

Also not surprising is the ideological rationale provided by Western economists for the postwar strategy followed, since they view social change from the government offices and universities of the center rather than from the rural and urban slums of the hinterland. More significant, however, is their implicit role in continuing underdevelopment (rather than in planning for development) by taking as given the existing class structure which in reality must be revolutionized for true social progress to be accomplished. Moreover, by failing to understand the historical forces operating on this part of the world and by mystifying the development process itself, Western economists create a false consciousness as to the causes of and remedies for underdevelopment which prevents alternative socialistic strategies from being considered, much less implemented.

In the postwar period the actual performance of these economies falls far short of their potential level. The difference can be most clearly seen by examining the contrast between actual and potential surplus generated and its effective use. The potential surplus may be defined as the output potentially producible, if there exists full utilization of resources, less essential consumption. This definition seems to be relevant for these countries in the sense that they should be engaged in a war against poverty, and in times of war there seems to be no problem in mobilizing resources or in defining essential consumption. However, for potential surplus to be realized there must not only be a full utilization of labor in producing material goods but also a change in the political and social structure to accomplish this reorganization of work activity.

The strategies followed so far have not properly integrated the sectors within the economy; indeed, they have led to industrial dualism, uneven development, and the dominance of the town over the country. To resolve these fundamental contradictions, a political organization must be developed which would see the economy as a social unit marked by inherent imbalances between agricultural and industrial development, consumer and capital goods expansion, and town and country. The experience of the last 25 years has shown that the ruling elites of these countries have neither the will nor the desire to accomplish this necessary reorganization of social priorities. Political and economic reform alone will not be sufficient to resolve these contradictions. What are needed are new leaders and new forms of organization.

An alternative strategy would have put as a primary goal the alleviation of the more obvious forms of human suffering by assuring minimum standards of health, education, food, and clothing. An effective use of the surplus would also have emphasized heavy industry rather than the proliferation of consumer manufactures, and a first priority would be the production of social goods such as education and medical supplies for all the people rather than the production of lawyers and heart surgeons for the rich. A proper government policy would have implied an all-out war on traditionalism and barriers to human development which "restrained the human mind within the smallest possible compass, making it the unresisting tool of superstition, enslaving it beneath traditional rules, depriving it of all grandeur and historical energies."[1] This would have led to a mass awakening of the people and their active participation in the economic and political processes of these countries.

These goals imply an output mix aimed at the many not the few, and this strategy is not feasible without disrupting existing groups and interests and creating new centers of political and economic power. The established classes are opposed to this as it implies a redistribution of privilege and of power. Moreover, any such change in the social structure of these countries would not be readily tolerated by the developed countries on whom the ruling classes are dependent. The economic and political realities of the international economy reflect the preferences of those in power, and to change the former implies a change in the latter.

In spite of the evidence of uneven development on both global and national levels throughout history, most Western economists continue to advocate policies which if anything only exacerbate this process of uneven development. Economists often misspecify the problem of underdevelopment by focusing solely on economic relationships which they assume can be analyzed independently from the political forces of a society. Their bias leads to a concern with the development of Southeast Asian economies rather than Southeast Asian people and, in reality, to policies and advice which serve the interests of a small class—they are, as Marx put it, "sycophants of capital."

Finally, the failure of economists to understand the historical determinants of underdevelopment and their concentration on the problem of development as an object outside the social relationships among men has resulted in a total preoccupation with "the goal of development" rather than with the nature of the social organization by which development is to be achieved. What is needed is a revolution of the mind which would allow work activity to be seen as a social product, thereby resolving dialectically this necessary task. Perhaps only China, North Korea, and North Vietnam have endeavored to accomplish this necessary task. But Western economists hardly consider these countries to be successful cases of development.

Just as it is clear that the common features of Southeast Asia were created by Western colonialism, it is also clear that whatever gains are to be made in the future will be in spite of, and not because of, the West. "Development fetishism" will rule the economists' paradigm as they continue to ignore the needs of two-thirds of the population by focusing on the requirements of the one-third. Unless there is a radical change in the center, Western development economists will have little to do with the needed revolution in the hinterland.

—1971

Corporate Dominance

In 1938 by joint resolution Congress established a Temporary National Economic Commission (TNEC) in response to a message from President Franklin D. Roosevelt, which said:

> Among us today a concentration of private power without equal in history is growing.
>
> This concentration is seriously impairing the economic effectiveness of private enterprise as a way of providing employment for labor and capital, and as a way of assuring a more equitable distribution of income and earnings among the people of the nation as a whole.

The President called for "a thorough study of the concentration of economic power in American industry and the effect of that concentration upon the decline of competition." He said that such a study, and measures to remedy the problem, would have the purpose and effect not of curbing but of restoring competition and would thus "preserve private enterprise for profit."

For scope, depth, and comprehension, the study conducted by the TNEC between 1938 and 1941 is without parallel. The focus of the TNEC was on competitive patterns in industry. Its analysis concluded that the concentration of production and ownership severely limited competition, controlled investment and technology, and preserved large-scale inequalities in the distribution of wealth and income. Its legislative recommendations were intended to reduce the pattern of concentration in order to stimulate competition and encourage higher levels of production and employment.

Since TNEC, studies of concentration have focused on market power, price, and output behavior. The Senate Subcommittee on Antitrust and Monopoly, chaired first by Estes Kefauver and since his death by Philip A. Hart, has been the principal forum for on-going analysis of these issues. In the late 1950s and early 1960s, when we experienced a period of simultaneous unemployment and inflation—similar, though far milder, than the 1973–1974 period—renewed interest was stimulated in the question. Gardiner C. Means, whose work was important in the 1930s studies, argued that we were subject to an inflation caused by administered prices. But this was a minority view; extended inquiry in 1959 into these questions by the Joint Economic Committee[1] gave little weight to market power factors.

In the 1960s the discussion shifted to the conglomerate, a new development. Here the old questions asked by economists are less useful. They look at each new metamorphosis in the corporate world with two questions in mind: (1) does it increase the concentration of market power? (2) does it increase or reduce the force of competition in markets? Conglomerates raise other, more fundamental questions. If we look, for example, at the absorption of major coal producers by major oil companies, then the relevant market sector becomes energy as a whole. It is possible that mergers of this kind will simultaneously increase competition among coal producers—by strengthening weaker ones—and strengthen concentration in the energy market as a whole. It is, further, likely that conglomerates increase the concentration of ownership independent of their effects on market structures. The definition as well as the locus of economic power changes. Gus Tyler described the role of the conglomerate:[2]

> The conglomerate acquires anything and everything that fits into its game plan. It buys profitable enterprises to take the profits or to assimilate a competitor. It buys unprofitable enterprises to show losses for income tax purposes. It buys related companies—horizontal or vertical—or totally unrelated companies for reasons of finance or taxation or just to project images for the money market.
>
> The conglomerate commotion of the last two decades has its funny side. A kosher food company picks up a copper mine; a copper mine picks up a knit-goods factory; a knit-goods factory picks up a realty company; and sometimes one company does all of these things under the occult aegis of Free Enterprises Inc. Consider just one real—not fictional—conglomerate, as described by Harrison F. Houghton, former assistant to the director of the Bureau of Economics for the Federal Trade Commission before the Senate Subcommittee on Antitrust and Monopoly in 1964:
>
> "In all, Textron has acquired nearly 70 different companies outside the textile industry. As a matter of fact, there are so many different industries . . . that . . . it was necessary to separate out some 37 different industrial categories, ranging all the way from aircraft . . . to watch bracelets."

The list included a passenger liner, the *SS La Guardia;* two poultry farms where the chickens were fed by Textron's very own home-grown feed; several pharmaceutical houses; shoes, glue, paint, plastics, aircrafts, and electronics.

The 1969 study paper produced for the Cabinet Committee on Price Stability summarized much of the postwar record and took account of conglomerate and other new forms of corporate transformation; it serves as a good exposition of the facts and their significance. But not everyone agreed that we need be concerned; a House study said,[3]

> All authorities do not share the concern reflected in the Studies by the Staff of the Cabinet Committee on Price Stability, and in the Staff Report to the Federal Trade Commission, about the relation-

ships of aggregate and market concentration and the trends asserted to exist. A responsible body of opinion asserts that the economy is not endangered by increases in aggregate concentration, and that market concentration, while competitively significant, either remains stable or, in fact, may be lessening. In support of these positions, the critics of the FTC Staff Report point to the substantial growth and achievement of the American economy throughout the period that increases in aggregate concentration were noted. Increase in size of the operating units has been accompanied by a continual growth in the Gross National Product. National incomes in terms of current prices have grown 12 times since 1890. The American economy is vigorous, productive, and profitable. This vitality is attributed to management of resources by large-scale operating units.

This study brought together the record of acquisitions, and the goals and strategies behind them, of such modern conglomerates as International Telephone & Telegraph, Gulf & Western Industries, Leasco Data Processing Equipment Corp., Ling-Temco-Vought, Inc., and Litton Industries. The data were revealing. They demonstrate the central role played by major financial institutions, particularly the trust departments of key banks. They show how rising market values of common stocks made it possible for the merger architects to achieve major changes in corporate control with relatively small funds and at the same time weakened the financial structure of acquired firms. They stress the importance of inside dealings that enabled individuals and banks to take advantage of anticipated merger decisions from which others, including the owners of target firms, were unable to benefit.

The more one digs, the more the evidence points in the direction of a pattern of concentrated holdings and voting power— with banks playing the central role, through their trust departments and through dummy corporations closely associated with them. One Congressional study showed that 324 of the 373 members of the boards of the fifteen largest commercial banks held more than 1,500 positions as managers or board members in other banks, insurance companies, and industrial firms. More than half of the total assets held by bank trust departments are held by 49 banks whose representatives sit on the boards of 300 of the largest 500 corporations. In 1968 a House Committee observed:

> Many major banking institutions [have] become by far the largest holder and voter of stock in some of the largest industrial and commercial corporations in the United States. The situation has led in many cases to both direct and indirect representation on the boards of these corporations by banks. Companies which have previously been characterized as "management controlled," are probably controlled either by banks or by a combination of minority control through bank trust department stockholdings and management control.[4]

The 1956 Bank Holding Company Act was intended to prevent such control, but it included a loophole—the exemption for the so-called "one bank holding company"—which has enabled the largest banks to circumvent the intent of the law. By 1969 one-bank holding companies had been formed by 34 of the 100 largest commercial banks. Adolf A. Berle told the House Committee on Banking and Currency:

> The one-bank holding company, left unlimited, can go in all directions, and there is no limit. It crystallizes around itself, first, a concentration of financial power, and second, a concentration of industrial power beyond belief in the United States. There is no question that a one bank holding company, with the resources of its bank, with the stockholding power in the bank's trust department, and especially if it also acquires control of mutual funds which have further stock interests, can probably attain control of any corporation in the country it really wants to get, aside from a few of the very giants that are too large. This is already beginning to happen.

Recently it has become possible to look at ownership and the pyramid of control more closely, and to pierce the veil of anonymity which conceals the identity of the owners and ultimate claimants to the power and wealth represented by bank trust departments and dummy corporations. Senator Lee Metcalf has provided some of the information which goes behind the scenes, in a document released with virtually no public attention in 1974.[5] The focus is on the role of bank trust departments which hold major blocks of stock as nominees for others. They in turn represent portfolios or holding companies about which little is known, with names like Cudd & Co., Pitt & Co., Cede & Co., and others. Cede & Co., for example, was the largest stockholder in 36 major corporations, holding between 10 percent and 39 percent of the common stock. Stock owners may divide their holdings among several of these holding companies, and existing disclosure laws fail to show the results. The report pinpoints the enormous concentration of voting power which rests in the hands of 50 bank trust departments, which exercise voting rights for significant—and often controlling—blocks of stock of major corporations in every area of economic life: airlines, oil, life insurance, steel, chemicals, utilities, automobiles, etc. Among the corporate names which dot this list are Chrysler, IBM, Xerox, ITT, Textron, Gulf, TWA, Merck, Boeing, Eastman Kodak, General Dynamics, McDonald's, etc.

The 50 banks themselves hold quite unequal proportions of the total stock they control. While all 50 hold 24 percent of the stock of TWA, for example, the 4 largest alone hold 18 percent, the eight largest 23 percent. A similar pattern is seen in many other major corporations.[6] In essence, while the attention of economists, the anti-trust division of the Department of Justice, and the Federal Trade Commission has been fixed on market power and behavior,[7] the upper tiers of control have been almost wholly ignored, though they constitute the basic reality of economic power uniting the banking and business sectors as a whole, and showing close patterns of interaction between the largest banks and the largest corporations in all key sectors of economic life.

John Blair, who served for many years as chief economist of the Senate Antitrust and Monopoly Subcommittee, offered his assessment in 1965 of the relationship between bigness and technological progress in a series of industries—automobiles, bread baking, and drugs:

> In none of the three important new technologies in steel—oxygen conversion, continuous casting or the planetary mill—did any of the largest producers make any significant contribution in research or

development, invention, or innovation, or in any of Novick's four stages. The same is true of the continuous process in bread baking. It was also true for the many innovations conceived and introduced into their models by the smaller automobile manufacturers in the days when they were still extant. Such important classes of drugs as the corticosteroids, tranquilizers, and antibiotics stemmed from discoveries and ideas of independent scientists, some of whom were fortunate in receiving from the drug companies financial support. The major contribution of the drug companies, however, has been in the "development" or "innovation" stages, or more particularly in Novick's step IV of developing new modifications of existing products which in some cases represent important therapeutic advances but in others were criticized as lacking any therapeutic advantages as well as involving the waste of scientific resources.

The information developed during the course of the subcommittee's inquiry into administered prices thus provides no support for the thesis that concentration is essential for invention, and only limited support for the idea that it is necessary to produce development and improvement.[8]

Given the fact that great power does adhere to major corporations, how is it used? In the large, this group sustained the capital goods expansion, which was a key factor in the boom from the late 1950s through the late 1960s. Measured in constant prices, capital expenditures grew every year but one between 1958 and 1967. Expenditures for aircraft, trucks, and buses were among the highest, and utilities and communications firms expanded at a high rate. As the capital goods boom slowed, the economy began to slow also. Industries old and new, in which concentration is high, led both the boom and the slowdown.

The scrutiny of individual corporations is also rewarding. One of the most controversial examples was that offered in Bradford C. Snell's 1974 study, "American Ground Transport," which appears in the record of hearings held by the Senate subcommittee on antitrust and monopoly. It traces the role played by the General Motors Corporation in the replacement of electric by diesel locomotives on several railroads, of electric trolley lines by buses in urban and suburban transport in some places, the replacement of buses by automobiles in other areas, and the replacement of rail by truck transport for goods.

The argument made in Dollars and Sense and in my own article that concentration and inflation go together is one not often discussed, at least since Means more than a decade ago.

The relationship between the corporate sector and the state sector is the real key to understanding both the power of business and the limits of efforts to curb or control it.

Aspects of the interplay between the two sectors are profiled in the articles on the auto industry and the federal safety bureaucracy, as described in *The Wall Street Journal* by John Emshwiller and Albert Karr. One would also want to look at the role of the Interstate Commerce Commission, the collapse of the Penn Central Company, and the persuasive presence of oil company representatives in the structure of federal advisory committees and commissions.

Tracing the role of farm policy in furthering corporate interests, Stanley Aronowitz dissects the industrialization of agriculture and its impact.

The speech by the Chairman of the Federal Trade Commission, Lewis A. Engman, reveals the long-standing fabric of collaboration between state agencies and business needs, much of it built in the wake of the Depression and designed to preserve businesses just as labor and welfare laws sought to protect other groups.

The House Antitrust Subcommittee
INVESTIGATION OF CONGLOMERATE CORPORATIONS

At the beginning of the investigation, the Subcommittee was interested particularly in information that would shed light on motivations that generated the merger movement in the post-war period. Were the generating forces financially oriented, or were the motivations managerial attempts to increase production or marketing strengths? Even before documents were produced by the sample companies there was a popular consensus that financial considerations and not productivity goals were predominant. A number of public officials pointed to the relationship of the financial markets to the merger movement. Remarks of Hamer H. Budge, Chairman of the Securities and Exchange Commission, on February 25, 1969, are typical. He said:

> Until the last three or four years the acquisition and merger move-ment, although extremely important from the standpoint of overall competition, did not carry with it or have associated strong financial implications. In the last three or four years and particularly this last year, more and more the basic reason for the merger or combination seems to be essentially a financial reason. That is, companies are buying other companies or merging with other companies because there are substantial immediate financial advantages to the surviv-ing company in terms of increases in per-share earnings, in terms of the liquid assets which can be obtained by acquiring other compa-nies and because of, what is perhaps the more important, apparent improvements in per-share earnings that can often be obtained.

Information about the mergers of the sample companies sup-port this conclusion. Participation by bankers in the mergers and takeover attempts was a characteristic of all companies. The rela-tionship of Chase Manhattan and its "imaginative lending" to Gulf & Western's growth is the clearest example. Carter, Berlind, & Weill's machinations with both Leasco and National General in their takeovers of insurance companies provide another example of the dominance of financial speculations in merger transactions.

A disquieting relationship appeared in three companies that involved use of trust fund moneys and trust fund personnel in merger activity. Chase Manhattan's trust department was deeply involved in attempts by Resorts International to accumulate shares of Pan American World Airways. Gulf & Western's officials also were related to this speculative "investment." In its battle to beat off Leasco's attempted takeover, Chemical Bank's trust depart-ment was active in strategy and battle plans, and trust fund port-folios were analyzed to locate stock holdings for future use against Leasco. LTV, in its acquisition of Wilson & Company, used $5 million made available from the LTV retirement trust fund. This transaction was questioned by the trustee.

· · ·

From the inception of the investigation, the Subcommittee sought information that would bear upon the contention that conglomerate organizations, through superior management, and institutional relationships, could produce more than the sum of their parts. A name, reputedly coined in Litton Industries, for this highly touted phenomenon was "synergism." This concept has its basis in physiology where it describes cooperative action of a mixture of drugs such that the total effect is greater than the sum of the effects taken independently. In other words, two and two make five. No support for this concept was found in the materials supplied by the sample companies. In fact, management difficulties with newly acquired companies showed, if anything, that combination frequently had injurious effect on efficiency, productivity and corporate values.

The experience of all the companies in the sample, particularly Litton and National General, shows the lack of substance in the synergism concept. Litton is giving up the word, according to *Forbes* magazine, which reported the following [October 15, 1967]:

Conglomerators love to talk about "synergism"—two plus two equal five. "It makes them sound so good," says Roy Ash, "but it is a bad word now and we are giving it up."

In actual practice, "synergism," to the extent that the word is used in business jargon as reflected in documents submitted to the Subcommittee, was employed to identify situations where the business of an acquired company could be used to reinforce "in house" markets, or to add strength in external markets. "Synergism" identified practices that breed malpractices associated with aggregate concentration problems. ITT's use of Avis and Sheraton to exploit "in house" markets and captive external markets are examples. Similarly, another example is the use of Levitt's housing sales to reinforce and create markets for the production of other ITT subsidiaries.

—1971

Dollars & Sense
MONOPOLY AND INFLATION: WHY PRICES NEVER GO DOWN

In the economy as a whole, 78 giant corporations own 43% of all manufacturing assets, and get 49% of all manufacturing profits.

There's more to it than that, of course. It would be wrong to blame inflation entirely on the power of large corporations. But it would also be wrong to forget business and blame inflation on everyone else—an approach often taken by the news media, government, and (of course) business representatives. The other leading suspects in the great inflation mystery—Arab countries, U.S. government spending, crop failures, "wasteful" consumers, "greedy" workers, etc.—can't do the job alone. (Some have nothing to do with it at all.) Big business is at the very least a willing accomplice, always found at the scene of the crime.

Monopoly power, the control of an industry by a few companies, is widespread. This power allows companies to resist pressures for price decreases, while taking advantage of all pressures for price increases. The resistance to market pressures works in only one direction. If a neighborhood laundry suddenly had [spectacular] price and profit increases, someone would open another laundry across the street, undersell them, and drive prices back down. But almost no one can raise the huge amounts of money needed to open a new oil or sugar refinery, especially when interest rates are as high as they are today. And even a business that could raise the money might think twice before taking on such powerful opponents. So the oil and sugar companies don't have to worry much about their skyrocketing profits' attracting more competitors.

In the 1800's, when the U.S. economy was still fairly competitive, prices went down as often as they went up. During times of scarcity, such as the Civil War, prices shot up; but afterwards, they returned gradually to their previous levels. Overall, prices were no higher at the end of the century than at the beginning.

Monopoly power started to be important in the economy around the beginning of the 1900's. And so did long-run inflation. Prices doubled from 1914 to 1920, and never returned to 1914 levels, even in the depths of the great depression of the 1930's.

Since 1940, consumer prices have fallen in only two years: in 1949, by 1%, and in 1955, by less than 0.5%. 1975 will set a new record in American history: 20 years of consecutive price increases.

The usual cure suggested for the ills of monopoly is a "vigorous antitrust policy," breaking up big corporations and restoring competition.

Between 1950 and 1960, the government won 39 anti-trust cases, requiring the separation of recently merged companies. But only 10 of these cases *ever* resulted in a company breaking up in a way that increased competition. In the other cases, it was either impossible to separate the company's assets into two independent units, or there was no buyer outside the industry interested in purchasing part of the company. The same problem has occurred again in the last few years: the government ordered ITT to sell Avis Rent-A-Car, but they have been unable to find a buyer, so ITT still owns it. If you meet anyone who wants to buy a rent-a-car company, call the Justice Department.

Monopolies don't just contribute to inflation through their own pricing policies. They also make government attempts to control inflation less effective. The classic capitalist answer to inflation has been recession. By throwing workers off the job and reducing consumer incomes, a recession forces down total demand, and thus undermines the upward pressures on prices. But with the expansion of monopoly power and its resistance to price decreases, the recession required to stop any given level of inflation must be more severe.

"Conglomerates" such as ITT make the problems of stopping price increases even more difficult. Recession usually hits specific sectors before spreading throughout the economy. A company that sells products in several different industries will be able to resist downward pressure on prices in any one industry because they make profits in many industries. They won't really feel the pinch of recession until their profits are down in several sectors. Recession still does a great job of squeezing the competitive sector of the economy, as any construction company or gas station owner, cattle farmer, or independent trucker can tell you. But that's not where most inflation comes from.

Wage and price controls won't help much either. Somehow the controls are always applied more vigorously to wages than to prices. Even when the government tries to control prices, big corporations have ways of resisting. For instance, they can move production or sales abroad to escape control. Oil companies have been expanding their refinery capacity in the Caribbean islands faster than in the U.S. to escape regulation. And any company selling price-controlled products would rather export them at uncontrolled prices than sell them at home under controls.

Monopoly power isn't the only cause of inflation, of course, but whenever inflation starts, for any reason, monopoly power keeps it going and makes it worse. And government anti-trust and anti-inflation policies aren't much of a solution. If you wait for the government to fight big business for you, you'll be waiting a long time.

—1974

Sumner M. Rosen
THE INFLATIONARY BIAS OF CORPORATE INVESTMENT CONTROL

Keynesian economics is much concerned with the determinants of the level of investment as a major component of the level of aggregate demand. But the *amount* of investment is only one part of the question. The *composition* of investment is equally important. Investment decisions at one point in time determine the composition and the level of output in later periods; today's investment becomes tomorrow's production capacity. Investment decisions affect an industry's future price structure. Large firms set target prices which are intended to realize a desired level of cash flow and rate of return, based on projected sales. The break-even point is determined by price-times-volume on the one hand and total costs on the other. Fixed costs of capital investment are an important component of total costs. The higher the fixed cost total, the higher the price needed to break even at projected levels of sales volume and the more important become marketing and advertising efforts intended to assure that sales meet this minimum volume *without having to lower price to do so*. Thus, today's investment commitment becomes tomorrow's fixed cost, to be recovered from the market through a price-volume combination which yields revenue sufficient to meet or exceed the break even target. This sequence operates as a built-in upward lever on the price level.

For firms which have the market power to generate a cash flow sufficient to meet costs and provide still further funds for investment, investment funds are costless. This process enlarges the capital base of concentrated industries and increases the burden of overhead costs which must be met through sales; if volume does not rise, then price must. This is an important inflationary bias inherent in the market power of large firms in oligopoly markets.

—1974

John Emshwiller and Albert Karr
AUTO MEN USE SLUMP TO SEEK LOWER SAFETY

Since the mid-1960s, the government has written ever-tighter auto safety and pollution rules, mandating everything from stronger bumpers to extensive engine changes. Auto makers, in turn, have resisted almost every new rule, often predicting that production would be disrupted or sales crippled. Yet in the end, new standards seemed inevitably to be met—sometimes even embraced—by the auto companies. During most of the past decade, production didn't falter and sales kept rolling in, topped by three record years in a row in 1971–73.

Now, however, the auto makers are mounting perhaps their most ambitious campaign yet against federal safety and pollution regulations, and they are making more headway than ever. For the auto industry is in one of its deepest slumps in years. And while it's far from clear what role, if any, federal regulation has had in that, the plunge in car sales and the layoff of thousands of auto workers are creating strong sympathy in Washington for the industry's view that the added costs imposed by the regulations hurt auto sales.

"The Detroit situation concerns everybody in the administration. The economic situation has changed dramatically in the past few weeks," says James B. Gregory, head of the National Highway Traffic Safety Administration, the Transportation Department agency that writes the auto-safety rules. "The President has highlighted the administration's concern, and I'm trying to be responsive to that concern." One official, who sees the administration reacting to "a state of panic" in Detroit, says the Transportation Department "is reconsidering its full regulatory structure."

Capitalizing on what they view as long-overdue recognition of their side of things, the auto makers are seeking a three- to five-year delay on all new auto safety and pollution standards, including some that have already been delayed before. Such a freeze would delay, in some cases into the 1980s, a wide range of planned regulations, including tougher pollution-control rules now set for 1977 and 1978, more sophisticated protection of motorists in crashes, and less flammable seats and interiors. Some auto men are even urging that several existing features, such as head restraints and reinforced doors, be stripped off future cars.

So far the outcome is in doubt. Even if President Ford wanted to, the former Michigan Congressman couldn't give Detroit all it is seeking. As far as pollution is concerned, the Environmental Protection Agency can grant one-year postponements, but Congress would have to vote on any further relaxation and the new Congress may be more environment-minded than the outgoing one. Regarding safety, relaxation could be accomplished administratively without Congressional action, but any such move would almost certainly cause an uproar in Congress. Sen. Vance Hartke, Democrat of Indiana, chairman of the Senate panel's Surface Transportation Subcommittee, says a moratorium on safety is already in progress within the Executive Branch. "They're starting to turn the clock backward," he says, and he promises his subcommittee will soon hold hearings on the matter.

It is true that the auto makers have already scored some victories on safety. A few months ago, Congress voted to scuttle the device that prevents cars from being started before front-seat belts are fastened. In late December, federal safety regulators acted to relax tough rules on damage protection by bumpers. And the safety officials have been persuaded to consider a long delay, or even outright shelving, of the automatically inflating air bag proposed to protect passengers in auto crashes; under the latest plan, the air bag was to have been required in 1977 models.

At the same time, the Administration plans to add its voice to the auto makers' pleas for putting off new emission rules. President Ford is expected to propose this month that in exchange for a pledge from auto makers to achieve 40% better gasoline mileage by 1980—and thereby help the U.S. achieve greater independence from foreign oil—Congress delay for five years the carbon monoxide, hydrocarbon and nitrogen-oxide limits planned now for the 1977 cars. He is expected to propose this even though the Environmental Protection Agency and the Department of Transportation recently published a report contending that President Ford's goal of a 40% mileage improvement could be obtained by 1980 without easing any pending regulations other than a tough 1978-model standard for nitrogen oxides, a key smog ingredient. Auto makers call the two agencies' report too optimistic, though one General Motors executive concedes his company could come close to 40% under these conditions.

As far as Detroit is concerned, nothing less than the economic health of the nation and its ability to cope with the energy problem hang in the balance. Auto men argue that most future standards, and some current ones, cost more than they are worth and interfere with the orderly development of potential long-term solutions to auto-safety, pollution and mileage problems. New standards "will give a big new push to inflation, depress sales and employment in our industry even farther, increase gasoline consumption substantially—and do hardly anything for public health and safety," contends Lee A. Iacocca, president of Ford Motor Co.

To many who have battled Detroit for a decade on these issues, the newest campaign is less than convincing. They worry that the quality of the air and the safety of millions of motorists could be jeopardized. They also point to a long-standing Detroit credibility gap ("sins of the past," one auto man acknowledges).

For example, auto makers for years predicted disastrous consequences if they were forced to use catalytic antipollution devices
on cars; but now they are not only using them; GM, at least, is
even extolling their virtues in full-page newspaper ads.

"This is the most blatant power play they've tried to pull in
the last 10 years," charges the consumer advocate Ralph Nader.
Like others, he contends that the industry's cost estimates on
present and future standards are inflated and that safety and pollution gear have played an insignificant role in the current auto
slump. He claims that by linking federal regulations to sagging
sales, auto makers "are hoping to find a scapegoat" for their
current troubles.

All this frenetic activity by the auto men has won some new
and powerful converts. Most notable so far has been the United
Auto Workers Union, long a supporter of tough safety and pollution rules. Now, with thousands of its members jobless, the UAW
has thrown its weight behind a moratorium. Thus, some liberal
Congressmen may have to choose between two sets of backers: on
the one hand, environmentalists and auto-safety advocates; on the
other, job conscious union members.

Ironically, a safety and antipollution freeze isn't likely to do
anything to help the current auto slump; the most important scheduled standards are still a year or two away. Although Rodney
Markley, Ford Motor's top Washington lobbyist, says that the
heavy layoffs in the industry will force Congress to "see the
realities of the problems," he concedes when pressed that a freeze
won't "directly" help 1975 sales or layoffs.

—1975

Stanley Aronowitz
BUTTER FROM BOEING, HAM FROM ITT

Of all the "crises" we've experienced in the past two years, it was
the food crisis that held an aspect of terror. Even for many persons
in lower income brackets the plentitude of food and its relative
variety constituted an important source of psychological security.
As if to underscore the disintegration of the assumptions of daily

life, food became not only expensive but some types of food were actually becoming scarce. Hoarding meat became a commonplace. People began to shop in bulk rather than run to the nearest grocery store for a bottle of milk and a loaf of bread. Shopping now became a serious life activity for many who simply never considered the problem of getting nourishment as something to be planned.

Meanwhile, agriculture, *Business Week* concluded in April 1973, was America's "greatest growth industry" of 1972. The huge profits in agriculture that began to be earned in late 1972 and 1973 are the other side of the coin of high food prices.

As William Appleman Williams has argued, the tendency for farm surpluses to outrun consumption has been the primary impulse toward U.S. expansion in the twentieth century.[9] In the 1890s, 24 percent of all agricultural production went for export and this tendency to produce for the world market has been central to the fortunes of the American farm sector ever since the 1930s. The export of farm goods was facilitated by government subsidies when New Deal diplomacy attempted to accelerate the disposal of farm surpluses through foreign trade agreements which provided for the import of manufactured goods and such cash crops as coffee. The heart of government agricultural policies has not only been price supports for domestic production, but also the two-price system, whereby prices for exports are lower than the price in the domestic market.

Food growers have always fought the railroads, the "middlemen," and the banks that often controlled intermediate businesses. But the solution to both the problem of surpluses and the dwindling share claimed by farmers of the retail price of farm goods turned out not to be a larger share for farmers at the expense of corporate interest. Instead processors and the government offered another way out—overseas markets.

Even the yeoman farmer eventually became convinced that American imperial expansion was really in his interest. The populist movement against railroads and the so-called middlemen who used their monopolistic position to squeeze the small farmers was a significant political development in American history. In the 1870s and 1880s many farmers were persuaded that their economic destiny was antagonistic to the interests of the large trusts which were establishing their domination over transportation and the marketing of food and cotton. But even as agrarian radicalism was waging a powerful, but ultimately rear-guard, action against the trusts, strong forces were forging an alliance with the same hated giants.

The coalition between financial and agricultural businesses was cemented firmly as the small farmer gave way to the corporate farm in the years after World War I. Factories in the field (farms), owned and often controlled by large banks and insurance companies, became integrated within the larger corporate nexus that pressed for new capital and commodities markets overseas. Thus it is no exaggeration to claim that the export of agricultural products has been a significant component of favorable U.S. trade balances throughout this century.

American industry not only gathered its initial strength from the productive farm sector, but has relied upon it for currency stability and, to a lesser extent, for the extension of its world political influence. Thus, food is much more than the material substratum of industrial development, insofar as cheap prices insure relatively low wages and high profit rates that can be translated into investments in new manufacturing industries. Agriculture has become a vital component of foreign economic policy and an extraordinary political weapon to sustain a favorable atmosphere for U.S. investments in poor nations.

The fundamental reason for the sudden jump in food prices was that agricultural surpluses and basic stocks were pressed into service when the value of the dollar slipped in the late 1960s and began to tumble rapidly in the first two years of this decade. Farm businesses, long restive about the serious decline of their share of the consumer dollar, put powerful pressure on the Administration to move swiftly to insure a high rate of return on their investments. The price of machinery was higher, the power of processors, wholesalers, and retailers was growing, and Congress was threatening to remove price supports after nearly 40 years of artificially inflated prices.

Competition between growers and processors, wholesalers and retailers, and within the farm sector itself intensified in the 1950s, leading to an unprecedented era of mergers and combinations.

By the first years of the 1970s, many of the largest farms were owned or controlled by food processors. Key processor-farm owners such as Del Monte, Libby Foods, and Seabrook Farms dominated fruit and vegetable production in the United States. These and other corporations controlled 85 percent of retail vegetable sales and 69 percent of food and nut sales in 1969, indicating the emergence of what is called "vertical integration" as the characteristic feature of the food industry since 1960. The control over farms by relatively few large processors, which in turn are dominated by banks and large holding companies, means that price fixing in agriculture has become as feasible as in the auto and steel industries. Corporate farming, which really began on a large scale in the thirties, has reduced the number of farms by 300 percent in 40 years.

Government price-support policies are oriented to the largest growers who have accumulated millions of dollars in price supports. In 1959, Senator John Williams (R-Del.) estimated that the three largest farm corporations received more price-support money from the federal government than the states of Pennsylvania, New Jersey, Delaware, and Maryland combined; 56 percent of the farms received less than 7 percent of all supports.

As early as 1967, economist Ben Seligman advanced the point of view that monopoly control over retailing, especially the growth of supermarket chains and involuntary "independent" grocery cooperative buying arrangements, was driving prices upward.[10] By 1963 the top four chains controlled half the food sales in 218 metropolitan areas, while the top eight had 62 percent of these sales. Seligman pointed out that the profit margins of the major chains such as Safeway, A&P, Acme, and Kroger rose by more than 35 percent each, while the increase for the retail food industry as a whole was 28 percent between 1949 and 1965.

Control by the national and regional chains over food retailing has made them extremely powerful in their relations with processors and agribusinesses. Ownership of disparate functions in the food business is not the only means of achieving vertical integration. Sometimes the retail chains control all aspects of the food industry through the device of the exclusive contract, which subordinates other aspects of the industry to its rule without direct ownership. Or a large processor, such as Consolidated Foods, will enter the retail chain business and achieve integration through its position as a wholesaler. But the retailers seem to have achieved the most sophisticated level of vertical integration. In 1967 Seligman estimated that some of them were able to supply as much as 65 percent of their own needs through control over processing and contracting out food growing.

—1974

Lewis A. Engman
SPEECH TO FINANCIAL ANALYSTS FEDERATION

There are some, myself among them, who believe that inflation can be reduced by purging the economy of anticompetitive behavior. The FTC and the Justice Department's Antitrust Division are both looking with especial care for the types of trade restraints, collusion, and unfair marketing practices which reduce competition and lead to higher prices for consumers. Some have suggested that import duties and quotas be lifted to permit entry of more lower priced foreign goods. Others cast their vote for the reimposition of controls or, at least, for some form of guidelines. But the suggestion enjoying perhaps the greatest vogue at the moment is that inflation can be curbed by reducing the government's involvement in the economy; more specifically, by reducing its regulatory role.

It is not just the survival-of-the-fittest, every-man-for-himself free-marketeers who make this suggestion. It has the support of many people generally viewed as liberal and interventionist in their approach to the economy. It has received the blessing of Ralph Nader. And it is about to be endorsed by Lew Engman.

Here's the reason. Though most government regulation was enacted under the guise of protecting the consumer from abuse, much of today's regulatory machinery does little more than shelter producers from the normal competitive consequences of lassitude and inefficiency. In some cases, the world has changed, reducing the original threat of abuse. In other cases, the regulatory machinery has simply become perverted. In still other cases, the machinery was a mistake from the start. In any case, the consumer, for whatever presumed abuse he is being spared, is paying plenty in the form of government-sanctioned price fixing.

The airline industry provides an example. Under the Federal Aviation Act, the Civil Aeronautics Board controls the entry of new carriers to the market, controls the distribution of routes and has the power to disapprove or modify an airline's rate change proposal after hearing complaints from the so-called competition. The result is that in the areas of rates and routes for all intents and purposes there is no competition at all. Competition, where it exists, is concentrated on the one unregulated aspect of airline activity, customer service. That is why the average airline commercial looks like an ad for a combination bawdy house and dinner theater.

Any doubt that one consequence of the CAB's control over rates and routes is higher prices, is dispelled by what happened some years ago in California when Pacific Southwest Airlines, an intrastate carrier not subject to CAB rate regulation or entry restrictions, entered the San Francisco/Los Angeles market with rates less than half those being charged by the interstate CAB certified carriers TWA, Western, and United. What happened? After attempting to ignore PSA's lower fares, the CAB carriers were forced to cut their rates to meet the competition. Even today, to fly from L.A. to San Francisco costs only about half as much on a per-mile basis as it costs to fly from Washington to New York.

Another instance of prices being pushed up by regulation is that of the Interstate Commerce Commission, created back in 1887 supposedly to protect shippers against the monopolistic power of the railroads. But by 1935, the nation had sprouted a network of highways, and the trucks which rolled over them were biting deeply into the market power of the railroads. With the trucking field still wide open to new entrants, this might logically have been the time to dismantle the ICC. The railroad monopoly was broken, competition could take its course. However, instead of freeing the railroads from regulation, Congress, in the Motor Carrier Act of 1935, just cast the regulatory net wider to include the interstate truckers as well. As a result, today we have a situation in which market entry by new trucking firms is restricted by the ICC at the same time that rates are being fixed by the carriers who are given antitrust immunity to do so. Though the ICC has authority to investigate rate findings by the carriers, according to testimony given before a House Committee two years ago the Commission was doing so in less than 1 percent of the cases.

And what is the result? Well, when the Supreme Court held some time ago that fresh dressed poultry was an agricultural commodity under the ICC Act and thus not subject to regulation, the average rate for shipping it fell by 33 percent.

I have given you just a couple of examples. But, when you take all of the industries subject to direct federal regulation—that's air, rail and truck transport, power generation, television, radio, the securities industry and others—it works out to a substantial fraction of the economy. In fact, it is estimated that these regulated industries account for 10 percent of everything made and sold in this country. What makes them even more important from the point of view of inflation is that they tend to be industries whose prices show up as costs buried in the prices of hundreds of other products. Take transportation for example. When you change the price of hauling freight, that change is going to show up not just once but again and again. By the time you get a piece of meat from the pasture to the plate, it carries with it numerous transportation charges.

These industries subject to direct regulation are only part of the story. There are, in addition, the dozens and dozens of federal and state regulations, prohibitions, proscriptions and requirements all of which subvert competition in the name of a greater objective—though sometimes it is hard to see exactly what that greater objective is or on whose judgment its greatness rests. I refer to things such as:

• state laws against advertising the prices of eyeglasses or prescription drugs;

• the Jones Act forbidding foreign competition in the shipping business between U.S. ports;

• the federal government's own "buy American" procurement preferences which can allow domestic producers to charge as much as 50 percent more than foreign sellers for some items. I should add that many states have similar preferences;

- an agricultural price support program which asks the consumer to buy with his tax dollars what he does not want, cannot use and will never eat;
- an agricultural export subsidy program which asks the consumer to pay the farmer to sell his product to some foreign buyer at a price lower than that at which the consumer himself can get it.

The effect of some of this regulation may perhaps be seen in some recent events in California. This summer the California Milk Producers Association dumped 420,000 gallons of fresh skim milk into Los Angeles harbor. The dairy co-op said that it was necessary to dump the milk "because no market could be found for it." At what price, I might ask? I suspect that more milk could be sold if it were not for the elaborate government programs designed to maintain higher than competitive prices on the producer, processor and on the retail levels.

I mention only a few. Former Council of Economic Advisers' member Hendrik Houthakker has compiled a list of 45 regulatory policies that contribute to inflation. To me, the most distressing development is the pervasive and well-accepted dishonesty that pervades the government's approach to regulation. The existing crazy quilt of anticonsumer subsidies embodied in the intricately woven fabric of federal and state statutes and regulations is pernicious because: (1) The subsidies are deliberately hidden from public view. (2) The government has irresponsibly lost track of the actual cost of these subsidies. (3) In most, if not all, cases, we have adopted the least efficient form of subsidy with the purpose of hiding the subsidy from the public and obfuscating its true cost.

From time to time, proposals have been made to provide direct cash subsidies in lieu of the patchwork of regulatory subsidies that now pervade our economy. Opponents rise indignantly to object that hard-working individuals and businesses don't want handouts. Well, a rose by any other name . . . Our airlines, our truckers, our railroads, our electronic media, and countless others are on the dole. We get irate about welfare fraud. But our complex systems of hidden regulatory subsidies make welfare fraud look like petty larceny.

I have no way of knowing what the numerous regulatory measures cost the consumer each year. I have seen private estimates indicating that the annual costs in the transportation area alone may exceed $16 billion. I invite students of this kind of thing to come up with their own figures. Whatever they are, I think we can all agree on this: the costs are too high.

—1974

Multinationals

In their new study,[1] Richard Barnet and Ronald Müller call the multinational corporations "the globalization of oligopoly capitalism" which produces "a new concentration of political power in private hands." These are correct statements but their generality limits their usefulness. More to the point is their view that multinational corporations cannot be effectively influenced, much less controlled, by even the powerful national governments, including ours. The results are several:

1. A reordering of production and market relationships which shifts employment and wages to the developing countries. As a result the economic role of the United States increasingly shifts to services performed on behalf of the multinationals. The U.S. balance of payments relies more heavily on agricultural exports.

2. Concentration of international as well as national control over economic affairs in the hands of the U.S. banks which hold

decisive blocks of shares in the multinationals. These in turn are dominated[2] by the Rockefeller-Morgan group.

3.   Control over the U.S. balance of payments by multinationals in two aspects: their predominant role as ultimate buyers and sellers of U.S. exports and imports, and the large share of international movement of goods represented by intracompany transactions.

4.   Private international control over a significant section of market prices beyond the power of official agencies to affect by monetary or fiscal policies. This control extends also to key money flows themselves. Because of the close connection between the major banks and the multinationals, a significant share of all business loans are made by one to the other and are almost wholly resistant to official efforts to curb or expand credit.

5.   Minimal tax liabilities to the U.S. for activities controlled from this country and benefiting predominantly Americans.

Most debate about multinationals has focused on their direct employment effects. Unions claim that job losses have been substantial and that multinationals, by utilizing modern technology outside the United States, have also reduced the share of skilled, better-paying jobs in domestic industry. Other studies[3] claim that multinationals increase domestic employment and upgrade the domestic component of the multinationals' payrolls. Unions have clearly experienced difficulties in securing any leverage over the location or production decisions of multinationals and cannot fall back on federal action to help out, as they could when the problem was moving production from North to South, city to countryside. The International Metalworkers Federation and the International Chemical and General Workers Federation have taken the lead in trying to develop international cooperation among domestic labor unions dealing in different countries with the same firms, but this effort is still in its infancy, with uncertain prospects at best. The governments of the European Economic Community have developed somewhat more advanced patterns of joint policy-making, but these structures too are relatively primitive and weak compared to the strength and sophistication of the multinationals.

It is not surprising that the viewpoint of Ralph Nader on the multinationals is critical and pessimistic, while other writers stress the benefits they see from the accelerated development of an "international economic system." Illustrating some current dangers is the short piece in *The Wall Street Journal* which summarized a Tariff Commission study about the possible role of multinationals in international currency movements, a danger which had been created long before the oil crisis and OPEC currency accumulations caught our attention; the $268 billion in short-term assets held by private organizations, many of them multinationals, dwarfs even the $40–$50 billion accumulated in 1974 by the OPEC countries and held largely as short-term balances.

But we should note that while multinationals may reduce jobs for workers, they appear to offer full-employment prospects for economists; introducing an article on the subject in the July 1973 issue of *Financial Executive,* the editor observed that at Harvard alone the ongoing study of multinationals had already "contributed to the completion of about 15 doctoral theses, nearly 60 articles in various journals, a 500-page compilation of basic data, and seven books," and the second phase of the investigation had hardly begun!

Ralph Nader
STATEMENT AT THE UNITED NATIONS

A most serious international problem caused by "worldcorps" is the way they manipulate or play off nations, governments and rulers against each other. Since they operate globally, and nation-states do not, they can exploit weaknesses in the policies or laws of specific countries. Just as the state of Delaware is a corporate Reno (Nevada), so are Panama, Liechtenstein and Switzerland, in their ways, global Delawares.

The result is that some nations are becoming dumping-grounds for products and facilities that multinationals have trouble selling elsewhere. So Pepsico sells its inventory of cyclamates abroad after they have been banned as hazardous to human health in this country. So Parke, Davis and Merck and Company sell Choloromycetin and Indocin, respectively, abroad without the cautionary contraindications of danger required in the United States. And firms which seek out the cost-free method of waste disposal known as pollution end up residing in the countries with the most lenient environmental regulations.

Unions are especially frustrated by this playing-off of nations, since striking an International Telephone and Telegraph subsidiary in Spain simply means that ITT increases production elsewhere or lets the strikers cool their heels while its empire suffers little. The leverage enjoyed by striking workers, which was one of their only points of power in corporate contests, is vitiated. Worse, firms are attracted to places with low wages and strong anti-labor laws. And those countries which do try to emulate our labor movement's efforts to upgrade working conditions and pay are met with the threat of corporate flight.

Taxation, the balance of payments, and the international monetary system also allow the multinationals to display their global creativity. First, firms seek out tax havens, Taiwan and the Cayman Islands being examples, for the promise of a decade or two of tax-free production. When a worldcorp has subsidiaries in many countries, it can manipulate pricing to disguise accurate earnings and minimize its tax payments. Accounting gimmickry permits firms to pass on costs to host countries where taxes are low, or to those countries with sound currencies and little inflation. Thus the worldcorp becomes a pump primer for instability and inequality— often alternatively described as the rich getting richer and the poor getting poorer.

The cost of these maneuverings becomes glaring when one looks closely at multinational corporations which dominate their host countries. The problems, first of all, are sheer size, external control, and escape from responsible political control by the host country. The largest 10 worldcorps (by sales) are bigger than some 80 nations (by GNP), and the largest 40 firms are larger than some 65 nations. Complicating size disparity is the obvious conflict between a worldcorp seeking profits and the nation-state seeking public welfare. The two quite obviously do not invariably overlap. Consider the following choices facing a country: should there be investment in future producer goods or present consumer goods; should emphasis be on the military or civilian sector, the public or private sector; should it stress human resources or physical assets, full employment or no inflation; should there be more or less automation, higher or lower prices; how is economic growth to be balanced against environmental preservation; should a worker's benefits be based on value or welfare; should we have a state-run or a competitive economy; should economic policy emphasize licensing and loans over controlled technology and equity investment by these worldcorps? The answer to each varies with the development, culture, and demography of each country. What is right for the United States is not necessarily right for China, or Sri Lanka. The cardinal standard is that the choices should belong to the people who live in each country and not to a tiny number of anonymous and distant corporate executives in the West and Tokyo, whose power vastly exceeds their accountability to these people they so deeply affect or afflict.

But who is to decide all these questions? The issue is one of control: who, in fact, controls an economy when a dominant multinational firm can pick up and leave if the local rules are changed to its displeasure? "Increasing numbers of a poor country's economic actors become responsible to superiors . . . who are citizens of other countries," observed Peter Evans in a recent book, *Transactional Relations in World Politics*. "If a similar chain of command existed in public organizations, the peer country would be deemed a colony." This point is most applicable to Third World developing nations, but it is not only applicable to them. Canada, nearly half of whose industry is owned by United States firms, understands what it means to be a branch plant economy. So does Chile, 40 of whose largest 100 industrial firms are foreign-owned. Even the United States is not immune to a firm contemptuous of national borders or authorities. When the Federal Trade Commission recently brought an action against Xerox, the firm at first would not even meet with Federal Trade Commission representatives, saying, "We don't believe that the Federal Trade Commission is the appropriate forum for the resolution of the problems of multinational corporations." They did not explain what was the appropriate forum.

The profits of worldcorps are often lush. Ronald Müller studied the rate of return on net worth for 15 pharmaceutical subsidiaries in Latin America, and found that it ranged from a low of 44.2 percent to a high of 962.1 percent, with the average return being

136.3 percent. Looked at more broadly, in 1950 and 1965 the profit inflow to the United States from Third World investments was 264 percent of its capital outflow, while the equivalent percentage for Western Europe was 71 percent. Such profits could not exist with the competition that multinational firms can frustrate. Exacerbating this exploitation is the fact that so much after-tax profit is repatriated to the domestic Unied States, as multinational firms indirectly admit. If their investments help the United States balance of payments because of repatriated profits, as they claim, the surplus must come from somewhere, and the somewhere is the developing nations. This exchange can also regressively distribute income—from the relatively poorer class who produce the goods to the relatively rich foreigners who own the stock of these firms.

With returns so large, it is predictable that worldcorps should often take political measures to protect their investment. Just as du Pont has turned Delaware into a company state, International Telephone and Telegraph apparently could not resist trying to shape Chile in its own image. Where investment goes, so does well-planned, behind-the-scenes politics, often with the close assistance of the United States or other governments of worldcorp domicile. Thus multinational enterprise can move a Trojan horse to developing countries. Alluring at first, it can undermine local investment, dominate technological development, exploit cheap labor and pervert local politics.

It is altogether fitting, then, that the United Nations, a multinational entity, should scrutinize multinational corporations. The time is late, but the opportunity remains to finally hold these firms accountable to more than their profit statements.

A basic way to hold corporations more structurally accountable, even international corporations, is by building controls into their birthright—the corporate charter. The charter is effectively a contract between the state and the firm; you can incorporate to provide a service or product, the state says, if you follow certain conditions in the public interest. But many nations have weak chartering laws in order to induce corporations to remain or locate there. Thus, all are driven down to the lowest common denominator in the "competition" for corporate business. As a preliminary course, nations could be encouraged, under United Nations initiatives, to formulate parallel and strict terms in their chartering mechanism, covering such areas as corporáte disclosure, antitrust, shareholder rights, management liabilities, and affirmative duty to report on a wide variety of matters to all nations where the firm is doing business. A "law corporate" can be developed, much as the "law merchant" evolved in the past, only much more quickly.

—1974

The Wall Street Journal
CURRENCY CRISIS "CAN BE EASILY TRIGGERED" BY MULTINATIONALS

Multinational corporations control such vast quantities of money that they can precipitate international monetary crises by moving only small portions of their funds from country to country, a government study concludes.

The big companies and banks can outgun even the world's central banks in international currency dealings, the massive study by the U.S. Tariff Commission contends. And though the study absolves most multinational concerns of "destructive, predatory motives," in their currency dealings, it says that much of the speculative money surge during currency crises, such as the current turmoil in exchange markets, stems from the multinationals.

The 930-page study of the economic impact of multinational concerns on trade, investment and employment was made by the Tariff Commission at the request of the International Trade subcommittee of the Senate Finance Committee. It's certain to add fuel to the growing debate in Congress on the effects of the multinationals, which have been under attack by organized labor as "exporters" of U.S. jobs and technology.

The study estimates that some $268 billion of short-term liquid assets were held at the end of 1971 by "private institutions on the international finance scene," and that the "lion's share" of this money was controlled by U.S.-based multinational companies and banks.

The $268 billion, the study reports, "was more than twice the total of all international reserves held by all central banks and

international monetary institutions in the world at the same date."
It adds: "These are the reserves with which the central banks fight
to defend their exchange rates. The resources of the private sector
outclass them."

Due to the immensity of the multinationals' assets, "it is clear
that only a small fraction . . . needs to move in order for a genuine
crisis to develop," the Tariff Commission concludes. This money
"can focus with telling effect on a crisis-prone situation—some
weak currency which repels funds and some strong one which
attracts them." That's what has happened in the past two weeks as
speculators dumped dollars and bought German marks and Japanese yen in hopes of profiting on future changes in their exchange
values.

Since only a "small proportion" of the multinationals' money
is needed "to produce monetary explosions," the study says, "it
appears appropriate to conclude that destructive, predatory motivations don't characterize the sophisticated international financial
activities of most multinational corporations, even though much of
the funds which flow internationally during the crisis doubtlessly is
of multinational corporation origin."

In assessing the aims of big companies in currency crises, the
report offers two possible conclusions: either that the multinationals "react protectively" with moves to protect the value of their
assets or, alternatively, that most multinationals "hardly react at
all, while a small minority, capable of generating heavy, disruptive
movements of funds, do so." The study said the latter group
includes companies that may actually "speculate" in the sense of
betting on exchange-rate changes in hopes of a swift profit.

The study found that U.S. concerns invest abroad primarily to
reach new markets, rather than to find lower-cost production. The
search for low-wage labor is a "secondary" consideration except
in a relatively few industries, including consumer electronics, foot-
wear, toys and apparel, it says.

The study doesn't resolve the question of whether multinationals have caused major job losses in the U.S., as American
unions contend. It presents three alternative explanations—two of
which will please unions and one which companies will like.

The commission estimates that the presence of American-owned plants abroad represents a net loss of 1.3 million jobs in America if it's assumed foreigners would otherwise import the plants' entire output from the U.S. If foreigners imported only half of such output, and produced the rest themselves, the job loss would be calculated at 400,000. A third set of quite different assumptions produces an estimate that the multinationals have produced a net gain of roughly 500,000 jobs in the U.S.

The study concludes that the multinational corporations "played no role" in the sharp deterioration of the U.S. balance-of-payments position during the late 1960s.

—1973

The Military Economy

We ended mass unemployment in the depression by arming for World War II. We relied on military spending in large measure to reverse economic declines in postwar years, most notably during the first months of the Kennedy administration. Presidents claim that we can prosper without arms—while they continue to increase military budgets. Military contractors say that they would prefer ploughshares to swords—but they continue avidly to seek ever larger contracts for weapons.

The major aerospace producers are as highly specialized, and as vulnerable, as the dinosaur. Their survival depends on the perpetuation of the military budget and the constant replacement of older weapons systems by new ones. They and the Pentagon have a symbiotic relationship; each depends on the other, each cleaves to the other, both unite to resist and repel efforts to reduce military spending.

There have been dramatic shifts in the international climate— the destruction of the myth of a monolithic communist menace, for one—yet the military fixation persists as a core feature of the economy.

The National Security Summer Research Project showed that the problems of conversion remain difficult, and the relationship of the aerospace industry and the Pentagon as close as ever. One approach might be to focus not on the firms themselves—let Lockheed go if necessary—but on the groups of scientists, engineers, technicians and workers who might well be creatively deployed into needed civilian work.[1]

The system of military procurement violates almost every convention of traditional economic analysis. It is not competitive; it minimizes risk to the contractor; it provides excess profits; it permits massive cost overruns; and it does all these things in secrecy, hidden from the public eye. On occasion a determined investigation can reveal some of these realities. A persistent feature of the arms economy is pinpointed in Mary Kaldor and Alexander Cockburn's analysis of the 1975 defense budget. They show how small beginnings grow to enormous proportions while depriving Congress of any option but to accept them. They demonstrate the connection between strategic doctrine and economic decisions which assume a momentum that requires extraordinary mobilization of effort to stop, an effort seldom possible.

Arms sales abroad, once a sideline, have now assumed a central role in arms budgeting and international economic policy. Michael T. Klare shows what this means. Finally, Seymour Melman summarizes some of the things we've been missing in our 25-year addiction to arms spending.

National Security Summer Research Program
DEFENSE INDUSTRY: THE FOURTH BRANCH OF GOVERNMENT[2]

The military market supports the largest single industry in the country today, providing more than $40 billion in sales each year and involving in total over 20,000 firms. In fiscal year 1969 there were more than $24 billion in prime contracts for new weapons systems and components, in addition to more than $6 billion for military research and development. The industry is remarkably concentrated, with the 100 largest contractors receiving two-thirds of the total contract funds, and the top 25 receiving half these funds.

Negotiated contracts are the rule rather than the exception in the defense industry, accounting for 58 percent of all military prime contracts in 1968, with advertised competitive bidding accounting for only 11.5 percent of the total procurement dollars. This industry is one of our least competitive. Firms seldom if ever suffer a financial loss in their defense business. The Defense Department acts to insure that the firms which do business with it remain financially healthy. Through the widespread use of negotiated contracts and "change orders," to aid a firm when it is in financial trouble, a profitable return on company investment is almost automatic. And the investment which a defense firm must make is considerably smaller than that of a firm doing business with the public. The Federal Government will often provide the building and much of the capital equipment at no cost to the firm (roughly half of the capital assets controlled by defense firms are government property), and it will make "progress payments" even before it receives the finished product.

There also appears to be an informal policy within the Defense Department to provide an automatic share of military business to each of the large defense firms, rationalized by a belief that these firms represent a necessary part of our national security and must be kept financially healthy. As one industry official put it to us, "Everyone feeds at the trough, even though it isn't planned that way." Any idle industrial capacity is filled by new programs. When the Fast Deployment Logistic Ship program was cancelled by the Congress, the Division of Litton Industries which had begun building shipyard facilities for this program instead received a contract (expected to total over a billion dollars) for construction of the new Helicopter Assault Ship. The result of this policy is a striking entrenchment of the major defense firms in their successful profit positions; 21 of the top twenty-five defense firms in 1966 were also in the top twenty-five a decade earlier. Furthermore, no large defense firm has folded and few have significantly reduced their military business in the last decade.

A recent sampling of the views of industry leaders indicated that they are quite satisfied with this situation and have no intention of gambling its future on risky ventures in the civilian market. While much industry advertising refers to their potential contribution to solving the nation's social ills, in fact there has been little industry funds invested in this area, and defense firms have shown little capacity for participating successfully in the civilian market. It is therefore important to them that the market of defense contracts continue active and that their firm receives a significant share of the defense business. This requires an all out effort to be involved with the weapons decision process itself, and these firms have been highly successful in this effort.

Industry efforts are aimed at winning contracts for the actual production of hardware or, in the words of one representative, "the pot of gold." However, this does not mean that they wait for the procurement decision. Rather, industry must "buy in" early in the research and development phase to gain the specialized information that will make it a "sole source" when the procurement award is made. As an officer of General Dynamics told us, "You have to get in on the ground floor or forget it." Or, as Murray Weidenbaum, Assistant Secretary of the Treasury, put it, "At the present time, typically, the key competition is for the relatively small development contract, and the winner of that virtually automatically gets the large so-called 'follow-up' procurement contracts."

Industry representatives are in continuing contact with government officials, where they can influence new research and development decisions, suggest ideas for new systems and for system improvement, and establish in the minds of the government official the special competence of their firms to carry out the job. As one sales representative told us, "If you wait around until the RFP [request for proposal] comes out, you're dead." Such close contact is viewed as essential by these firms, if they are to be prepared to suggest and then carry out the specialized tasks required in any weapons systems development. As an official of North American Rockwell told us, "Any company which would go by all the rules would have no idea what the government wants and would be developing things that would be completely out of line."

Industry attempts, as much as possible, to staff its sales force with engineers, so they can deal as professional colleagues with their government counterparts, rather than acting merely as salesmen looking for the government's money.

Industry takes advantage of the insistence of each service that it remain on the frontier of advanced technology. The contractor is free to come up with a design that exceeds the initial requirements, and in most cases such a proposal will be enthusiastically received. As an official at LTV remarked, "Several companies may come up with a good design, but what makes you better is what else you might come up with, what added component you have, what possible breakthrough you stimulate." Since the pressure for technological sophistication is far greater than any pressure to keep costs down, this results in rapidly rising costs and, even more important, a direct and powerful influence by defense contractors on the weapons which the military wants and procures.

Defense firms maintain active research and development programs supported by overhead receipts on prior contracts. Through these efforts they develop ideas and products which can then be sold to the government on a sole-source basis. By this means they can, in industry jargon, "create a need," that is, generate the demand they alone can meet. As a representative of North American Rockwell informed us, "Your ultimate goal is to actually write the RFP, and this happens more often than you might think." Another, from Pratt and Whitney, boasted, "We have the technical superiority and are on the offensive. We spoon-feed them. We ultimately try to load them with our own ideas and designs, but in such a way that, when they walk away from the conference table, they are convinced it was their idea all along."

Peter Schenck, an official of the Raytheon Corporation and former president of the Air Force Corporation, put it this way: "Today it is more likely that the military requirement is the result of joint participation of military and industrial personnel, and it is not unusual for industry's contribution to be a key factor. Indeed, there are highly-placed military men who sincerely feel that industry is currently setting the pace in the research and development of new weapons systems."

(Research by David Sims)

The National Security State. This report is not intended as another attack on the "military-industrial complex"—we do not see America as a victim of an insidious conspiracy emanating from this power bloc. It appears to us more accurate to say that American society is becoming what we have chosen to call a national security state, whose dominant institutions and ideology are focused upon the military establishment and military solutions to national policy problems. The issues which have recently made news: the cost-overruns on weapons systems; the extent of our chemical and biological arsenal; the clandestine practices of the Green Berets—and the new material which we present in this report are not accidents or exceptions. They are all part of the operation of a total system which was laid down in the immediate postwar era by the Truman Administration and strengthened by each successive administration.

In the immediate postwar years, a number of bills were passed which had the effect of transforming ad hoc wartime arrangements into law. All the essential institutions of the National Security State were created in that period. The draft was resumed. The National Security Act of 1947 coordinated the Armed Forces under the Office of the Secretary of Defense, created the National Security Council, and established the Central Intelligence Agency and the Joint Chiefs of Staff. James Forrestal, soon to become the first Secretary of Defense, told the Senate:

> This bill provides . . . for the coordination of the three armed services, but what is to me more important, it provides for the integration of foreign policy with national policy, of our civilian economy with military requirements.

The Armed Service Procurement Act of 1947 created the basic structure for the close relationship that has developed between the military and American business. It established the legal standards for the procurement process, including the provisions allowing the Defense Department to offer contracts by direct negotiation with a single contractor. It asserted that "all purchases and contracts [are to be made] . . . by advertising . . . except [that they] may be negotiated . . . if"—and then it provided seventeen exceptions, including "for supplies for which it is impracticable to secure competition" and, most especially, if it is "in the interest of the national defense that any plant, mine, or facility or any producer, manufacturer, or other supplier be made or kept available."

The result, of course, has been the growth of a condition in which little more than a tenth of all defense contracts are let by competitive bidding, and in which a small number of large corporations dominate the military business.

The Atomic Energy Commission was formed in 1946 with, in President Truman's words, "civilian direction, which will serve the military needs." The President was empowered to appoint the AEC Commissioners, but the act also established a Military Liaison Committee to advise the AEC on military research and empowered to appeal any Commission decision:

> If the Committee at any time concludes that any action, proposed action, or failure to act of the Commission on such matters is adverse to the responsibilities of the Departments of War or Navy derived from the Constitution, laws and strategies, the Committee may refer such action to the Secretary [of Defense]. If he concurs, he may refer the matter to the President . . .

Congress also delegated to the President the right to develop in secret any size stockpile of nuclear weapons which he feels desirable. He was given the power to direct the AEC to "deliver such quantities of fissionable materials or weapons to the armed forces for such use as he deems necessary" and "to authorize the armed forces to manufacture, produce or acquire any equipment or device utilizing fissionable material or atomic energy."

(Research by Bob Borsage)

—1969

Mary Kaldor and Alexander Cockburn
THE DEFENSE CONFIDENCE GAME

The most conspicuous feature of the FY (fiscal year) 1975 defense budget is its colossal size. "A policy," Schlesinger remarks, "requiring us to maintain our military strength and alliances while we are actively pursuing détente with the Soviet Union and the People's Republic of China may appear to some as incongruous." The incongruity, expressed in round figures, amounts to this: the DOD has requested budgetary authority to spend $99.1 billion (the largest ever, with the exception of 1942 when the figure was $99.5 billion) and the DOD's estimated outlay is $85.8 billion, the largest sum ever to be spent by the Defense Department. This, despite DOD claims to the contrary, represents an 8 percent real increase on the outlays for FY 1974.

The substantial increases in this year's budget are not due to a sudden change of heart toward the Soviet Union, or to a striking shift in strategic thinking. They are, rather, consequences of past decisions. The jumps in the Procurement and the Research, Development, Test and Evaluation (R&D) budgets of 6 percent and 12 percent respectively are logical outcomes of hasty projects started within the last five years to compensate for the collapse of the Vietnam war boom. The rise in the R&D budget is particularly significant, for it represents additions to military know-how. All of it goes toward the *enhancement* rather than the *maintenance* of military capacity. Since the early Sixties the R&D budget has been constant or falling in real terms.

Its rise this year, just as in the early Sixties—and indeed in the early Fifties—represents a new phase in the arms race, a quantum leap in future arms spending consequent upon decisions taken to solve the industrial difficulties of 1968–1972. The R&D appropriation reverberates throughout the entire budget of which it seems merely one small part. An increase in R&D of 12 percent this year implies a much larger increase in total spending in the future. These increases flow from the decision to preserve a capacity to make armaments; such a decision is also a decision to expand that capacity indefinitely.

What has come into being is the system known as the follow-on. The system started in the late Forties when new procurement decisions were taken to prevent the total collapse of specialized defense companies such as Boeing, Raytheon, and Bath Iron

Works of Maine. Boeing began to develop the B-47 bomber and Raytheon the Sparrow and Hawk missiles which have kept it going to this day. The full impact of these decisions was obscured by the Korean War. After the peak of that war the defense budget has never fallen below $40 billion.

These projects were followed by others in expensive succession. For Boeing, the Minuteman followed the B-52 strategic bomber, which followed the B-47. Lockheed developed a notorious (for cost over-runs and allied misfortunes) series of heavy transport planes, the most recent being the C-5A.

The idea that each weapons system must have a follow-on has become self-perpetuating. Each corporation has a planning group whose sole function is to choose suitable successors for weapons currently being produced and which maintains close contact with consorts in the military. The planning procedure is supposed to be an exercise in prediction. In actual fact, because of the intimate relationship with the armed services it becomes a self-fulfilling prophecy. Even so the system has not worked smoothly, and it has taken periodic industrial crises to initiate the full range of new projects.

The first wave of weapons production after the Second World War began to subside in the late Fifties. In the resulting trough a plethora of new projects was introduced, hence promoting the difficulties experienced by Kennedy and McNamara when they made some efforts to control defense spending in the early Sixties. A decade later large cuts in the space budget coincided with recession in civil aviation and merchant shipping. The second great wave of postwar military boondoggles was subsiding: the time was propitious for a new set of decisions.

Between 1968 and 1972 aerospace employment fell by 42 percent. Shipbuilding employment showed a decline of 10 percent. The situation in naval yards had been exacerbated by McNamara's decision to contract navy work to new aerospace-managed yards, e.g., Litton, and to avoid the traditional parceling out of naval work among several contractors.

In this situation it was not surprising that the Pentagon should have precipitately fostered a number of new projects. We are now witnessing the consequences. For example, the new strategic bomber, the B-1, gets $500 million for development funds in this year's budget. It follows on from early North American (now Rockwell International) projects—the wartime B-25; the Korean War B-45, and the attempt to produce B-70, strangled by McNamara. That strangulation seemed to most people to mark the end of the vulnerable strategic bomber. North American was in a serious situation. The famous series of Sabre fighters was coming to an end and North American's attempts to get into the missile business in a big way had failed.

Boeing, the creator of the B-29, the B-47, and the B-52, had also hoped to construct the B-1, particularly in view of its own crisis at the end of the Sixties. Instead it received some consolation prizes: the B-1 "avionics" (i.e., airborne electronic equipment), and a strategic cruise missile which some people hope will provide an alternative to the B-1 bomber, among others. Boeing, of course, has continued to oversee the production of Minuteman, and the budget proposal for the development of a new follow-on ICBM opens up limitless prospects for land-based strategic missile production.

All this amounts to a mere $2.2 billion in the 1975 budget, not including $155 million for converting the jumbo 747s for emergency military airlift purposes. Altogether the Pentagon plans to convert 110 jets (747s, DC-10s, and Lockheed Tristars) at a cost of over $1 billion—about half as expensive as rebuilding the same planes from scratch.

Boeing and North American are not the only beneficiaries of the post-1968 crisis. The F-15 Eagle ($1 billion in the budget) and the F-14 Tomcat ($700 million in the budget) keep McDonnell Douglas and Grumman in funds.

There is also a cornucopia for the shipyards—over $1 billion for Trident (not including missiles); $500 million for a nuclear-powered submarine; $240 million for nuclear-powered missile-firing frigates; $100 million for patrol hydrofoils. Lockheed along with minor contracts gets the money for submarine-based missiles—making for a $1.5 billion total.

To soothe those appalled by such expenditures the Pentagon

applies a salve called the High-Low Mix: the addition to many expensive projects of many relatively "cheap" projects. This satisfies defeated competitors for the big contracts and gives congressmen a saucy whiff of military parsimony. The Narwhal submarine and the strategic cruise missile fit this category as does the A-10 close air support aircraft, which costs $270 million.

Of course the Procurement and the R&D appropriations are not the only items in the budget. They jointly account for 30 percent of it. But a weapons system means much more than just its acquisition cost. It takes fifty men, for instance, to make up a field organization to repair and service a single military aircraft. The cost of a submarine will be multiplied several times over in repair and overhaul costs during its lifetime. Every new generation of weapons costs more and more to maintain. This is the reason why the Operation and Maintenance budget increased 10 percent this year. And then we must not forget the sailors and the pilots and the planners. For the air force and navy "force structures"—the term used to indicate the composition, size, and hierarchy of various sections of the armed forces—are built around particular weapons systems.

The intense battle to maintain force structures is in fact an industrial battle, since the maintenance of a particular military function—such as strategic bombing—supports a whole host of weapons systems, which in turn keep the industry alive. Grumman is a navy corporation; Boeing is an air force corporation. Competition between them, based on different "capabilities," gets translated into interservice rivalry ostensibly about differing weapons specifications. This in turn appears before the public as arguments about strategic doctrine.

In the United States the power of the defense industry and of the military combine to make arms production the mechanism for maintaining a sufficient level of demand, in that a higher level of federal spending is required to avert the crises of over-capacity which the US experienced before World War II. Schlesinger admitted, both to the Joint Economic Committee and the House Appropriations Committee, that his budget request exceeded minimum military requirements by somewhere between $1 billion and $4 billion, and that this sum was needed to stimulate the economy. In theory such crises could be averted, without recourse to arms expenditure, by the kinds of planning undertaken in the USSR, since central decision making should be able to eliminate the disparities between what people want and what competing individual manufacturers decide to produce.

Pentagon strategists and military analysts approach the defense budget from the outside in, as it were. They ponder strategic balances, which are impossible to assess objectively in peacetime since the only confirmation of a balance is a war which no one wins. They see the flowering of new missile systems and the busy hum in the armaments factories as somehow the result of their strenuous conclusions about options, about parity, about the Indian Ocean. Yet their conclusions are closely circumscribed by the military build-ups of the past, and their doctrines are conditioned by the atmosphere that the arms build-up has created.

"Advances" or "setbacks" in political détente have no effect on the growth of the world's military arsenals. These have a momentum of their own and keep on growing. The Indian Ocean and NATO defenses keep Newport News and McDonnell Douglas in business. The doctrines build up around the weapons, not the reverse, and military arsenals have more to do with strategy than do the ruminations of the defense analysts.

Schlesinger's posture in the era of peace he doubtfully welcomes is not one to be viewed with any equanimity. His huge budget parallels the great leap forward in defense spending of the early Sixties. Then as now the economy needed stimulation. Under Kennedy there were to be new flexible options. NATO conventional forces were to be reinforced and then as now this reinforcement was seen as an argument for consolidating American hegemony in Western Europe. Forces in the Far East then received the emphasis that the Indian Ocean is getting today. The Sixties ended in the Vietnam war. As a portent, this year's defense budget does not fill one with much optimism about the end of the Seventies either.

—1974

Michael T. Klare
THE POLITICAL ECONOMY OF ARMS SALES

Increased U.S. arms sales to the Third World has become a central component of [our] military and economic policies. Even the poorest countries like South Korea and the Philippines are being pressured into buying weapons for their defense.

The military rationale for arms sales is complemented by pressing economic and political considerations:

Balance of Payments. Ever since October 1971, when America's foreign-trade balance showed a net deficit for the first time since 1893, the Nixon administration regarded the balance-of-payments problem as a major foreign policy issue. As one solution to the problem, the Department of Defense launched an intensive campaign to expand sales of U.S. military equipment abroad. The Pentagon's hard-sell tactics have not been without success: while foreign sales of most U.S. manufactured goods have declined in recent years due to stiff competition from Europe and Japan, U.S. aerospace exports are rising and in 1972 were the only commodity to show a positive trade balance. In order to sustain these gains, Pentagon salesmen are continuously eying the Third World (and particularly the Persian Gulf) for new export opportunities. *Aviation Week and Space Technology* reported in June, 1973, that "Representatives of both the Navy and the Air Force, and U.S. contractors building aircraft for the services, have ranged widely in pursuing new markets, with increasing movement into Africa and the Middle East." Among the firms now represented in Iran, for instance, are Northrop Corporation, Hughes Aircraft Company, Westinghouse, Computer Sciences Corporation, Bell Helicopter, Honeywell, Inc., McDonnell-Douglas, General Electric, and Motorola. This strategy has already begun to pay off: Iran is now the leading customer for U.S. weapons, and Kuwait and Saudi Arabia have placed substantial orders for American military hardware.

Aerospace Production. When Vietnam-related defense expenditures began to decline in the early 1970s many U.S. aerospace firms experienced significant cutbacks in defense contracting and were forced to order massive layoffs of skilled and semi-skilled personnel. Some companies—particularly producers of attack aircraft and military helicopters—predicted that termination of the war would precipitate the closure of entire production lines or even corporate bankruptcy; many companies launched intensive export drives designed to find foreign customers for their Vietnam hardware. This effort has been successful in rescuing several production lines scheduled for termination or sharply reduced output.

Political Influence. Arms sales, like military assistance grants, are considered an effective tool for strengthening the bonds of dependency that tie Third World arms recipients to their suppliers among the advanced industrial nations. The more advanced and expensive the weapons traded, the more dependent the buyer becomes on the training, spare parts, ammunition and credits that are only available from the supplier; these in turn provide the supplier with considerable political leverage, as demonstrated during the October, 1973, Arab-Israeli war when both the United States and the USSR used their status as the principal arms suppliers to the key belligerents to compel their clients to accept a cease-fire settlement attractive to neither. The leverage obtained from arms sales is also viewed as a negative sanction; thus, when several congressmen voiced concern that U.S. jets sold to Saudi Arabia would ultimately find their way into the hands of Israel's adversaries, Secretary of State William P. Rogers replied that such transactions were unlikely because "if the planes were transferred it would only be a short period of time before they have problems because the planes require spare parts and maintenance that can only be done by our experts."

Arms sales are also considered particularly useful for winning and preserving the loyalty of foreign political and military elites, which in many Third World countries have a substantial—if not decisive—role in determining national policies. These leaders are increasingly eager to acquire the modern aircraft and other advanced hardware that they consider primary symbols of power and success—a phenomenon the U.S. arms dealers have been quick to exploit.

The Pentagon argues that increased arms sales are necessary to preserve American influence in areas where arms competition is brisk and particularly in the Persian Gulf, where British and French officials are energetically promoting sales of their weapons in order to secure long-term contracts for deliveries of petroleum supplies.

Spurred by these intertwined political and economic considerations, U.S. arms salesmen are flocking to the Persian Gulf in efforts to increase the variety, complexity and number of weapons being sold. The defense capabilities of the principal Gulf states are being transformed at a very rapid pace. Indeed, the Iranian military budget is reportedly increasing at a rate of 50 percent a year, and a similar rate of increase can be ascribed to Saudi Arabia.

U.S. government spokesmen frequently assert that the Pentagon's arms sales campaign is not intended to foster a weapons race in the Third World. "I am not urging in any sense an attempt to have an arms race by the developing countries," Deputy Secretary of State Kenneth Rush told Congress in 1973 while testifying on behalf of liberalized credit sales to the Third World. Nevertheless, the cumulative impact of administration policies has been to quicken the pace of militarization in underdeveloped areas and to help fuel an upwardly spiraling "balance of terror" in certain key areas—particularly the Persian Gulf—that could lead to an unending series of local wars or even a major world war.

Cost-Sharing.   As aircraft and other military systems incorporate increasingly advanced technological improvements, the costs of research and development and production engineering consume a larger share of total acquisition costs. R & D expenditures on the C-5A jumbo transport jet, for instance, amounted to well over $1 billion. In order to pass on some of these mounting costs, Defense Department officials are increasingly willing to overlook cold war restrictions on the transfer of advanced armaments containing classified devices. The administration's cost-sharing strategy is perhaps most evident in the sale of F-14 Tomcats to Iran: by purchasing 30 F-14s, a navy jet whose production costs have consistently surpassed every ceiling set by the Pentagon, the Shah will help reduce overall development costs to the U.S. government and thus help ease continued F-14 appropriation requests through the Congress, where opposition to their procurement is stiff.

Dollar Accumulations. With increased U.S. purchases of petroleum from the Persian Gulf and the rising prices of crude oil, the supply of dollars in Arab hands has been growing at a spectacular rate. "The biggest long-range problem facing the U.S. in the Middle East," a Pentagon official told me in 1973, "is finding a way to get the Arabs to spend their dollars without letting them get control of our economy." A somewhat more cautious assessment of this problem was offered by Assistant Secretary Sisco in 1973:

> The Saudis and other oil rich [Arabian] Peninsula states have begun to accumulate large foreign exchange reserves well beyond their needs. They have now indicated that if [oil] production is to rise beyond their income requirements, they must find productive outlets at home or abroad to invest their surplus revenues. This is a challenge to the consumer countries generally and to our American businessmen specifically.

U.S. arms sales were over $4 billion to Iran, Saudi Arabia and Kuwait alone in fiscal 1973–74.

Other countries, including both the Soviet Union and China as well as the NATO powers of Europe, have been compelled by similar reasons to boost their own weapons exports. The United States, in turn, has been obliged to liberalize its export policies so as not to lose its customers in the Middle East, where the competition is keenest. This competition between the arms producers has naturally induced a parallel and complementary competitiveness between the arms recipients. When one nation obtains supersonic jets or modern tanks, its neighbors and rivals naturally feel a need to obtain equivalent or superior weapons in order to protect their security. This process perpetually threatens to precipitate armed conflict, for when one country feels that it has a temporary advantage in firepower it will naturally be tempted to invade its weaker rival (as, for instance, when India invaded Pakistan in 1971); conversely, when a nation suspects that pending arms transfers will shift the balance of power in favor of a rival, it will naturally consider immediate invasion in order to preclude a future attack by a stronger opponent (as demonstrated by the Israeli attack on Egypt in 1967). And since, as a supplier increases its investment in a local regime through credits advanced, training personnel deployed, etc., its stake in the survival of the client expands proportionally, there is an increasing danger that local Third World conflicts will precipitate a clash between the great powers. This danger became all too real in October 1973 when military personnel of both the United States and the USSR were sent to the edge of the Israeli-Egyptian battlefield to supervise deliveries of advanced armaments.

Our stated policy has been to try to promote regional cooperation of Gulf riparians with the Iranian-Saudi relationship the key factor. That relationship is fragile at present and is based on negative rather than positive considerations: a common vision of kings surviving in a sea of ex-kingdoms, a common distrust of the Soviet Union—and a common dislike for the policies and actions of some neighbors. Such matters can create only lukewarm bonds, especially against a background of deep-seated religious, tribal, cultural, and political legacies that fuel an undercurrent of tension and suspicion between Iran and Saudi Arabia. Representative Lee H. Hamilton stated: "one of our prime challenges in the Persian Gulf will be to avoid any confrontation between our two close friends."

Even if war is averted, the growing sales of costly military hardware will strengthen the rule of authoritarian governments while at the same time diverting scarce resources from the social and economic development programs that alone can redress the inequities prevalent in these societies.

—1974

Seymour Melman
GETTING THE BIGGEST BANG FOR THE BUCK

[Following is a list of some civilian and military trade-offs adapted from the book *The Permanent War Economy*. The author is professor of industrial engineering at Columbia University and national co-chairman of SANE.]

66 low-cost houses	=$1 million	=1 Huey helicopter
Unfunded housing assistance in Arkansas	=$100 million	=1 DD-963 destroyer
257 apartments in New York City	=$9 million	=1 Navy A6-E Intruder plane
Impounded Federal housing funds, 1972	=$130 million	=8 F-14 aircraft
Vetoed Environmental Protection Agency plan to depollute the Great Lakes	=$141 million	=1973 request for new airborne nuclear-war command post
1973 unfunded Housing and Urban Development water and sewer requests	=$4 billion	=cost excess on F-111 aircraft
National water-pollution abatement, 1970–75	=$38 billion	=cost excesses for 45 weapons systems
National solid-waste-treatment program	=$43.5 billion	=B-1 bomber program
Total environment cleanup	=$105.2 billion	=new weapons systems in development or procurement
1 high school in Oregon	=$6.25 million	=paid by 1 Oregon county to support military
Unfunded program to upgrade rural American life	=$300 million	=5 C-5A aircraft
Unfunded 1973 rural health care	=$22 million	=50 per cent of Lockheed Cheyenne helicopter funding increase, 1973
Child-nutrition programs funding cut	=$69 million	=2 DE-1052 destroyer escorts
Special Milk Program funding cut	=$1 million	=1 Main Battle Tank
Health, Education and Welfare public assistance cut, 1973	=$567 million	=3 nuclear attack submarines
To bring all poor Americans above poverty line, 1971	=$11.4 billion	=B-1 bomber program, low estimate
To eliminate hunger in America	=$4–5 billion	=C-5A aircraft program
Vetoed child-care program	=$2.1 billion	=Development excess on B-1 bomber program
Philadelphia 1971 schools deficit	=$40 million	=1 B-1 bomber
Reopening New York Public Library weekends and holidays	=$900,000	=1-year operation 6 Huey helicopters

For each of 250 communities, 3 equipped schools; also, 1-year salaries for 35,714 teachers	=$6 billion	=6,000 aircraft lost in Indo-china by October, 1969
Graduate fellowships funding cut, 1973	=$175 million	=1 nuclear attack submarine
New Orleans unfunded urban development, 1973	=$94 million	=2 months' Laos bombing
1972 housing funds impounded	=$50 million	=3 F-14 aircraft ($57.6 million)
1973 Newark needs for urban renewal	=$125 million	=4 DE-1052 destroyer escorts
1973 cities' needs to rebuild blighted areas	=$3 billion	=1 nuclear aircraft carrier, equipped, and escorts
1971 Detroit city deficit	=$30 million	=3 F-15 fighters ($27 million)
1972 Federal health budget de-ficiency	=$2.3 billion	=overruns on C-5A aircraft and Main Battle Tank
1972–73 cut in Federal mental-health budgets	=$65 million	=1 C-5A aircraft ($60 million)
1972–73 funds reduction for training health personnel	=$140.9 million	=1 DE-1052 destroyer escort, and 1 DD-963 destroyer ($134 million)
1973 unfunded medical school construction	=$250 million	=cost excess on M-60 Sheridan tank

—1974

Unequal Shares,
Unfair Taxes

Economists have long debated the degree of inequality which prevails in the distribution of both wealth and income, and what it means. These issues assumed special sharpness in 1973–74, as corporate profits, led by the oil companies, increased in the face of stagnant wages and increasing unemployment.

The First National City Bank argues the traditional position that profits fuel growth and jobs:[1]

> The need for higher profits is twofold: to provide the means of replenishing and improving the nation's capital stock—to replace equipment that is worn out or made obsolete by changing technology—and to provide the incentive for such investment. It is through this process that industry is able to achieve the increases in productivity that lead to higher incomes and improved living standards for workers, management and shareholders alike.
>
> Without rising profits and higher levels of investment, the growth of all types of income will eventually slow. It would avail

Percent of Income

Fifths	All consumer units			Families			Unrelated individuals		
	1964	1970	1971	1964	1970	1971	1964	1970	1971
Lowest	4.2	4.6	4.8	5.8	6.4	6.6	3.2	3.9	4.1
Second	10.6	10.7	10.8	11.8	12.0	12.1	8.0	9.0	9.3
Third	16.4	16.4	16.4	16.7	16.8	16.8	14.0	14.4	14.6
Fourth	23.2	23.3	23.3	22.5	22.6	22.5	22.9	22.6	22.6
Highest	45.5	44.9	44.6	43.1	42.3	42.0	52.0	50.1	49.4
Total	100.0	100.0	100.0	100.0	100.0	100.0	100.0	100.0	100.0
Top 5%	20.0	19.2	19.1	18.8	18.0	17.8	24.2	23.0	22.5
Top 1%	8.0	7.6	7.5	7.5	7.0	6.9	11.1	10.3	9.9
Median	$6,459	$9,067	$9,428	$7,354	$10,527	$10,968	$2,761	$4,208	$4,527

Source: Survey of Current Business, October 1971.

196

labor little to demand an ever-increasing share of a dwindling pie. Meany might well ponder the advice of an illustrious predecessor, Samuel Gompers, who said: "The worst crime against working people is a company that fails to make a profit."

Not reproduced here are charts showing profit and employee compensation patterns for the post war period, with the heading: "Profit recovery disappointing, while wages soar." Most bank and business journals regularly offer the same arguments.

Three issues should be disentangled in this debate: *First,* do corporate profits and workers' wages directly compete for the same income? In a sense they do, but other claimants on total business incomes also count, particularly the owners of debt instruments; payments to them are counted as a cost, not income, but they and shareholders are part of the same small proportion of the population which directly or indirectly receive most non-wage and salary income payments. There is in addition the division of employee compensation between wage and salary-earners. The latter include clerks, foremen and others whose incomes are likely to stay close to those of wage earners, but they also include middle-level and upper-level management. The other important distinction to be made is between the results when the economy— and business sectors generally—are growing and when they are not. In the first case, relative shares may not change but wage incomes can nevertheless increase; in the second case this will not be possible. Thus the issue of income shares is most important when the economy is in most trouble.

Second, are corporate profits "functional" in the sense that the First National City Bank describes them? The Introduction to this book argues that the social and economic functions, which in theory and tradition justify profit-making and accumulation on the scale that has been true in the United States, no longer hold true.

Third, what is the connection between corporate earnings and wages on the one hand, and patterns of total income distribution on the other? Here the facts provided in the Introduction speak for themselves, though the summary data from the survey of Current Business, reproduced here, show that change does take place over time.

The data are one thing; their interpretation another. For example, Sanford Rose argued[2] that the figures overstate the degree of inequality, and that the record shows "a pattern of sizable fluctuations around a trend line of gradually declining inequality" in the postwar period, but concludes that "a dramatic decline in inequality is not in the cards." Irving Kristol, by contrast, has argued[3] that the egalitarian impulse itself is profoundly misguided and self-defeating, that significant redistribution could only occur at the expense of the middle class and would be far more socially disruptive than any gains for the low-income population would justify. He would be willing to prohibit the inheritance of large fortunes but accepts no other serious redistributive or equalizing social policy goals.

In this debate much attention focuses on the tax system. The size of the tax burden is one issue; its fairness is another; its effects in changing income and wealth shares is a third. S. M. Miller and Paolo Roberti showed that our total tax levy of 30 percent of GNP is relatively low among industrial countries.[4] We need to recall that with the 1964 tax cut we chose to meet the need for economic stimulus by lowering taxes rather than increasing social expenditures.

A study comparing tax payments made and transfer payments received, by income groups, showed[5] that the biggest tax burden falls on those in the $10,000–$25,000 class and declines for *both* higher and lower income groups.

In their *Washington Report* for June 12, 1972, the United Automobile Workers summarized an estimated total of $58 billion in tax concessions included in the internal revenue code. The biggest categories are those to personal income, business, state and local governments, home-owners, and capital gains. Within the personal income group the major items are tax exemptions for the elderly ($2.95 billion), for self-employed pension plans ($3.075 billion), and for charitable contributions ($3.55 billion); the first benefits many older lower income receivers, the second and third are largely helpful to those with high incomes. Homeowners tax exemptions ($5.7 billion) benefit many middle income people, few low income receivers. The other major categories are mainly for the benefit of business and upper income groups.

The most careful recent study of tax incidence was done by Joseph A. Pechman and Benjamin A. Okner.[6] The most striking of their findings is the low degree of progressiveness of federal taxes even under the most favorable assumptions, the wide variations in tax liability of people and families at the same income level, and the negligible degree to which taxes reduce income inequalities. Specific features of the tax code have long attracted the ire of critics and reformers. Philip M. Stern was one of the first and most perceptive of these; his two books, *The Great Treasury Raid* and *The Rape of the Taxpayer,* broke new ground in public understanding. His article in *The New York Times Magazine* added fuel to the fire for tax reform. But changes in recent years have been in the other direction; Arnold Cantor of the AFL-CIO illustrates some of the results of the 1971 Revenue Act in deepening inequalities and preserving inequality. The AFL-CIO has been a consistent advocate of tax reform.

The selection from the *First National City Bank Monthly Economic Letter* offers rebuttals to these views, particularly the liberal attack on capital gains preferences in federal tax law; preferential tax rates are defended on grounds of both equity and functional purpose.

Philip M. Stern
UNCLE SAM'S WELFARE PROGRAM FOR THE RICH

Most Americans would probably be intensely surprised to find, in their morning newspaper, headlines such as this one:

> Congress Sets $16-Per-Year
> Welfare Rate for Poor Families,
> $720,000 for Multimillionaires

Or this one:

> Nixon Asks $103-Billion
> Budget Deficit, Doubling
> Previous Red-Ink Record

The story behind the first of these headlines (the second will be explained later) might read this way:

WASHINGTON, April 16—Congress completed action today on a revolutionary welfare program that, reversing traditional payment policies, awards huge welfare payments to the super-rich but grants only pennies per week to the very poor.

Under the program, welfare payments averaging some $720,-000 a year will go to the nation's wealthiest families, those with annual incomes of over a million dollars.

For the poorest families, those earning $3,000 a year or less, the welfare allowance will average $16 a year, or roughly 30 cents a week.

The program, enacted by Congress in a series of laws over a period of years, has come to be called the Rich Welfare Program, after its principal sponsor, Senator Homer A. Rich. In a triumphant news conference, Senator Rich told newsmen that the $720,000 annual welfare allowances would give America's most affluent families an added weekly take-home pay of about $14,000. "Or, to put it another way," the Senator said, "it will provide these families with about $2,000 more spending money every day."

The total cost of the welfare program, the most expensive in the nation's history, amounts to $77.3-billion a year.

Political analysts foresee acute discontent not only among the poor, but also among middle-income families making $10,000 to $15,000 a year. For them, welfare payments under the Rich plan will amount to just $12.50 a week, markedly less than the weekly $14,000 paid to the very rich.

Reporters asked Senator Rich whether wealthy families would be required to work in order to receive their welfare payments, a common eligibility requirement with many welfare programs. Senator Rich seemed puzzled by the question. "The rich? Work?" he asked. "Why, it hadn't occurred to me." Congressional experts advised newsmen that the program contains no work requirement.

Admittedly, the above "news story" sounds implausible, if not unbelievable. Yet the story is essentially true. The facts and figures in it are real. Such a system is, in fact, part of the law of the land. Only the law isn't called a welfare law. It goes by the name of

"The Internal Revenue Code of 1954, as Amended"—the basic income-tax law of the United States.

Since a tax law takes money from people, rather than paying money to them, what connection does the tax law have with the topsy-turvy welfare system in the news story? The connection lies in the way Congress has played fast and loose with the 16th Amendment to the Constitution, and with the principle of basing taxes on "ability to pay."

The 16th Amendment, which authorized the first United States income tax, empowered Congress to tax "incomes, *from whatever sources derived.*" (Italics mine.) That expresses the Gertrude Stein-ish notion that a dollar is a dollar is a dollar and that, regardless of its source, the dollar endows its lucky recipient with 100 cents of "ability to pay" for food, shoes for the baby, a fraction of a yacht—or for taxes. Hence, in fairness, all dollars, no matter what their origin, should be taxed uniformly. But Congress has decreed differently. It has decreed that dollars earned in an oil or real-estate venture, in a stock market bonanza, or in interest on a state or local bond, while undeniably effective in buying food, shoes or yachts, are somehow reduced in potency when it comes to paying taxes—for Congress has exempted such dollars, in whole or in part, from taxation.

The American tax system, which stipulates that rates rise as a person's affluence grows, also holds that a billionaire like oilman John Paul Getty—with a reported income of $300,000 *a day*—is better "able to pay" taxes than an impoverished Kentucky coal miner. In fact, under the tax rates supposedly applicable to all citizens, Mr. Getty's $100-million annual income endows him with an "ability to pay" about $70-million to the Internal Revenue Service (on the premise that he should be able to make do on the remaining $30-million each year). But since Mr. Getty's dollars come largely from oil ventures, they are not, by Congressional fiat, taxed like other dollars. In consequence, according to what President Kennedy told two United States Senators, Mr. Getty's income tax in the early sixties came nowhere near $70-million. It amounted to no more than a few thousand dollars—just about the amount a middle-income engineer or professor would pay.

Now compare the notion of excusing John Paul Getty from paying $70-million in taxes—taxes that an equally wealthy non-oil man would legally have to pay—with the notion that Mr. Getty is receiving a $70-million Federal welfare check. In both cases the consequences are that:

Mr. Getty is $70-million richer.

The United States Treasury is $70-million poorer than if the full tax had been paid.

The rest of the taxpayers are obliged to pay an added $70-million to make up the difference.

Thus the net effect of a "tax forgiveness" is identical to that of a direct Federal handout.

A Brookings Institution study[7] concludes that of the $77.3-billion in tax "handouts," just $92-million goes to the six million poorest families in the nation, while 24 times that amount—$2.2-*billion*—goes to just 3,000 families (those with incomes of more than a million dollars a year). Coincidentally, that $2.2-billion is just the same amount Congress voted last year for food stamps for 14.7-million hungry Americans. Moreover, five times that amount in the form of "tax welfare" went to families earning more than $100,000 a year.

The disparity between the "tax welfare" for the wealthy and that granted the poor is even more breathtaking in the case of the "tax preferences" involving so-called "capital gains"—the profits on sales of stocks and bonds, land, buildings and other kinds of property. When a person cashes in such profits during his lifetime, he pays no more than half the usual tax. Even more striking, all the gains in the value of property a person holds until death are not taxed at all. Some $10-billion entirely escapes taxation in that manner every year.

Since to have capital gains you have to own property (i.e., have the surplus cash to buy same), it's not surprising that only one taxpayer in 12 is able to report any gains, and that three-quarters of such gains are enjoyed by the wealthiest 9 percent of America's taxpayers. Thus, all but the super-rich have a right to be envious, if not startled, by the Brookings figures on the "tax welfare" payments—the average per-family tax savings—granted capital-gains recipients:

Yearly income	Yearly "tax welfare" from capital gains
Over $1,000,000	$641,000
$500–1,000,000	165,000
$100–500,000	23,000
$20–25,000	120
$5–10,000	8
$3–5,000	1

These Federal handouts to the wealthy reach the astounding total of nearly $14-billion a year. But even that sum is dwarfed by the tax benefactions that Uncle Sam bestows on all but our poorest citizens the instant they are pronounced man and wife, a happy moment that carries with it the privilege of filing a joint return. The Brookings study reveals, startlingly, that the annual total of this giveaway to married couples comes to $21.5-billion.

Some, noting that the Environmental Protection Agency will only be permitted to spend one-fourteenth that amount next year, have difficulty discerning how this $21.5-billion matrimonial "tax dole" benefits the national welfare. If it is supposed to be an incentive to marriage, it is a strange one indeed, since it shows a total indifference to the marital status of the poor, who derive no financial benefit from this tax giveaway whatever. Instead, it offers increasingly generous benefits the higher a couple's income goes, in brackets where it matters little whether two can indeed live as cheaply as one. Two-thirds of this marital "tax welfare" goes to taxpayers making more than $20,000 a year, and less than 3 percent goes to the hardest-pressed married couples—those making less than $10,000 a year. These are the average per-family matrimonial tax savings:

Yearly income	Yearly "tax welfare" to married couples
Under $3,000	$0
$3–5,000	72 cents
$5–10,000	$24
$25–50,000	$1,479
$100–500,000	$8,212
Over $1,000,000	$11,062

Dramatically top-heavy tax largesse flows to the super-rich via the fiction, in the tax law, that the $5-billion of interest on state and local bonds is totally nonexistent. Not only is such interest income untaxed; it doesn't even have to be reported on tax returns. Ownership of such bonds is, understandably, reserved to financial institutions and wealthy individuals, in part because only they have the spare cash to buy such bonds, and in part because these bonds bear comparatively low interest rates that are attractive only to persons in high tax brackets.

As a result, the per-family tax benefactions from this loophole are almost insultingly low for the un-moneyed: an average of only 80 cents a year for families earning $5,000 to $10,000, and just $24 a year even for those in the $25,000–50,000 bracket. But the financial blessing is handsome indeed for the wealthy—$36,000 a year for families with incomes of over $1-million—and it is even more spectacular for the big banks. In 1970 this tax feature saved the Bank of America an estimated $58-million.

All these profligate handouts to the unneedy would be far more publicly apparent if the billions lost to the Treasury through the loopholes came to be regarded in the same jealous, penny-pinching way as the direct outlays that the President requests and Congress votes every year. If that had been the case this past January, newspapers might well have carried a news story such as the following:

> WASHINGTON, April 16—President Nixon today sent Congress the most startling budget in history, calling for a Federal deficit of no less than $103-billion, more than twice as high as any previous deficit in American history.
>
> This colossal deficit resulted from Mr. Nixon's inclusion in his annual budget, for the first time, of not only direct outlays from the Treasury but also what the President calls "tax expenditures." These are sums the Treasury does not collect because of various exceptions and preferences embedded in the nation's tax laws. For the current year, such sums amounted to more than $77-billion, Mr. Nixon said.
>
> "It is time the American people faced up to the truth," Mr. Nixon said in his budget message. "Every dollar in taxes that some

individual or industry is excused from paying is just as much of a drain on the Treasury, and contributes just as much to Federal deficits, as a dollar appropriated by the Congress and spent directly from the Treasury.

"For example," Mr. Nixon said, "nearly $10-billion in 'tax expenditures' is granted every year to stimulate home ownership. This sum ought to be part of the budget of the Department of Housing and Urban Development if we are to get an honest picture of how much we, as a nation, are really spending on America's housing problems."

Of course there was no such fiscal candor in Mr. Nixon's January budget message; nor had there been in those of his predecessors in both parties. But the housing example is a good one, for almost assuredly, few, if any, of the housing specialists in HUD— and few of our elected representatives—are aware that a tax-subsidy program Congress has enacted for homeowners operates in the following manner:

Three families—the Lowlies (who make $7,000 a year), the Comfortables (with a $50,000 income) and the Opulents (they make $400,000 a year)—ask HUD for help in paying the 7 percent mortgage interest on homes that each family wants to buy. HUD's response is different in each case.

• To the Opulents, HUD replies: "HUD will be delighted to pay 5 percent mortgage interest for you, so that when you buy your mansion, you only need pay 2 per cent mortgage interest."

• To the Comfortables: "HUD will pay half the interest charges, so you can borrow toward your house at 3.5 per cent."

• To the Lowlies: "We're terribly sorry, but the most we can do is pay 1 per cent interest for you, so if you want to borrow to buy that house, you'll have to pay 6 per cent."

That seemingly inhumane result, which flows from the tax deductibility of mortgage interest payments, is inherent in the nature of any tax deduction in a tax system such as ours where tax rates get higher as income rises. It works this way: say Mr. Opulent has a taxable income of $400,100. This puts him in the top tax bracket of 70 per cent and it means that he has to pay a tax of $70 on the top $100 of his income. Mr. Lowly, on the other hand, has a taxable income of $7,100, placing him in the 19 per cent tax bracket; this imposes a tax of $19 on the top $100 of his more modest income.

Now suppose that each spends $100 on mortgage interest which, being tax-deductible, reduces the taxable income of each by $100. That step lowers Mr. Opulent's tax by $70; that is, $70 that would have gone to Uncle Sam, were it not for the tax deduction, has been diverted to Mr. Opulent's bank account. Uncle Sam has, in effect, footed the bill for $70 of Mr. Opulent's mortgage interest. But in the case of Mr. Lowly, the $100 deduction only lowers his tax by $19. Only $19 is diverted from Uncle Sam to Mr. Lowly's bank account.

Not only does Mr. Opulent get a bigger bang for each tax-deductible buck than Mr. Lowly does, but also Mr. Opulent far outstrips his counterpart in the *number* of bucks he spends yearly for tax-deductible purposes. Mr. Opulent's average annual deductions for mortgage interest, for example, are about $4\frac{1}{2}$ times as large as Mr. Lowly's. According to the Brookings study, the benefits from the various "tax preferences" enjoyed by homeowners (over home renters) come to just 66 cents a year for the least pecunious taxpayers. But the benefits amount to 10,000 times as much—over $6,000 a year—for the nation's wealthiest and best-housed families.

The price tag attached to this inverted subsidy program is enormous: $9.6-billion a year. This is more than twice HUD's total budget and more than 50 times HUD's direct outlays for housing assistance. Clearly, if the $9.6-billion were part of HUD's budget, HUD officials would be embarrassed if they tried to justify a program that gave 66 cents of aid to the neediest citizen and $6,000 to the wealthiest. But since the inequity is embedded in the tax laws, involving no visible outlays, HUD, the President and the Congress are all spared the embarrassment of annually accounting for this expensive and irrational subsidy.

The same is true of the tax favors enjoyed by oil companies and investors, which entail an annual "expenditure" of a billion and a half dollars (supposedly to encourage development of our oil resources). But that sum appears nowhere in the Interior Depart-

ment's natural resources budget. Perhaps if it did, Secretary of the
Interior Rogers C. B. Morton would be spurred to cut back or end
this huge "outlay," especially since a recent Government-commis-
sioned study showed that the returns on the $1.5-billion were a
meager $150-million in additional oil exploration. Any direct sub-
sidy program with a 90 per cent waste factor would hardly warm
Congressional hearts when it came up for annual approval; but
oil's multibillion-dollar tax subsidy is spared that discomfiture.

Translating tax loopholes into "tax expenditures" (i.e., treating the revenues that leak out through the loopholes as if they were
direct outlays) can make even the most unexceptionable feature of
the tax laws seem questionable. Tax expert Stanley Surrey has
explained the effect of that most worthy of all tax features, the
deduction for contributions to charity:

Suppose that one Horace Pauper writes the Government as
follows: "I am too poor to pay an income tax, but the Salvation
Army helped me in a time of need and I am contributing $5 to it.
Will the Government also make a contribution?" The response:
"Dear Mr. Pauper: We appreciate your generosity and sacrifice,
but in this situation we cannot make the contribution you request."

Suppose that at the same time, Herman Greenbacks, nouveau
millionaire, writes to say that of his $500,000 income, he has
decided to send $3,000 to the Society for the Preservation of Hog-
Calling in Arkansas. He wants to know if the Government will
help. Reply: "We will be delighted to be of assistance and are at
once sending a Government check for $7,000 to the Hog-Calling
Society."

Here again, this strange situation results from the fact that
when a taxpayer in the 70 per cent bracket such as Mr. Greenbacks
gives $10,000 to charity, it reduces his tax by $7,000—i.e., it
diverts $7,000 from the United States Treasury to the charity. But
for Horace Pauper, who has no taxable income to be affected by
his generous deduction, there is no tax saving and the Government's role is zero.

As if the Greenbacks-Pauper contrast weren't irrational
enough, the charitable-deduction feature of the tax law could even
give rise to a third situation. Let us say that Roger Croesus, heir to

the huge Croesus fortune, writes the Government to say that he is selling $2-million in stocks inherited from his grandfather, since he wants to raise cash to pay his taxes and also to buy a yacht. Croesus adds that he feels the Antique Car Society of America is a worthy institution, and that while he has decided not to contribute to the Society himself, he is writing to inquire if the Government has any interest in doing so. In this case, the Government writes as follows:

"Dear Mr. Croesus: We will be delighted to send a $2-million contribution to the Antique Car Society and we will be glad to say that the contribution is in your name. Moreover, in appreciation of your thoughtfulness in suggesting this fine idea to us—and confident that your new yacht will need outfitting—we are sending you a check for $100,000, tax-free, of course."

That unbelievable feat could be accomplished if Mr. Croesus, a taxpayer in the 70 per cent bracket, were to give to the cause of antique cars $2-million of stock that was virtually valueless when he inherited it. His tax saving (i.e., the Treasury's contribution) includes $1,400,000 of income tax from the deduction, plus the avoidance of $700,000 in capital gains tax, for a total of $2,100,-000—or, $100,000 more than his $2-million gift. The result: even after the Treasury has, in effect, paid for his entire contribution, he still enjoys a $100,000 cash profit.

Capital gains represent by far the most gaping escape hatch for the very rich, allowing them to pay, on the average, only half what the Federal tax rates indicate they should. Ending the capital-gains preference would at one stroke narrow, or close, a variety of tax escape-routes available to only a few selected taxpayers guided by ingenious tax lawyers. Examples of such escape routes are corporate executives' stock options, and tax shelters for high-salaried doctors and other professional men who invest in—but usually never see—cattle farms, or kiwi-nut groves, and the like.

Finally, the dire predictions about the drying up of capital that invariably greet any proposal to alter the taxation of capital gains are, at the least, greatly exaggerated. This is evidenced by the economy's apparently tremorless adjustment to a 10 per cent increase in the capital gains tax enacted in 1969, as well as by the fact that 95 per cent of corporations' capital needs are met through plowed-back profits and borrowings, and only 5 per cent from stock issues.

It's likely that there will be increasing pressure to end or modify the tax exemption of state and local bonds. While zealously cherished by hard-pressed governors and mayors as an inexpensive means of public borrowing (the tax-free status allows these bonds to carry below-average interest rates), the tax exemption is a grossly inefficient means of subsidizing state and local borrowing costs. Students of the subject calculate that about half this annual $1.2-billion "tax expenditure" is, in effect, wasted, and that both tax justice and governmental economy would be served by replacing the tax exemption with a direct-subsidy program.

The inefficiency of the bond-interest exemption is typical of such "tax expenditures," which, ironically, are spared the traditional scrutiny for "efficiency" that pinch-penny Congressmen usually require of direct-spending programs. For example, in 1971, in enacting multibillion-dollar tax "incentives" for corporate exports and plant investment, Congress wastefully granted the incentives to exports and to plant outlays that most corporations would have made anyway—rather than confining the benefits to *increases* in those activities. Thus, those tax subventions are windfalls to corporations that merely export or invest as usual. Similarly, the oil-depletion allowance, supposedly designed to reward risk-taking, not only goes to the venturesome oil driller but also is freely dispensed to the fortunate landowner—who permits a successful well to be drilled on his property, but who risks absolutely nothing in doing so.

Tax favors granted to the lowly as well as to the mighty often produce both inequity and inefficiency. Take, for example, the additional $750 personal exemption that Congress has voted the aged and the blind. For nonagenarian Charles Stewart Mott, who is said to be worth more than $300-million, that exemption allows him a saving of $525 a year. But for a retiree in St. Petersburg who qualifies for the lowest tax bracket, it saves only $105. And the exemption gives no relief whatsoever to, say, an ancient and impoverished sharecropper whose meager income would not be taxable anyway.

That same perversity applies to the regular exemption available to each taxpayer and his dependents. While its supposed purpose is to spare poor families from being taxed on what they need to meet "some minimum essential living costs," the exemption nonetheless confers some $4-billion in tax handouts to families making over $15,000 a year. Some Congressional reformers have proposed replacing the exemption with a flat $150 cut in *taxes* for each dependent. This would be applicable equally to the St. Petersburg bench-sitter and to the nonagenarian multimillionaire. That step alone—which would increase the taxes of those who earn $10,000 or more, while reducing the taxes of those who are less affluent—would increase Federal revenues by nearly $2-billion a year.

Other long-standing "loopholes for the many" are rarely examined with a critical eye, even though they represent immense "tax expenditures" justified by little rhyme or reason. For example, about $10-billion in interest accruing on life-insurance policies is exempt from taxation; this annual "tax expenditure" amounts to $2.7-billion. Nonbusiness personal itemized deductions (for major-medical expenses, charitable contributions, taxes, interest and the like) excuse another $10-billion from taxation, and the price tag for this is over $4-billion annually. Another rarely discussed but major untaxed item is the return on a homeowner's investment in his own house; this takes the form of rent the homeowner is spared paying to a landlord, rent which the homeowner, in effect, pays to himself. The total of this untaxed "income" amounts to an estimated $15.5-billion annually; failure to tax it represents an unconscious decision on the part of Congress to "spend" more than $4-billion annually on aid to homeowners—with, as usual, far more comfort to mansion-dwellers than to Levittowners.

The basic question raised by the Brookings study is whether the unreviewed annual "tax welfare" of over $77-billion makes sense in a time of budgetary deficits averaging $30-billion a year, and in a time when we are plagued with "social deficits" (in housing, health and the like) of vastly greater proportions. The Brookings experts propose an essentially preference-free, or "no-loophole," tax system. That would open up some choices that the present sieve-like system forbids: it would make it possible to raise added revenues that could be applied to the nation's social needs. Or it could make possible a massive tax-rate reduction; the study says that in a no-loophole system, the present levels of Federal revenues could be collected with tax rates ranging from 7 to 44 per cent, instead of the present 14 to 70 per cent. Or there could be a combination of both revenue-raising and rate-reduction. But whatever the choice, a preference-free system would put an end to irrational multibillion-dollar "tax expenditures" that continue to be perpetuated as long as Congress fails to act.

—1972

Arnold Cantor
TAX JUSTICE: A GIANT STEP BACKWARD

It will take years to evaluate the full impact of the Revenue Act of 1971, which placed billions upon billions of potential tax dollars beyond the reach of the federal government. It amounts to a decimation of the tax base; it could place severe limitations on the government's ability to function. In a nation faced with glaring and obvious needs for sharply increased public investments in schools, hospitals, medical facilities, housing, mass transit and pollution controls, a tax-cutting spree is a luxury we obviously can ill afford.

The act did not simply limit the money-raising ability of the federal government. The tax breaks, windfalls and enlarged loopholes were engineered to swell the treasuries of big businesses and corporations and the bank accounts of their wealthy stockholders. It increased the share of the tax load borne by wage and salary earners. It sharply reduced the business community's contribution to the costs of running the nation.

Unfortunately, the tax provisions which underlie the Administration's 1971 program are not temporary expedients, for their damaging effects will continue long after this Administration's dismal record of economic mismanagement ceases to be news. For the 10-year period through 1981, the total cost to the American people in terms of foregoing sorely needed public investments will be some $100 billion. Of that $100 billion, individuals will receive $17 billion in income tax breaks while businesses will receive over $83 billion—a ratio of almost 5:1 in favor of business.

Business groups have been extremely successful in reducing their share of the cost of running the nation. In 1960 the corporate share of the federal income tax was 35 percent; individuals paid the balance. Although the ratio bobbed and weaved in the early 1960s, a sharp decline began in the latter half of the decade. In 1968 and 1969, when corporate profits skyrocketed to all-time peaks, the corporate contribution to the income tax burden slipped below 30 percent. Over the decade the corporate share will probably range around 26 to 27 percent. Thus, if estimates prove correct, corporations will have their share of the tax burden reduced from roughly one-third in the early 1960s to only one-fourth by the late 1970s. Individuals, of course, will be making up the balance.

A similar shifting of the tax burden away from business and onto individual workers and consumers has also occurred in the states and localities.

Between 1957 and 1967, according to a study by the Advisory Commission on Intergovernmental Relations, the business share of the state and local tax burden dropped from 34.2 percent to 29.4 percent. This means that if businesses had kept paying their relative share of the tax burden, another $4 billion annually, at 1967 tax rates, would have been available to help ease the fiscal pressures faced by most states and virtually every local government.

On property taxes, the subject of much recent controversy, the same study showed that in 1957 business property accounted for 45 percent of total state and local property tax burden. It fell to 42.8 percent in 1962 and down to 39.5 percent by 1967.

In the final analysis, of course, businesses don't pay taxes; people do. But the real issue in achieving a just tax structure is *which* people—low-income, middle, or wealthy.

Tax relief to a business is a direct and immediate boost in the income and purchasing power of the individual owner, the partners, or its shareholders. And the losses in government income and purchasing power are as immediate and direct. The benefits to workers and consumers, to the extent there are any benefits, occur only after a comparatively long process of trickling and filtering down. In short, reducing the business share of the tax burden is little different from adding new tax escape hatches for those of wealth and taxpaying ability—shifting the burden to those whose livelihood depends on a paycheck rather than on an interest receipt, a dividend, or an asset.

The new depreciation system. Under prior law, a business taxpayer could be called upon to demonstrate to the Internal Revenue Service that his depreciation write-offs had some relationship to reality. The tax write-offs had to be consistent with actual replacement patterns, measured by what was called the "reserve ratio test." If the firm failed this test, the Internal Revenue Service could disallow the excess depreciation deductions. Under the new law, however, the reserve ratio test goes by the board and the businessman gets an assurance that the depreciation deductions he claims will never be questioned. In effect, under this system a major business cost is to be determined by the whims of the Internal Revenue Service and the needs of the firm.

The depreciation speedup and the investment credit boil down to the addition of new loopholes in the tax structure. The benefits, in the main, will flow to the larger and wealthier businesses. And, like most tax incentives, large amounts of public revenues will be totally wasted since businesses will receive tax reductions whether they increase their rate of investment in machinery and equipment, decrease it, or carry on as before.

Both these so-called incentives to capital investment were touted as tax-relief provisions for the creation of jobs. In fact, the 7 percent investment credit was even called the "Job Development Investment Credit." Yet neither of these provisions includes any requirement—carrots or sticks—that a firm must add to its work force to receive the tax break. Nothing prevents a firm from using these windfall cash increases to buy machinery and equipment which in fact displace workers.

Obviously, attempts to induce business to significantly boost outlays for machinery and equipment through tax breaks are fantasy when over one-fourth of productive capacity is idle and over half is five years old or less. Businessmen don't invest money just for the sake of investing money and they're not going to buy machines merely for the sake of buying machines. In the short run, therefore, these investment incentives will be almost entirely a windfall to business and to major stockholders, with the probability that part of the tax bonanza will be exported for foreign subsidiary operations, with the loss of American jobs and displacement of U.S. production. Corporate after-tax earnings would rise as would dividend payments and opportunities for capital gains for wealthy stockholders.

Perhaps more important to the overall economic well-being of the nation are the longer-run implications of these investment incentives. As the economy gets back on its feet and begins to utilize its productive capacity, these so-called investment incentives will work—just at the time when artificial tax-spurred increases in business spending would rekindle the fires of inflation, presenting the serious danger of another lopsided, inflationary capital goods boom, as in the 1963–1969 period, followed by another, and perhaps much deeper, recession. In no small measure, the tax-spurred additions to our nation's productive capacity in the 1960s fueled the current inflation and led to the buildup in excess plants and equipment, which has contributed substantially to high levels of unemployment and precipitated draconian economic measures.

Another major tax loophole for business opened by the 1971 revenue act is the Domestic International Sales Corporation (DISC) gimmick.

This scheme was first proposed by the Administration early in 1970 after it failed to convince Congress to add a $1.6 billion corporate tax cut to the Tax Reform Act of 1969 and also failed in attempts to trim substantially the House-passed measures to grant relief to low- and moderate-income wage earners.

The original DISC proposal was part of the 1970 trade legislation that Congress did not pass. Under this scheme, corporations would be allowed to spin off into export subsidiaries and the entire export industry would in effect be exempted from the income tax. The provision that became part of the Revenue Act of 1971 trimmed the proposal until now only half the profits of these export subsidiaries are tax exempt. It was offered as an incentive to increase exports but this claim was never substantiated and companies will receive a tax windfall from DISC whether their exports increase, decrease or remain the same.

The gimmick actually serves to broaden an existing loophole for, under current law, profits of foreign subsidiaries of U.S. companies are not taxed until they are brought back to the United States—which may be never. The DISC extends this loophole to the export profits of domestic corporations and the major beneficiaries will be the large, U.S.-based multinational corporations that export semi-finished goods and components, which ultimately compete with U.S. goods. The losers will be the taxpayers—individuals and smaller businesses that cannot spin off into export subsidiaries and must make up the tax loss.

A just tax structure goes hand in hand with a flow of government receipts sufficient to provide needed and desired levels of public investment. You cannot, at least in a democracy, have one without the other.

The most obvious example of this relationship is the financial straits of the nation's state and local governments. In no small measure, the inability of these governments to provide adequate public services and facilities stems from their heavy reliance on unfair taxes on consumer sales and real estate. Inequitable tax systems have generated taxpayer hostility and mistrust and forced government officials to work against the overwhelming odds on shoestring budgets. And, of course, these factors have resulted in public school shutdowns and innumerable other examples of crisis situations which stem from drained budgets and cutbacks in public services.

If recent trends toward building more inequities into the federal tax structure are not completely reversed, there is the clear and present danger of the federal government's becoming similarly hamstrung.

—1972

First National City Bank

CAPITAL GAINS "REFORM"; FOREIGN INCOME TAXES

Of all the hobgoblins that haunt critics of the present tax system, none looms so large or elicits so much righteous indignation as the treatment accorded long-term capital gains. It is seen by some as a nefarious device by which the rich avoid paying very high rates on top-bracket incomes, the Treasury loses billions in revenues and the progressivity of the income tax is weakened.

Those who object to special treatment for capital gains claim that if long-term gains were taxed at regular income rates—instead of at half those rates as they are now—the result would be an impressive inflow of fresh tax revenue. One estimate puts it at more than $12 billion. But the base for the capital-gains tax is notoriously volatile and it might become even more so if capital gains were taxed more heavily.

The swings in this base are inherent in the very nature of capital gains. Income such as wages, rent, dividends and interest constitute a reasonably predictable flow of recurring cash payments. For example, rent is the income generated from the use of a building by its tenants. This income is sufficiently predictable to be specified in contractual form. A capital gain, by contrast, cannot be guaranteed. The gain arises from an increase in the value of an asset—an element of wealth. At any given moment, the asset's present value is based on the sum of the income expected to flow from its use in the future. For example, the anticipated rental income—and, thus, the value—of an office building will increase if the prosperity of the surrounding business community makes it a more desirable site. But in most cases, the owner of an asset seldom can foresee with certainty whether the asset's value will rise or fall.

Capital gains and losses are caused by changes in the economy—population movements that make certain locations more valuable, changes in taste that stimulate demand for antiques of certain periods, and even changes in government defense budgets that heighten or reduce demand for certain types of engineering skills. But though such changes are inevitable, their nature and repercussions are largely unpredictable.

Those who wish to alter the tax law see no convincing reason for it to distinguish capital gains from such sources of income as wages or dividends. The theoretical foundation for this view was popularized by Robert Haig and Henry Simons in the 1920s and 1930s. Both wrote that an individual's income for tax purposes is best defined as the increase in his command over economic resources. From this definition it follows that capital gains, seen as changes in the value of property rights, should be fully taxed as they accrue—that is, whether or not they are actually realized. This definition stands—and falls—on the judgment that an individual's tax bill should be based on the year-to-year increase in his power to direct the use of economic resources.

Another view is that, true to its name, an income tax should be based solely on income and not on a base that includes elements of wealth as well. Since capital gains represent simply the present value of future income, taxing them involves taxing wealth, not income. The fact that the gain is a part of wealth is underscored by the observation that a tax on the gain will prevent the taxpayer from obtaining as high a future income by reinvesting the proceeds of the sale as he would have enjoyed had he retained the asset.

Critics of the present capital gains provisions fuel their attack with statistics illuminating certain aspects of the present system. In particular, they spotlight the heavy concentration of capital gains in the upper-income brackets. In 1970, among all individuals reporting adjusted gross incomes of $50,000 or more, 43% listed net long-term gains, and the average gain listed was about $45,000. But among returns on incomes of less than $50,000, only 7% reported net long-term gains—and the average gain was $2,300. Because net long-term gains are taxed at half the rate for ordinary income, the heavy concentration of such gains in top brackets explains why the average effective tax rates at these levels fall well below the percentages printed in the rate schedule.

Those who seek a change in the tax law also assert that gains on corporate stock, which are the biggest source of capital gains, are not true gains in the sense discussed above. They argue that, insofar as the rise of a stock's value reflects an accumulation of retained earnings, gains are recurring and predictable. The tax treatment of capital gains is therefore said to permit stockholders to receive revenue they would otherwise have received as dividends without paying the full tax levied on dividends.

Any increase in taxes necessarily involves a reduction in private consumption or savings. But the striking feature of an increased levy on capital gains is that it is likely to have an especially heavy impact on savings—much heavier than an across-the-board increase in rates that would reap an equivalent increase in revenue. The impact of the capital-gains levy would be heavier, first, because investors show a marked tendency to reinvest capital gains, and, second, because most gains are realized at income levels where the ratio of current savings to current income is high.

The tax treatment of capital gains provides relief from highly progressive income-tax rates that otherwise might retard economic growth. It has helped to form and enlarge the great pool of savings that has financed private investment and fueled economic expansion for years. Removing this relief without changing any other feature of the tax law would sharply increase taxes on large realizations. Savings might shrink, and the result might be a significant reduction in investment, unless offset by government financing. Of course, if the top rates in the income-tax scale were cut sufficiently, the special capital gains provisions could be trimmed back without endangering the creation of private savings. But unless and until these high rates of income taxation have been adjusted downward, a bigger tax bite out of capital gains is likely to eat up the seed corn of investment.

Heavier taxation of capital gains might also dry up sources of venture capital. Typically, investments that have the highest potential for capital gains or losses have relatively low yields in terms of dividends or interest, while investments with relatively high current yields have a low capital-gains potential. Increasing the tax on gains would encourage investors to shift a portion of their commitments out of investments with capital-gain potential and into investments with high current yields. But investments with high capital-gains potential tend to be risky investments in innovative, untested ventures. The emphasis in such investments is on the future, not on the proven results of the past. Any diminution in this kind of investment would obviously be detrimental to the growth of the economy.

Finally, higher taxes on realized gains might deter realizations to such an extent that the functioning of capital markets would be impaired. And the tendency to postpone realizations might not be cured by such remedies as a tax on capital gains unrealized at time of death.

On balance, reform advocates overestimate the potential benefits from revising the current treatment of long-term capital gains. And they underestimate the potential cost in terms of reduced savings and slower growth. This does not mean present law can't be improved. But in formulating any revisions, Congress and the Administration should be mindful of the cogent reasons for providing relief when gains have been accrued over a period of years, when they are attributable solely to inflation, or when relief helps to redress the imbalance caused by the double taxation of corporate earnings. Most important, no change is likely to prove beneficial if it seriously impairs economic growth. It is essential, therefore, that appropriate reductions in tax rates accompany any package of tax revisions that would otherwise reduce savings and investment.

Even in the best of times, getting a new tax bill through Congress can require all the strategy and tactical maneuvering of a major military invasion. And these are certainly not the best of times. The House Ways and Means Committee hasn't even finished writing its tax proposal, and already the battle lines are forming. The liberal side opposes the committee's tentative decisions to reduce certain long-term capital gains taxes and boost tax credits to certain industries. The other camp stands ready to ward off any attempt to raise oil company taxes.

But considering the past victories of the committee, a major revision of the income tax laws—one that is acceptable to both sides—seems likely. Less certain is whether the revisions will pay enough attention to the ravages of inflation in dealing with personal and capital gains taxes. Nor is it assured that sufficient attention will be given to the heavy taxes already being paid to foreign governments in revisions affecting U.S. taxes on income earned abroad.

In the furor over capital gains tax revisions, scant attention is paid to the effects of inflation. In fact, this omission mirrors current law, which makes no allowance for the inflationary component of capital gains. Taxing the inflationary element in wages, interest and dividends may reduce after-tax real income but has no direct effect on pretax real income since the real value of the underlying capital (both human and non-human) is undisturbed. But taxing the inflationary element in a capital gain can reduce pretax income as well, since it impairs the taxpayer's ability to replace the asset sold with one that yields the same amount to real income.

Consider, for example, a 10% inflation rate that affects income, prices and capital values alike. An income of $10,000 will rise in value to $11,000 because of inflation, matching the increase in prices and leaving the real income unchanged before taxes. Yet taxing the capital gain of $10,000 that accrues to an asset worth $100,000 will reduce the real value of the tax-payer's capital and therefore lower his expected future pretax income from that stock. This consideration would seem a fairly compelling reason to adjust capital gains taxes.

All the arguments eventually boil down to either removing incentives or reducing disincentives. However, the whole issue seems overblown. There is a temptation to view the elimination of lock-in as an automatic means of freeing a store of capital that could then be used to provide needed investment. But it is the investor, not capital, who is locked in. While an investor might be more likely to exchange his titles to certain assets for cash if current tax laws were changed, he would not be adding to the supply of cash for use in financing investment but merely exchanging his assets for someone else's cash.

Thus, there is little reason to believe that the elimination of lock-in would contribute greatly to meeting the investment demands of the future, especially considering the vastly greater needs being created by the huge increases in the price of energy, imposition of expensive environmental protection laws, increased export requirements, and the shortages in certain basic industries. The tax system can help meet these demands by increasing the rewards available to savers and investors and by reshaping the tax structure to help increase private savings, capital consumption allowances, and other sources of corporate internal financing.

The House Ways and Means Committee's proposals include repeal of provisions that allow American citizens living abroad to exclude from U.S. taxes certain amounts of income earned over-seas, new restrictions on the foreign tax credit, and the termination of some provisions that allow deferral of taxes on income earned and retained in countries with relatively low tax rates. At the same time, the Treasury has released proposed regulations that would require many multinationals to attribute a smaller share of their earnings to foreign sources and more to U.S. operations.

The thrust of all these proposals now under discussion is to ensure that the foreign operations of a company do not become an avenue for avoiding U.S. taxes. But there is a tendency to view the issue as if it involved only two parties, the U.S. government and U.S. resident corporations with overseas operations. In fact, how-ever, a third party is very much involved, the foreign government that also taxes the overseas income of U.S. residents.

Failure to consider this third party is evident in those discus-sions that mislabel the foreign tax credit as a device for tax avoidance. The credit is not given for taxes avoided but only for taxes paid. Eliminating it would not merely raise taxes on foreign income to the level paid on domestic income, but would increase them well above this amount in those developed countries where the foreign activities of U.S. corporations are concentrated.

Many years ago, the U.S. tax law endorsed the principle that income from foreign operations would be taxed at the higher of U.S. rates or foreign rates. This result was accomplished by the foreign tax credit, under which income taxes paid to foreign gov-ernments reduce dollar for dollar the tax payments that would otherwise be due to the U.S. Treasury on the same income. In effect, this approach left it to foreign governments to decide how much of the tax on foreign income of U.S. overseas subsidiaries would be collected by them and how much would be left for the U.S.

If policymakers now feel that too little of the pie has been left to the U.S., the remedy lies in negotiations with the foreign governments. Unilateral actions will only catch the U.S. multina-tionals in a devastating squeeze. The overall tax rate on their overseas operations would rise sharply unless the foreign govern-ments involved voluntarily provided some offsetting relief. With-out such relief, competition with less heavily taxed foreign firms would become very difficult, while the value of extensive capital investments would plummet. The end result would be not just a shift from overseas to domestic investment, but rather a reduction in the real income of U.S. residents and a weaker dollar in international exchange markets.

—1972

Losers

Much of the material in this book deals with those who win and those who lose in our economy. How we deal with the winners depends in part on how much we know about the losers. Unemployment hurts people, some more than others. So does inflation. Those who work may also be those who hurt, particularly the unskilled in low-wage jobs. Most are black but many are white. Many are women but most are men. They work on farms, in mines, and in low-wage industries, in foundries, coke ovens, laundries, urban transit and meat packing plants. The readings of this section show the tip of the iceberg.

The official unemployment measures have several deficiencies. First, they do not show the wide differences in the effects on different groups. In December, 1974, the official rate reached 7.1 percent, the highest in years. But for black teenagers it was 18.3 percent and for all blacks 12.8 percent, while for married men it was 3.7 percent and for white adult men 4.7 percent. White collar workers showed less than half the unemployment rate of blue collar workers. Professional, technical, managerial and administrative workers showed less than 3 percent unemployment, compared with 10.6 percent for operatives and 13 percent for laborers. Unemployment in construction reached 15 percent and in manufacturing 8.6 percent, while in government it was 3.1 percent, and in transportation and utilities 4.0 percent. Any person's vulnerability to unemployment, or protection against it, depends therefore on (1) what occupation, (2) in what industry, and (3) in what area of the country he or she lives and works.

When the highest economic officials of the government argue that "if we were not at 'maximum employment' in 1973 we were at least very close to it" with 4.9 percent as the official measure, one must take strong exception, especially if, as Gross and Moses argue, we grossly undercount our unemployed, on purpose. Spring, Harrison and Vietorisz focus on the working poor.

It would be difficult to exaggerate the degree to which our social policies fail to respond to these and other needs. Henry Steele Commager eloquently summed up the case against the Nixon approach though he failed to give recognition to the fact that the "new federalism" was strongly urged during the Kennedy and Johnson periods as well. By 1973 official concern with the problems of the urban poor had shifted. Along with this came the new stress on "revenue sharing." The impact of recent inflation on the poor is vividly described in the report of the Community Council of Greater New York, on workers by Nat Goldfinger of the AFL-CIO, and on older people by Russell Baker. Coal miners and farm workers are losers of long standing.

More than Money.   When the cold war was at its height, most liberals and radicals agreed that military spending bulked far too large in the federal budget. If only we could get that down to reasonable size—there were important differences about what "reasonable" meant—we could, the argument went, free national resources and energies to meet social needs.[1] A point of view expressed by people close to the labor movement rejected the argument that it was necessary to choose between "guns and butter"; let us assure high rates of economic growth and the problem of choice need not arise.[2] But both sides agreed that higher levels of social spending were needed.

In 1960 defense-related purposes accounted for more than half the federal budget. A decade later they had been reduced to less than half, and now run, exclusive of interest and veterans' benefits, at about one third. The 1960's saw the enactment of important new social initiatives and federal funds were provided to carry them out. Yet our social problems now seem in many respects harder rather than easier to solve.

Until the Nixon administration attempted to curb the growth of social spending in 1973–74, the upward trend was well established: in 1972–73 it was 46 percent of the total budget. 1973–74 was also the year in which revenue-sharing first assumed significant size; these funds are allocated to the states with no special program purpose attached to their use. Including $6.6 billion of revenue-sharing funds, federal funds provided to the states for all social programs amounted to $26.6 billion, five times the amount provided them in 1955, and 60 percent above 1970.

Proposals to develop a revenue-sharing system go back to the early 1950's; in 1958 Melvin R. Laird introduced revenue-sharing legislation in Congress, and other bills were filed in the mid-1960's. The idea was picked up by the Kennedy administration; Walter Heller, Chairman of the Council of Economic Advisors, was its most prominent advocate in pre-Nixon times. Conservatives have supported the idea because it fits their view that centralized government should be reduced. Liberals supported it because of their desire to improve the performance of social programs which were widely seen as hampered by excessive rigidity, remoteness of central authority, and inappropriate fit to local needs and conditions. Students of public administration welcomed the idea because it promised to redress the fiscal imbalances among states and regions, and to supplement state and local tax revenues which rose more slowly than the expenditure needs for which they were required.[3]

The implementation of revenue sharing has in fact become the principal device to blunt the movement for the federal government to establish and carry out national priorities in the areas of social need. In fiscal terms, the highway program was a massive revenue-sharing program, but control always remained in federal hands. The response to the push for redressing social imbalances and economic hardship which was energized by the social unrest of the 1960's was precisely the opposite one. In the name of returning power to the people, revenue-sharing becomes the principal instrument for preserving the appearance of a social commitment, while diffusing responsibilities for assuring that the reality corresponds to the posture and, above all, for focusing accountability.

This Nixon initiative was justified by the argument that the centralized programs had failed. This assumes that the funds provided should do the job if they are used better. But in their analysis of the budget, the experts of the Brookings Institution point out that the domestic needs portion of the budget is dominated by funds which provide direct income to people or help them to buy essentials like food and housing; social programs in fiscal year 1973–74 were $14 billion, only 7.8 percent of the non-military share, and have never accounted for more than 9 percent of domestic spending even when they were growing most quickly.[4] Programs to develop people, social institutions like schools and health care systems, or to improve the social "infrastructure" have been short-changed despite the rhetoric of the past decade.

So the liberal argument remains to be invalidated; in effect it has not had a fair test. S. M. Miller once accurately characterized the approach of the Nixon administration to social problems as measuring success against stated goals; if the goals prove too high, then lower them and success follows.

Did "liberal" administrations do better? The evidence says no. Why? One problem is that ideas which merit serious attention are often dismissed or ignored. This can happen if those who propose them lack credentials which are credible to established authorities in the field. This was the fate of the "new careers" idea first advanced by Pearl and Riessman.[5] It was incorporated in federal anti-poverty legislation after the early experiments attracted Congressional attention, but it never received strong administrative support from federal agencies, or intellectual support from professional students of manpower problems. This had less to do with the merits of the idea than with the fact that its proponents were psychologists, social workers, and educators, not economists with reputations in manpower. As a result, these programs still lack competent, balanced analysis done by credible experts in the manpower field. Debate remains grounded on the claims—sometimes hyperbolic—of advocates and the dismissals—sometimes biased—of the skeptics.

A similar fate has so far met efforts to improve the upward mobility prospects of low-income workers by restructuring internal labor markets of large employers and revising civil service standards and procedures. As the developer of one of the more successful demonstrations of the applicability of this idea,[6] I recall vividly the skepticism with which municipal hospital administrators in New York City treated it when it was proposed. Ultimately the idea showed its worth, and was incorporated in the permanent personnel practices of the system because it had strong union support. But the professionals were unanimous in their view that it could not succeed. They had two reasons for this posture: (1) if it had merit, they would long ago have recognized it, (2) a union-based economist with no health credentials could not possibly propose a viable or credible approach to solving some of the vexing manpower problems of the hospital industry.

Conventional wisdom and its exercise by professional guilds is often a major obstacle to solving stubborn social problems. Most such problems have been submitted to, or appropriated by, the professions most concerned: health by physicians, education by teachers and administrators, social welfare by social workers. Their interaction with the federal bureaucracies which administer programs is intimate and pervasive, though less widely recognized than the similar interplay between the Pentagon and the aerospace industry.

Three considerations dominate their approach to a problem:
(1) its effect on the welfare of the profession;
(2) its consistency with accepted doctrine and dogma;
(3) its acceptability to funding and controlling agencies.
Thus the analysis of major social problems is entrusted to those who may lack the wit or the will to devise and execute effective solutions. They are, in effect, in collaboration with the dominant social and economic forces which play so important a role in creating the problems of ill health, poverty, hunger and want.

In an issue of *Social Policy,* looking at this phenomenon in the area of alcoholism, I speculated that failure may occur[7]

> because professionals whom we pay to work at curing, healing, and rescuing the victims of such afflictions enjoy a comfortable coexistence with those who profit from the products that cause the problem. . . . The comfortable coexistence which prevails between those who cure and those who profit assures that the professionals will never bring the issue to a head. As long as governments and foundations are willing to support some activity to treat alcoholics and some funds for research, the industry is free to go on in its accustomed, and highly profitable ways. And as long as they can get funds, even though protesting their inadequacy, the professionals in the field are quite willing to ignore the industry's role and responsibility. Why? Because their careers depend on the continuation of the problem, not its elimination or limitation. It's a nice arrangement: the healers and researchers perform socially useful and professionally satisfying roles, and the industry is free to exploit new generations of real and potential victims.

This pattern has another result. Particularly in the period following enactment of anti-poverty legislation, many new approaches were proposed to deal with problems of health and mental health, to provide better social and related services, to improve the quality of education and the performance of schools, and in many other areas. The social science literature of the period abounds with descriptions and assessments of these experimental programs. One of the most ambitious, cited because of its relevance to larger problems now under serious discussion, was the establishment by the Office of Economic Opportunity of comprehensive, neighborhood health centers; beginning in Watts, such centers were eventually funded by OEO and the Department of Health, Education and Welfare.

One cannot help being impressed by the results achieved in these experimental programs; some failed and others fell short, but many convincingly demonstrated the validity and usefulness of new approaches to major problems of human service delivery. But when one looks at their influence in changing the structure or performance of main-stream service delivery institutions—mental hospitals, general hospitals, clinics, departments of welfare, urban school systems—the results are close to minimal. The lesson is sobering but necessary to understand: our social and political institutions are highly tolerant, in fact encouraging, of experiments, and do not shrink from supporting even those which may be highly innovative. But they are able to contain them within the social laboratory; efforts to translate and institutionalize the results meet strong and effective opposition. Here again they get the best of two worlds; the established groups and institutions encourage efforts to make change, but seldom need to come to terms with the implications of these efforts.

Bertram Gross and Stanley Moses
MEASURING THE REAL WORK FORCE: 25 MILLION UNEMPLOYED

The annual average rate of unemployment, as reported "officially" by the Department of Labor, was 5.9 percent during 1971. Based on the "official" civilian labor force, which was reported as 84.1 million, this percentage represented a total of 4.99 million persons who were unemployed.

But this is far from being a complete and accurate picture of the real dimensions of unemployment in the United States. The official figures are calculated in relation to the official labor force. To be considered a part of the labor force, and consequently eligible for inclusion in the ranks of the unemployed, a person must be willing and able to work and in addition must have actively sought a job during the last four weeks immediately preceding the monthly Current Population Survey. There is no record, however, of the many people of different sexes, ages, and races who are willing and able to work but who, because they have concluded (quite rightly) that suitable opportunities do not exist, are not seeking employment. These millions of persons are the major focus of this article.

Our estimates reveal a "real," as contrasted with "official," unemployment rate of 24.6 percent for the nation and 25.3 percent for New York City. In other words, 25.6 million people are unemployed. Labor force definitions have been constructed so as to exclude millions of people in order to understate the dimensions of unemployment and the extent to which the economic system has failed to generate adequate and suitable job opportunities. The people who make up the unofficially unemployed must be considered in any attempts to provide meaningful and socially desirable work for these millions of Americans who are able and willing to work if suitable opportunities were presented.

What is involved here is a redefinition of full employment and a return to the intent of the proposed Full Employment Bill of 1944, before it became aborted into the Employment Act, calling upon the federal government to create and maintain conditions under which "there will be afforded useful employment opportunities, including self-employment, for those able, willing, and seeking to work, and to promote *maximum* employment, production and purchasing power."

The original Full Employment Bill used the words *regular, remunerative,* and *useful.* The first of these is still good. The second must now be interpreted in terms of decent wages with opportunities for advancement. The third needs substantial redefinition. Far too many jobs, including many in the human service sector, are useful only in the sense that they serve to augment profits, bureaucratic power, or careerist rat races.

Most recent debates on the number of additional jobs needed have revolved around a numbers game in which percentages of the so-called labor force are juggled around by so-called experts. The more liberal economists favor reducing official unemployment to 4, 3, or even 2 percent. This would reduce current official unemployment from 5 million to 3.4 million, 2.6 million, and 1.7 million, respectively. Others say that Nixonian full employment would exist when the number is reduced to 5 percent—or about 4.3 million. Some Nixon administration officials are even maintaining that current *real* unemployment is just a little over two million— since about three million of the reported unemployed are women and teen-agers, and women and teen-agers don't really count. Beyond these areas of dispute, official recognition is now given grudgingly to a *poverty undercount;* that is, about two million additional people who do not appear in the official statistics because the Census undercounted the population in poverty areas, because they had given up looking for jobs that are not there, or because they worked part-time at babysitting or minding a store.

The genuine undercount, however, is far more substantial. It stems from the very concept of officially defined unemployment, which includes only those actively seeking work. In contrast, the more logical, indeed the more human, definition of unemployment would be *all those who are not working and are able and willing to work for pay.* Whether someone is actively seeking a paid job would no longer be the important point. The question would be whether he or she *wanted* full- or part-time work and was able to do something that might be truly useful. Using this concept we would certainly find many millions of additional people now stamped "unemployable" or pushed out of the official labor market by one or another device.

Clarity on "real unemployment" is crucial to meaningful policy. If full employment is enacted as a goal of public policy within the limited association of unemployment with welfare recipients, we can be sure that the nature of employment will be undesirable and unsuitable. Only when full employment policy is discussed and understood in terms of the needs and abilities of people of all sexes, ages, and races will we be able to develop policies for all of the unemployed.

—1972

William Spring, Bennett Harrison, and Thomas Vietorisz
WORK WITHOUT A LIVING WAGE

What is wrong with the economies of America's big cities is at best poorly measured by the conventional unemployment rate published monthly by the U.S. Department of Labor and dutifully reported in the press and on television. The problem is that even those who work—or a very large proportion of them—do not and cannot earn enough money to support their families. They work for a living but not for a living wage.

The question of the line between decent poverty and destitution is clouded by the existence of an official poverty line. In 1964 when the Social Security Administration went about defining a poverty line for the War on Poverty, it began with a Department of Agriculture estimate of the absolute minimum needed to feed a family of four a survival diet and multiplied by three. Food, it figures, ought to be about one-third of a poor family's expenditures. The administration came out with a figure of $3,128 for a family of four at 1963 prices; it set the official line at $3,000. Since then, the poverty line has been adjusted annually upward in line with the Cost of Living Index. The level reached $4,000 in the fall of 1971, but, still, it does not represent a true measure of need.

The Bureau of Labor Statistics family-income figure of $7,183 is much sounder. That amount is based on actual minimum costs of living in the urban areas studied.

If we accept the B.L.S. figures of $7,183 as the least a family of four must earn to keep its head above water in New York City in 1970 (the B.L.S.'s national urban average for 1970 was $6,960), what does this require for the family's income earner? If he or she works 50 weeks a year, 40 hours a week (which is itself unlikely in the inner city), the answer is $3.50 an hour. Here is where we find the final link in our chain of employment statistics. For when we add those individuals who earn less than $3.50 an hour to the discouraged nonseekers, the involuntary part-timers, and the officially unemployed, the statistics take a horrifying leap. In the seven New York City sample areas, the subemployment rate rises to between 39.9 and 66.6 per cent of the labor force. Indeed, the average for all the sampled areas in the country comes to 61.2 per cent.

That the problem extends beyond the hard-core ghettos is demonstrated by statistics gathered for a recent New York City Planning Commission survey of industrial zones in all five boroughs of the city. The evidence shows that 60 per cent of all manufacturing establishments in the city pay median wages below the $3.50 threshold. If the median wage of an establishment is under $3.50, then more than half of its workers must be earning less than that amount.

Suppose—one may ask—that more than one member of the family works? Does each member need $3.50 an hour for the family to achieve the threshold of decent poverty? It is true that, nationwide, the *average* family has 1.7 full-time equivalent workers. But the majority of *low-income* families in America are unable to *find* enough work to occupy more than one "full-time-equivalent" member. In 1970, the average number of "full-time-equivalent" workers per low-income family was *less than one!* In other words, one person (usually the male head) worked nearly (but not totally) full time, or several family members worked, but very sporadically. It is therefore useless—and cynical—to tell those for whom jobs do not exist that they could relieve their poverty if only they would be more willing to work. Indeed, the proportion of C.E.S. four-person ghetto families—and just four-person families—with gross earnings of less than $7,000 in 1970 was also 60 per cent.

Even if we set the threshold level of subsistence at the official poverty line of $2 an hour, the Census Employment Survey shows that the seven New York City sample areas still had subemployment rates ranging from 19.3 to 25.9 per cent (the 51-city average was 30.5 per cent). Thus, even if we suppose that it takes only $2 an hour (or $4,000 a year) to hold a family of four together, we still have not solved the problem because the main reason for poverty in New York—and by extension elsewhere—is simply that not enough people can earn even this meager amount.

How do people in the central cities survive? They struggle for what income they can get: from jobs where possible; from welfare where necessary. They line up for manpower training programs, especially those that pay stipends. The money helps, but the training seldom leads to jobs at decent pay.

The Employment Service cannot make much difference either, given the structure of the job market; 40 to 60 per cent of Employment Service nonagricultural placements in 1970 were in jobs paying less, on the average, than the minimum wage.

Since "legitimate" pursuits do not yield adequate incomes, there is inevitably a good deal of economic crime. When great numbers of young workers are unable to earn enough to support wives and children in basic decency, they become demoralized and families fall apart and the welfare rolls soar. Property is not kept up, because it cannot be. Neighborhoods deteriorate, the circle of poverty and despair closes on itself, and this eventually creates an enormous drag on the entire economy.

This *is* the urban crisis. And it is the subemployment rate which helps us to see the connection between the structure of the labor market and continued poverty and despair.

It will not be easy to move beyond the rhetorical commitment to full employment at decent wages. But policies to achieve these ends have this advantage: Whereas welfare and other income-transfer schemes divide us—workers on one side and the poor with their intellectual and upper-middle-class supporters on the other— programs to achieve economic development and full employment at decent wages can unite us. Businessmen and workers alike stand to gain from them. We can aid the poor while helping the rest of the nation resolve its wide range of domestic problems, from the crises in the cities, to the lack of proper regional development, to techno- logical obsolescence, to foreign competition, to the general quality of American life.

In formulating an anti-poverty strategy, the government in the nineteen-sixties ignored the question of inner-city job supply, pay scales, and the labor market. Its programs were built on the assumption that the cause of poverty lay in the disadvantaged condition of individuals, not in the failure of the job market. Thus, Head Start for the children, antidiscrimination and legal services for the grown-ups, community health service for the sick, and, through Community Action and Model Cities agencies, a voice in city affairs for everybody. All these programs were expected to make more of a difference.

That they have made urban poverty somewhat less oppres- sive, that they encouraged the poor to organize, and that they provided help to thousands of individuals cannot be doubted. But they have not begun—and cannot begin—to reach to the heart of the matter.

—1972

Henry Steele Commager
PROBLEMS: INESCAPABLY NATIONAL

The notion that voluntarism and local authorities can deal effec- tively with the national and global problems which crowd about us is without support in logic or history, and is dangerous to the well being of the Republic.

The fact is that for a century and a half almost every major reform in our political and social system has come about through the agency of the national government and over the opposition of powerful vested interests, states and local communities.

It is the national government that freed the slaves, not the states or the people of the South, and there is no reason to suppose that these would ever have done so voluntarily. It is the national government that gave blacks the vote, guaranteed them political and civil rights, and finally—in the face of adamantine hostility from Southern states and bitter resentment from local communities—provided some measure of social equality, legal justice and political rights for those who had been fobbed off with second-class citizenship for a century. Ask the blacks if they could have "overcome" through voluntarism.

It is the national government which finally gave the suffrage to women and which, in the past decade, has so greatly expanded the area of woman's rights. It is the national government, too, which extended the suffrage to those over eighteen. And it is the federal courts that imposed a one-man, one-vote rule on reluctant states.

It is the national government which, in the face of the savage hostility of great corporations and of many states, finally provided labor with a Bill of Rights, wiped out child labor, regulated hours and set minimum wages, and spread over workers the mantle of social justice. Ask the workingmen of America if they prefer to rely on the voluntarism of private enterprise rather than on government.

It is the national government that first launched the campaign to conserve the natural resources of the nation and that is now embarked upon a vast program to curb pollution and waste, and to save the waters and the soil for future generations—a program which Mr. Nixon's new federalism is prepared to frustrate. Ask conservationists whether they can rely on the states, or on voluntary action, to resist giant oil, timber, coal and mineral interests for the fulfillment of their fiduciary obligations to future generations.

It is the national government, not the voluntarism of the American Medical Association that finally brought about social security and medicare—just as in Britain, France, Scandinavia and Germany it was government, not private interests, that established socialized medicine. It is the national government, not states or private enterprise (which did their best to kill it) that finally provided social security for the victims of our economic system. Ask the old, the poor, the unemployed, the "perishing classes of society" whether they wish to go back to the voluntarism of private charity or the haphazard of local welfare.

It is the national government, through national courts, which has imposed "due process of law" on local police authorities, and on the almost arbitrary standards of many states. We have only to compare the administration of justice and of prisons in local and federal jurisdictions to realize that many of the values of voluntarism and localism are sentimental rather than real.

It is the national government, not the local, which through its almost limitless resources has finally acted to ameliorate the awful inequalities in public education at all levels. And it is the national government which has, in recent years, given vigorous support to the arts, music, libraries, higher education and research in every part of the country.

Now these and many other achievements of nationalism in the arena of health, welfare, conservation, economic equality, and justice are not to be explained on some theory that those who work for the nation are more compassionate than those who work on the local level. The explanation is at once more simple and more practical; namely that as the problems we face are inescapably national, they cannot be solved by local or voluntary action. Pollution is a national problem, no one state can clean up the Mississippi River or the Great Lakes, regulate strip mining, or cleanse the air. Civil rights, medical and hospital care, drugs and mental health and crime, the urban blight, education, unemployment—these are not local but national in impact, and they will yield only to national programs of welfare and social justice. All of them are as national as defense, and all as essential to the well being of the nation, and not even Mr. Nixon or Secretary of Defense Richardson has proposed a return to the militia system, though that would be logical enough in the light of their philosophy.

Only the national government has the constitutional authority, the financial resources, the administrative talent and the statesmanship to deal with these problems on a national scale.

The Nixon-Richardson program is not a philosophy, it is an escape from philosophy; it is not a program, it is the fragmentation of a program.

—1973

Community Council of Greater New York

INFLATIONARY FOOD COSTS AND AID TO FAMILIES
WITH DEPENDENT CHILDREN

During the two-week period of October 21 through November 1, 1974, 73 recipients of AFDC (Aid to Families with Dependent Children) were interviewed to determine both how they were managing in light of rapidly rising food costs and the effects of inflation on their children. The study is in response to increasing alarm over the impact of inflation on low-cost foods and concern that the lowest income families might, as a result, be facing serious hunger and possibly malnutrition. Although malnutrition has not been completely and functionally defined in terms of the children of today's American poor, "a serious consideration of available health information leaves little or no doubt that children who are economically and socially disadvantaged . . . are exposed to massively excessive risks for maldevelopment."[8]

In addition to monies for rent and fuel, a family of four in New York City on AFDC currently receives $258 per month or approximately $2 a day per person to cover all needs, *i.e.,* utilities, clothing, school supplies, transportation, telephone, furniture purchase or repairs, household equipment and supplies, laundry and dry cleaning, as well as food.

Food purchasing power can be somewhat increased by the use of food stamps. For $95, a family of four may buy $150-worth of food stamps, thereby extending its food purchasing power by $55 a month.

Families receive two checks per month. Each check includes monies for one half of the monthly rent and for one half of all other monthly expenses including food. As the numbers of crises and expenses increase, particularly during winter months, it is difficult for families to save half of the money for rent from each check as well as saving the money required for food stamps. Difficulties increase if, in addition to paying the full rent from the first semi-monthly check, the family is also faced with a crisis requiring unforeseen expenses during the same two-week period.

From September 1973 to September 1974, "food at home" costs rose 11.5 percent according to the Consumer Price Index.

However, the cost of starch foods which have traditionally enabled poor families to stretch their food budgets increased even further; e.g., the cost of cereal products went up 26.9 percent; rice went up 79 percent; and dried beans went up 300 percent. The Consumer Price Index itself underestimates the impact of rising prices on low-income households because food represents a much larger share of a welfare household budget than it represents in the CPI market basket. Also, the low-cost food products consumed by welfare families are not greatly weighted in the CPI food groups.

There is a $90 gap between the current AFDC grant level and the New York State Standard of Assistance. An AFDC family of four in New York City now receives $258 per month, excluding money for rent and medical care. In September 1974, a family of four needed $348 per month to maintain New York State's own Standard of Assistance.

This Standard of Assistance is based on a modification of the Bureau of Labor Statistics' Lower Living Standard, eliminating budget items such as food away from home and car ownership. Items included in the Standard are food at home, household needs, public transportation, clothing, personal hygiene items, and gas and electricity.

Given the huge difference of $90 monthly between the State's Standard of Assistance and the actual AFDC grant level, it is not possible for an AFDC mother, even with very considerable sacrifice, to provide her family with an adequate diet. Nor is it possible for an AFDC mother to live up to minimum American nutritional and cultural standards even though she may be very conscious of norms accepted by the majority of our society.

Although food deficiencies could not be directly related to children's illnesses, mothers interviewed expressed deep concern about the health of their children.

Of the entire group of 73 AFDC recipients interviewed, 56 percent were spending less than the cost of the United States Department of Agriculture's (USDA) economy food plan.

Although AFDC mothers were aware of the value of proper nutrition and expressed a desire for a daily diet which would include appropriate amounts of meat, milk, vegetables, fruits, and juices, 78 percent indicated that they were not able to do so.

Even though grant levels were raised in June 1974, 63 percent of the families reported eating less and cheaper foods than in 1973. Considerable daily sacrifice was necessary to maintain even this inadequate diet.

A considerable number of families were forced into debt in order to maintain even this inadequate diet.

Even with maximum use of starch fillers, such as rice, beans, and potatoes, 41 percent of the families interviewed experienced varying degrees of hunger at all times. Eighty-six percent of the families ran out of food at the end of most check periods; of these, 15 percent had no option but to experience hunger during these last few days.

Of the mothers interviewed, 53 percent said that their children were frequently tired or sick, as well as underweight or over-weight. Many mothers reported that the poor health of their children was influenced by lack of money to provide an adequate diet. They expressed considerable frustration in being unable to correct this condition.

—1974

Nat Goldfinger
THE ECONOMIC SQUEEZE ON THE WORKER, 1974

The average wage and salary earner has been in an economic squeeze during most of the years since 1965. The squeeze was particularly severe in 1973 and 1974. By mid-1974 the buying power of the average worker's weekly take-home pay had dropped to about the level of 1965, nine years before.

The raging inflation of 1973 and 1974—which got under way in the second half of 1972, during the Administration's so-called wage-price controls with their one-sided hold-down on wages—has been a severe jolt to the living standards of most families and especially harsh for middle- and lower-income families with children.

In June 1974, the buying power of the weekly take-home pay of the average nonsupervisory worker in private, nonfarm employment was down 4.5 percent from a year before and nearly 7 percent below October 1972. This was the fifteenth consecutive month in which buying power was below the level of the same month in the earlier year. It was the sharpest drop in workers' buying power in the 27 years since 1947.

This situation, which has been a serious problem for the families of most wage and salary earners, has also depressed the national economy—the real volume of the nation's retail sales started to decline in the spring of 1973 and, by mid-1974, was about 4 percent below the year before.

The average wage and salary earner makes up nearly three-fourths of the total American workforce—the major group of consumers, as well as producers, in the American economy.

With gross weekly earnings of $154.71 in June 1974, a year-round, full-time worker would make $8,044.92 a year, before taxes. However, the Labor Department reports it cost $12,626, before tax payments, to maintain a modest standard of living—with amenities but few luxuries—for a family of four in an urban area in the autumn months of 1973; raging inflation brought the cost to about $13,700 in mid-1974. Even the Labor Department's "lower bud-

Average Weekly Earnings, Nonsupervisory Workers in Private, Nonfarm Employment

	Gross weekly earnings	Take home pay, after federal taxes, worker with 3 dependents	
		Current dollars	Constant 1967 dollars
1960	$ 80.67	$ 72.96	$ 82.25
1965	95.06	86.30	91.32
1966	98.82	88.66	91.21
1967	101.84	90.86	90.86
1968	107.73	95.28	91.44
1969	114.61	99.99	91.07
1970	119.46	104.61	89.95
1971	126.91	112.12	92.43
1972	135.78	120.79	96.40
1973	144.32	126.55	95.08
June 1974	154.71	134.57	91.48

get'' for an urban family of four—with some amenities and no luxuries—cost $8,181 before taxes in the fall of 1973 and an estimated $8,900 in June of 1974.

The result is that many workers' families supplement their basic earnings through the additional incomes of working wives or moonlighting. In fact, many families depend on some kind of supplement to reach middle-income status. The mid-point of before-tax family income was $12,051 in 1973, according to the Census Bureau.

Even for many of the skilled and technical workers, whose earnings are at such a level or better, maintaining it is often precarious. Frequently their higher yearly earnings include the effects of overtime work at premium pay. Elimination of such overtime can result in significant cuts in yearly earnings.

Moreover, many workers rarely work a full year, even in good times. As a result, hourly wage rates or weekly pay often give an exaggerated picture of many workers' yearly earnings.

The Consumer Price Index rose 5.9 percent between June 1972 and June 1973, followed by a rise of 11.1 percent in the next 12 months—sharply cutting the buying power of the average worker's weekly take-home pay and undermining living standards.

The average wage and salary earner's yearly earnings have come a long way since 1947. Between 1947 and 1974, the buying power of such a worker's weekly earnings, after deduction of federal taxes, rose about 37 percent. Even after accounting for the additional increases in state and local taxes on income and pay-rolls, buying power increased significantly.

But for a 27-year period, the improvement was very modest, indeed. And it did not come easily or steadily.

In addition, nothing in the years since the end of World War II approaches the sharp, precipitous drop in workers' buying power of 1973 and 1974.

So the average wage and salary earner has a lot of catching up to do. And there is a long way to go—to improve the buying power of his earnings sufficiently to be able to maintain a moderate standard of living for his family from his regular job.

—1974

Russell Baker
THE AGED, SHOPPING

Old people at the supermarket make you feel what's the use.

Staring at 90-cent peanut butter. Taking down an orange, looking for its price, putting it back.

Old turn-of-the-century babies with 1965 dollars, who remember Teddy bears, Teddy himself, Woodrow Wilson, Kaiser Bill, Arrow collar man, flaming youth, wandering among seven-dollar ribs, pausing at sugar that is 60 cents a pound and rising.

They shop like sappers going through a mine field, like Onassis looking at new corporations for sale.

Old people dress up to go to the supermarket, but their money becomes shabbier every day, and how do you put a gloss on those old 1965 dollars they dig out of their purses for the checkout clerk?

It is sad watching them fumble through antique old dollars, and hearing the clerk call for more.

"These ancient dollars, madam, have been heavily discounted since you were last in circulation and are quite worthless except in great bulk."

Clerks do not utter this advice aloud to old people. It is simply implied thunderously by everybody in the country and every mouthful of food in the supermarket. Old people have a way of laboriously counting their change at the cash register and trying to engage the clerk in sociable conversation, as though asserting a bit too defensively their right to be there despite their shabby old out-of-date dollars.

Maybe only because they have no place to arrive at in a hurry to pick up a batch of the new 1974 90-cent peanut-butter dollars.

Do old people at the supermarket care about Henry Kissinger's latest flight for peace? Does it matter to them that Republicans and Democrats are quarreling about whether the Democrats have a mandate?

And the latest economic program for ending inflation by 1977, is it of any interest to them at all?

Do they think of President Ford's meetings with Soviet leaders as news?

Perhaps so. News nowadays is largely an entertainment of flying professors, pointless quarreling among telegenic careerists, posturing theorists, and Presidential travelogues, and old people rely heavily on television for entertainment.

Perhaps they would turn it off if the news switched from entertainment to reality and dealt with the pain of not being able to afford an orange or the embarrassment of delaying the checkout line to take back the crackers 1965 dollars can no longer buy.

Old people at the supermarkets make you wonder about all those middle-aged people you see jogging the streets to preserve their vascular systems for another fifty years.

And about all the people of all ages all over the country who are eating less, drinking less, smoking less, driving safer, and in general looking for a deathproof safety suit to get them over the peak years and down into the valley of old age fit to enjoy the fruits of their abstention and labor.

Will anyone care when they get there?

Will they be able to afford an orange?

And if not, will professors quit flying for peace, politicians cease thumping their clavicles, theorists stop forecasting millennia for the next generation, and Presidents forgo red-carpet arrivals at distant airports long enough to say, "Hey, old people in this country still have a hell of a problem; let's close the circus long enough to do something about it"?

Old people at the supermarket are being crushed and nobody is even screaming.

Old people at the supermarket make you feel what's the use.

—1974

Tom Bethell
LOSING GROUND: ONE MINER'S STORY

Here is part of the coal miners' story, told from the point of view of one miner. The story is drawn from the experiences of many miners, but all the facts are true:

John Collier, let's call him, 38 years old, has been a coal miner since he got out of high school 19 years ago. He works the hoot-owl shift running a roof-bolting machine, and he has trouble sleeping during the day because his house is close to a steeply graded mountain road and the loaded coal trucks go through their gears outside his bedroom window all day long.

As a roof bolter, John Collier is classified in Grade 5 under the United Mine Workers of America contract. That's the second highest grade, and his straight-time pay is $5.91 per hour now (compared to an average of $5.63 for all UMWA members). He gets a 15 cents-per-hour differential for working the midnight shift, which brings his total hourly pay to $6.06.

Generally he works two or three hours overtime each week at time and a half. During the course of the year he also works a few Saturdays, also at time and a half. On his birthday, if he works, he gets triple time.

Thanks to the shift differential and the premium pay for overtime and Saturdays, John Collier was able to earn a total of $11,745 in 1973. (Under the contract, his hourly rate for more than ten months of the year was $5.47, until he received a scheduled increase in November.) After taxes, he had $9,631 left.

On that money, John Collier supports a wife, three children, a dog, a cat, a parakeet, a two-bedroom house that is too small for his family, and a two-year-old Pontiac GTO that has never handled quite right since the time he ran into a ditch when he fell asleep after doubling back to work a second shift. He runs the car 40 miles to work and back, 40 miles each way over mountain roads washboarded out by poor maintenance and overloaded trucks. The car will be paid for in another 12 months, but John Collier doesn't think it will last that long.

John Collier generally doesn't write letters much. But he wrote one to UMWA President Arnold Miller this year, after he heard something he didn't like on the evening news. What he heard was the president of the Bituminous Coal Operators' Association saying that "we must disagree with any suggestion that American coal miners are underpaid workers . . . the facts prove that the opposite is the case."

"If the opposite is the case, then I guess he means we are overpaid," John Collier wrote. "I hope he was joking. If he was not, I would like for him to work in my mine."

John has worked in his present mine as a roof bolter for five years. During that time two other roof bolters have been killed there in roof falls. Statistically, his job is more than four times as dangerous as the average manufacturing job, but he is not paid four times as much.

He has never suggested that he should be paid that much more, either, but the man from BCOA got him thinking. On the average, nearly 10 per cent of all the fatal accidents in underground mining happen to roof bolters, timbermen, and jacksetters—75 men out of the 830 who have been killed in the bituminous coal industry since the 1969 Federal Coal Mine Health and Safety Act was passed.

John Collier figures his job is about four thousand times as dangerous as a coal company president's. You don't get too many roof falls in the executive dining room and methane gas seldom ignites in a bank vault.

But John Collier doesn't want to run a coal company. He just thinks he ought to get a fair share of the profits. Mainly he would like to be able to buy a bigger home for his family, and he would like to be putting some money aside to help his children through college.

Consequently, he wants a wage increase. Not an "enormous" or "irresponsible" or "unreasonable" wage increase, but something to help him catch up with inflation and maybe get ahead of it.

In general, John Collier has definitely been losing ground. Since his increase in November, 1971, he has had two more wage increases totaling 16.7 per cent, and the cost of living over that same period of time has gone up more than 20 per cent. So both of those wage increases have been wiped out. He doesn't feel overpaid.

The people who speak for the coal industry like to talk about those high-paid miners who don't want to work. John Collier wants to work, and does work. He does a dangerous job and does it very well. He misses four or five days a year because of bursitis, which his doctor says comes from so much time spent working in water underground, and when he is at home sick he worries a lot. He has no sick pay, for one thing, and he is never very far away from the possibility of serious injury.

When he thinks about that mine he thinks about the roof falls and more than 10,000 injuries in the industry every year; he knows he could be next.

He doesn't have enough life insurance to carry his family, and his savings wouldn't buy groceries for six months. These things worry him. They likely wouldn't worry him so much if he were overpaid.

Occupational Injury Frequency*

Disabling injuries per million man-hours worked, 1973

40.92	Mining, underground coal
27.51	Meat packing
26.99	Air transport
25.26	Mining, underground, except coal
21.11	Lumber
18.34	Clay and mineral products
15.70	Food
14.23	Railroad equipment
13.59	Construction
13.43	Iron and steel products
12.70	Foundry
11.84	Glass
10.55	All industries
9.78	Pulp and paper
9.75	Surface mining
9.11	Cement
7.08	Shipbuilding
7.00	Rubber and plastics
6.93	Electric utilities
6.73	Petroleum
5.81	Machinery
4.45	Steel
4.25	Chemical
4.09	Textile
2.52	Electrical equipment
2.22	Aerospace
1.60	Automobile

Sources: National Safety Council, Labor Department (BLS), UMWA Research Department.
Excluding farmworkers.—Ed.

—1974

James M. Pierce
WORKING ON A FARM

There are almost as many definitions of farmworkers as there are government agencies dealing with the problems of farmworkers. Not surprisingly, then, there is an equal number of estimates of the numbers of farmworkers—ranging from two million to six million. The most reliable estimate is that provided by the Economic Research Service of the U.S. Department of Agriculture: 2,809,000 farmworkers in 1973.[9]

The problems of America's farmworkers arise uniquely from the nature of their work: low wages, seasonal work, limited coverage under protective labor legislation, increased mechanization, lack of alternative job opportunities, few marketable skills, poor education, and critical health and housing needs.

The typical farmworker:
- Is a male head of a family, 23 years of age;
- Is poorly educated, with about 8.5 years of schooling;
- Is involved in nonmigratory farmwork;
- Works an average of 88 days at $13.20 per day for an annual wage of $1,160;
- Works for an average of 39 days doing nonfarm labor for an additional $698.

Fewer than one-fourth of the farmworkers were employed full time and these farmworkers earned an average of $4,358.[10] Considering the average size of the farmworker's family, the farmworker's income is far below the poverty line.

These poverty wages are paid by an industry which is the nation's third most hazardous and the nation's largest employer, hiring one out of every seven Americans.[11]

The poverty of farmworkers goes beyond substandard wages to include the worst housing in the country, which they share with other rural residents. Rural America has only one-third of the nation's population, but nearly 60 percent of the nation's substandard housing.[12] The Housing Assistance Council, a nonprofit organization dealing with low-income housing problems, has documented the extent of the rural housing crisis:

- Rural areas have two-thirds of the American homes that lack plumbing;
  - In rural areas one home in five is substandard;
  - 90 percent of all farmworkers' homes lack a sink;
  - 95 percent of all farmworkers' homes lack a flush toilet;
  - The average migrant home consists of two rooms for an average family of 6.4 people;
  - More than half of the rural housing units in the South are valued at less than $5,000;
  - Nearly two-thirds of all black-occupied rural housing is substandard; and
  - In rural Appalachia nearly one out of four families lives in substandard housing.[13]

Since the 1930s, much social legislation has been enacted to enhance the life of American workers, but farmworkers have been systematically excluded from most of these legislated benefits:

- Federal Unemployment Tax Act: Farmworkers excluded in all states except Hawaii.
- Workmen's Compensation Laws: Twenty-nine states exclude farmworkers.
- Farm Labor Standards Act: Establishes a minimum wage for farmworkers at $1.30 per hour;[14] excludes farmworkers from overtime provisions; covers only an estimated 35 percent of the farmworker population.
- Child Labor Laws: Eighteen states specifically exclude farmworkers from restrictions on child labor.[15]

In addition to these specific legislative exclusions, farmworkers have for all practical purposes been administratively excluded from food stamp programs and public assistance programs.

Approximately one-sixth of the people in rural counties suffer debilitating health conditions.[16] This is particularly true of farmworkers; and the physical limitations on their activities further add to the economic problems of workers whose income stops when they are unable to work. Funds provided under the Migrant Health Act, which attempts to provide health services to farmworkers, reach only 3 percent of the nation's farmworkers.[17]

According to the U.S. Public Health Service, the average migrant lives only to age 49, while the average American lives to be

72 years old. A Washington State report shows that the average Mexican-American migrant in the states dies by age 38.[18] The infant and maternity mortality rates for migrants are 125 percent higher than for average Americans.[19]

Some 800 to 1,000 field workers are killed and 80,000 to 90,000 are injured by pesticides annually, according to the Food and Drug Administration. Ironically the ban on DDT may make the pesticide health problem even worse. Farmers who once relied on DDT are now turning to organophosphates, especially methyl parathion, one of the deadliest poisons known. Just one drop on the skin can cause convulsions and death.[20]

An estimated 184,000 migratory farmworkers were employed in U.S. agriculture in 1973.[21] Migrant workers share the disadvantages of other farmworkers—they suffer low wages, poor housing, poor health, and are by and large ignored by legislation. The chief distinguishing characteristic of migrants obviously is that they travel from their home county to work in areas beyond daily commuting distance. Major streams of migratory farmworkers flow northward from Texas, Florida, and California. Too often these hardworking people leave the northern states at the end of the harvest in as shameful a state of poverty as when they arrived.

—1974

Our Long-Run Fate: What Choices? Who Chooses?

The steady deterioration of the U.S. international position, accelerated and dramatized by the oil crisis, forces us to face squarely the long-run question of the kind of society we want and can have, and our future relationships with other societies and economies.

The need for basic reexamination is reinforced by the fundamental questions of energy and resources. Lester R. Brown's comprehensive look at resource questions—and at the limitations of economic analysis in dealing with them—is sobering and inescapable.

The debate on whether environmental and ecological pressures will become parameters limiting our exploitation of the earth still divides economists. John Hardesty weighed the merits of the two sides and concluded that we have no choice but to accept the necessity of the no-growth stationary state with all that this implies:

> Key technical questions in favor of the stationary-state position are increasingly settled: resources are becoming increasingly scarce;

social costs of production (imposed on the environment) are pervasive, large, and related to output of goods and services; and funda--
mental change rather than ad hoc taxes are required to deal with the
problem.

A stationary state for the U.S. and world but for the United
States first and foremost, and not for the less-developed nations for
some time to come—this implies an investment rate equal to the
rate of depreciation of the capital stock; a birthrate equal to the
death rate; and that these rates, representing flows, be minimized
consistent with the desired level of human well-being. Included
must be a relentless effort to minimize the differences in living
standards between the over-developed and the less-developed
countries, perhaps by including in our constant flow a certain
quantity of output to be transferred to those nations whose
resources helped us become developed in the first place.

In a nongrowing economy there must be essential income and
wealth equality, with differentials based primarily on need; as
contrasted with the present system that is based, by definition, on a
substantial inequality that is irremediable (that is, a few own the
means of production and most do not).[1]

Gar Alperovitz thinks through some of the social and economic changes that would be required in shifting away from our
centralized, industrialized mode of economic organization. James
O'Connor sharpens some of these questions—while E. F. Schumacher invokes a radically different world. But that we possess the
power to imagine and to choose is, I believe, the message we need
to hear and to believe.

Lester R. Brown
ECOLOGICAL ECONOMICS

One of the most important questions that we need to be asking is
why we have not done a better job of anticipating some of the
resource scarcities which have affected us so dramatically in recent
months. And I would like for a moment to speak from the vantage
point of the economics profession and suggest some of the reasons
why I think we have missed the mark so badly.

One is that within economics as a profession we are somewhat
arrogant. We tend, for example, to think of ecology as a subdisci-

pline of economics. In reality, I suspect it would be more accurate to think of economics as a subdiscipline of ecology. Those of us in economics forget that all of the economic activities in which we engage are entirely dependent on the earth's natural resources and cycles. This is most evident in agriculture, where you cannot produce anything without the functioning of the nitrogen cycle, the sulphur cycle, the hydrological cycle, and others.

Within economics, we have reached a degree of abstraction in our thinking where all too often we think that economic activity is independent of the natural systems upon which it is dependent.

Also, within economics we have often made the point that we need not worry if commodity A becomes scarce because we will substitute commodity B or C for it. And that is quite true. But, if we had turned over that coin and read what it said on the other side, I think we would have been much better off, because the other side says beware, commodity scarcity may be contagious. And this is the situation in which we find ourselves today. We are seeing a domino effect of resource scarcity begin to operate. Natural gas becomes scarce, so nitrogen fertilizers become scarce, and the price of food soars.

Fresh water becomes scarce, and we find that, although we have enormous reserves of coal in the Northern Great Plains, there are already court battles under way to see who gets control of the limited available water supplies: whether it will be the energy interests, who want to develop the coal resources and coal gasification resources, or whether agriculture will continue to control the water resources.

With petroleum being in short supply, synthetic fibers have become scarce. The price of cotton has climbed and cotton is beginning to compete with soybeans for land, particularly in the southern Mississippi Valley. The result is that our soybean prices have climbed.

I think that within economics, we have become unduly impressed with what technology can do, and that is in part because most economists today have lived during a generation, or roughly the period since 1940, in which technological advances have been most impressive, beginning with splitting the atom and extending through new contraceptives, breakthroughs in agriculture, control of polio, and finally to landing a man on the moon in 1969. And we began to think that we could do anything with technology if we set our minds to it. There were quick fixes. All we had to do was identify the need, put the scientists to work, and within a very short time they would be back with the answers to the problem.

But what we are now beginning to discover is that there are some very important problems facing us to which there are no quick and easy technological fixes. Most of us would like to turn back the clock to the cheap energy prices of just a couple of years ago. But the scientists tell us that the prospects for cheap energy are probably at least the better part of a generation away. And that is an assumption predicated on a breakthrough in fusion power that can, by no means, be taken for granted.

We are hopeful that we will make that breakthrough. We cannot be certain.

A further problem which I think has hindered economic analysis of resource scarcity is that we have said we do not have to worry if a commodity becomes scarce, because the price will rise, and that rise in price will encourage additional production. And in most cases that is certainly true. But we forget to look at what happens on the demand side when the price rises. And in the world now we are faced with a situation where all of the basic resources used to produce food, land, water, energy, and fertilizer are in short supply. None of these can be described as abundant today. In order to get more land or to establish more irrigation projects, we have to move further and further out on the marginal return curve, and we are now in a situation where our idle capacity has disappeared—where in order to get more of these resources, we have to keep raising the price to get new water supplies, new energy supplies, additional land under cultivation. And as the world price of food goes up, we have forgotten that there are several hundred million people who are already spending 80 percent of their income on food. As the price of food begins to go up, it simply moves out of their reach. And what this will lead to is a period of political instability in the world, perhaps unlike any we have seen in our lifetime.

We are now seeing these economic forces beginning to override the traditional concerns of national security. We are in a situation where political instability is rising from basic economic change—particularly inflation, and particularly among the poor people throughout the world. These instabilities resulting from inflation and energy prices may offset the billions that we have spent in the military field in trying to maintain some semblance of political stability throughout the world.

I mentioned this because these relationships are complex but terribly important. At the rate at which things are unfolding, it leads me to think that it is going to be increasingly difficult for political decisionmakers, whether in the business world or in the political world, to make responsible, intelligent decisions.

During the third quarter of this century, the global economy expanded about 4 percent per year. In 1970 dollars it roughly tripled from $1 trillion in 1950 to about $3 trillion at present. The addition of that third trillion dollars has brought with it untold resource scarcities and ecological stresses.

Anyone who thinks that the final quarter of this century simply is going to be an extrapolation of the third is going to miss the boat by a very wide margin. I doubt very much that the global economy can continue to expand at 4 percent per year between now and the end of this century. If it did, it would mean going from a gross world product—GWP—of $3 to $9 trillion in real terms. I do not think that this is in the cards, and I think that it is time we began to recognize this and ask ourselves what some of the alternatives are.

I think a similar kind of discontinuity is in prospect demographically. Existing projections of world population show roughly a doubling within a generation span to $6\frac{1}{2}$ billion by the end of the century—and at sometime during the latter part of the next century to 10 to 16 billion. I do not think that is in the cards either. I simply do not think we can stay on our present demographic path without incurring costs that will become far greater than those we will be prepared to pay. And those costs mount, whether they be rise in unemployment in Mexico, political disintegration in India, or collapse of the oceanic fisheries; I believe we are going to turn from this path.

Another major discontinuity that I see between the third and the final quarter of this centry is a shift in emphasis from production to distribution. During the third quarter of this century, the name of the game has been growth, and it has been production on which we have been focusing. The expansion of production has become an objective of every government in the world. The only difference is in the rate of economic growth to which national governments aspire. For some it is only 4 percent per year, for others it may be 7, 8, or even 10 percent.

A further major discontinuity that flows from this change between man and the natural systems of resources on which economic activity depends is a shift in political power in the world. From the beginning of the industrial revolution until quite recently, political power in the world has been concentrated in those hands which controlled capital and technology, including importantly the United States in that group of early industrial countries. But what we are now seeing is the transfer of a substantial degree of political power to countries which control raw materials, who historically have not had any leverage at all in the international and political system. Not only are they gaining political leverage, but a great deal of economic leverage as well.

And I would suggest that we are only on the edge of this fundamental shift in political power. While we have been concerned with it and have been experiencing the international, economic and political convulsions that derive from that shift, I do not think we have yet begun to fully comprehend it. We have begun to understand what happens when someone begins to turn off the tap on our energy supplies. We have not yet begun to grapple with the problem of what happens when a small handful of countries, the oil exporting countries, gain control of a disproportionately large share of the world's liquid capital.

Another major shift that I see between the third and fourth quarters of this century is in the emphasis on the traditional way we have balanced supply and demand. The emphasis has been almost always on expanding supply as rapidly as possible. We are now moving into a situation where we must continue to expand supply without question, but where we will also begin to pay much more attention to demand conservation. We see one example of this coming from the Council on Environmental Quality on the energy front. The idea that the earlier projected growth in energy consumption can now be met, half by expanding energy supplies and half by practicing demand conservation, indicates a new period.

The final point in terms of these discontinuities is whereas since the end of World War II the overriding objective of national trade policy, including our own trade policy, has been to assure access to markets abroad for our exports, whether industrial or agricultural products, we now suddenly see this issue beginning to shift. Increasingly, international trade relations will be governed not so much by the question of access to markets abroad for exports as by access to supplies abroad of needed imports.

We have to be very careful that in this period of rapid change we do not end up treating symptoms rather than causes. That is as risky in the economic field as in medicine, because if you are not careful, sometimes you end up exacerbating the illness. And that is, I think, a very real risk. It is very difficult now for us to view this problem in national terms. We must start first with an international or global framework and work back to our national policies within that.

Whether or not you have a capital shortage depends very much on what you assume about the desired future rate of economic growth. If you are thinking of the 7 percent rate of economic growth, you need much more capital than if you are thinking of a 3 percent rate of economic growth. The question I would raise is, what should be our future rate of economic growth?

Someone in the political arena should tell Americans that the consumer joyride is over. The notion that we can consume more and more of everything is not going to hold up for much longer. I think we need to seriously reexamine the link between the level of material goods consumption and our actual well-being. That is to say, if you and I and others double our consumption of material goods, will we be twice as happy as we are now, will we be 20 percent more happy, or will our happiness increase at all? I think we have reached the point where for many of us in this society we may need to ask that question.

The question of how resources are shared among countries is going to dominate international affairs for years to come: the question of how to accommodate ourselves to this worldwide situation will loom large in the years immediately ahead. The time has come to examine some of the fundamental values that we hold and some of the fundamental principles underlying our economic system.

—1974

E. F. Schumacher
THINKING DIFFERENTLY: BUDDHIST ECONOMICS

"Right Livelihood" is one of the requirements of the Buddha's Noble Eightfold Path. It is clear, therefore, that there must be such a thing as Buddhist economics.

Buddhist countries have often stated that they wish to remain faithful to their heritage. So Burma: "The New Burma sees no conflict between religious values and economic progress. Spiritual health and material well-being are not enemies: they are natural allies." Or: "We can blend successfully the religious and spiritual values of our heritage with the benefits of modern technology." Or: "We Burmans have a sacred duty to conform both our dreams and our acts to our faith. This we shall ever do."[2]

All the same, such countries invariably assume that they can model their economic development plans in accordance with modern economics, and they call upon modern economists from so-called advanced countries to advise them, to formulate the policies to be pursued, and to construct the grand design for development, the Five-Year Plan or whatever it may be called. No one seems to think that a Buddhist way of life would call for Buddhist economics, just as the modern materialist way of life has brought forth modern economics.

Economists themselves, like most specialists, normally suffer from a kind of metaphysical blindness, assuming that theirs is a science of absolute and invariable truths, without any presuppositions. Some go as far as to claim that economic laws are as free from "metaphysics" or "values" as the law of gravitation. We need not, however, get involved in arguments of methodology. Instead, let us take some fundamentals and see what they look like when viewed by a modern economist and a Buddhist economist.

There is universal agreement that a fundamental source of wealth is human labor. Now, the modern economist has been brought up to consider "labor" or work as little more than a necessary evil. From the point of view of the employer, it is in any case simply an item of cost, to be reduced to a minimum if it cannot be eliminated altogether, say, by automation. From the point of view of the workman, it is a "disutility"; to work is to make a sacrifice of one's leisure and comfort, and wages are a kind of compensation for the sacrifice. Hence the ideal from the point of view of the employer is to have output without employees, and the ideal from the point of view of the employee is to have income without employment.

The consequences of these attitudes both in theory and in practice are, of course, extremely far-reaching. If the ideal with regard to work is to get rid of it, every method that "reduces the work load" is a good thing. The most potent method, short of automation, is the so-called "division of labor" and the classical example is the pin factory eulogized in Adam Smith's *Wealth of Nations*. Here it is not a matter of ordinary specialization, which mankind has practiced from time immemorial, but of dividing up every complete process of production into minute parts, so that the final product can be produced at great speed without anyone having had to contribute more than a totally insignificant and, in most cases, unskilled movement of his limbs.

The Buddhist point of view takes the function of work to be at least threefold: to give a man a chance to utilize and develop his faculties; to enable him to overcome his ego-centeredness by joining with other people in a common task; and to bring forth the goods and services needed for a becoming existence. Again, the consequences that flow from this view are endless. To organize work in such a manner that it becomes meaningless, boring, stultifying, or nerve-racking for the worker would be little short of criminal; it would indicate a greater concern with goods than with people, an evil lack of compassion and a soul-destroying degree of attachment to the most primitive side of this worldly existence. Equally, to strive for leisure as an alternative to work would be considered a complete misunderstanding of one of the basic truths of human existence, namely that work and leisure are complementary parts of the same living process and cannot be separated without destroying the joy of work and the bliss of leisure.

From the Buddhist point of view, there are therefore two types of mechanization which must be clearly distinguished: one that enhances a man's skill and power, and one that turns the work of man over to a mechanical slave, leaving man in a position of having to serve the slave. How to tell the one from the other? "The craftsman himself," says Ananda Coomaraswamy, a man equally competent to talk about the modern west as about the ancient east, "can always, if allowed to, draw the delicate distinction between the machine and the tool."[3] It is clear, therefore, that Buddhist economics must be very different from the economics of modern materialism, since the Buddhist sees the essence of civilization not in a multiplication of wants but in the purification of human character. Character, at the same time, is formed primarily by a man's work. And work, properly conducted in conditions of human dignity and freedom, blesses those who do it and equally their products. The Indian philosopher and economist J. C. Kumarappa sums the matter up as follows:

> If the nature of the work is properly appreciated and applied, it will stand in the same relation to the higher faculties as food is to the physical body. It nourishes and enlivens the higher man and urges him to produce the best he is capable of. It directs his free will along the proper course and disciplines the animal in him into progressive channels. It furnishes an excellent background for man to display his scale of values and develop his personality.[4]

If a man has no chance of obtaining work, he is in a desperate position, not simply because he lacks an income but because he lacks this nourishing and enlivening factor of disciplined work which nothing can replace. A modern economist may engage in highly sophisticated calculations on whether full employment "pays" or whether it might be more "economic" to run an economy at less than full employment so as to ensure a greater mobility of labor, a better stability of wages, and so forth. His fundamental criterion of success is simply the total quantity of goods produced during a given period of time. "If the marginal urgency of goods is low," says Professor Galbraith in *The Affluent Society,* "then so is the urgency of employing the last man or the last million men in the labor force." And again: "If . . . we can afford some unemployment in the interest of stability—a proposition, incidentally, of impeccably conservative antecedents—then we can afford to give those who are unemployed the goods that enable them to sustain their accustomed standard of living."

From a Buddhist point of view, this is standing the truth on its head by considering goods as more important than people and consumption as more important than creative activity. It means shifting the emphasis from the worker to the product of work, that is, from the human to the subhuman, a surrender to the forces of evil. The very start of Buddhist economic planning would be planning for full employment, and the primary purpose of this would in fact be employment for everyone who needs an "outside" job: it would not be the maximization of employment nor the maximization of production.

While the materialist is mainly interested in goods, the Buddhist is mainly interested in liberation. But Buddhism is "The Middle Way" and therefore in no way antagonistic to physical well-being. It is not wealth that stands in the way of liberation but the attachment to wealth; not the enjoyment of pleasurable things but the craving for them. The keynote of Buddhist economics, therefore, is simplicity and nonviolence. From an economist's point of view, the marvel of the Buddhist way of life is the utter rationality of its pattern—amazingly small means leading to extraordinarily satisfactory results.

For the modern economist this is very difficult to understand. He is used to measuring the standard of living by the amount of annual consumption, assuming all the time that a man who consumes more is better off than a man who consumes less. A Buddhist economist would consider this approach excessively irrational: since consumption is merely a means to human well-being, the aim should be to obtain the maximum of well-being with the minimum of consumption. Thus, if the purpose of clothing is a certain amount of temperature comfort and an attractive appearance, the task is to attain this purpose with the smallest possible effort, that is, with the smallest annual destruction of cloth and with the help of designs that involve the smallest possible input of toil. The less toil there is, the more time and strength is left for artistic creativity. It would be highly uneconomic, for instance, to go in for complicated tailoring, like the modern west, when a much more beautiful effect can be achieved by the skillful draping of uncut material. It would be the height of folly to make material so that it should wear out quickly and the height of barbarity to make anything ugly, shabby, or mean. What has just been said about clothing applies equally to all other human requirements. The ownership and the consumption of goods is a means to an end, and Buddhist economics is the systematic study of how to attain given ends with the minimum means.

Buddhist economics tries to maximize human satisfactions by the optimal pattern of consumption; while modern economics tries to maximize consumption by the optimal pattern of productive effort. It is easy to see that the effort needed to sustain a way of life which seeks to attain the optimal pattern of consumption is likely to be much smaller than the effort needed to sustain a drive for maximum consumption.

Simplicity and nonviolence are obviously closely related. The optimal pattern of consumption, producing a high degree of human satisfaction by means of a relatively low rate of consumption, allows people to live without great pressure and strain and to fulfill the primary injunction of Buddhist teaching: "Cease to do evil; try to do good." As physical resources are everywhere limited, people satisfying their needs by means of a modest use of resources are obviously less likely to be at each other's throats than people depending upon a high rate of use. Equally, people who live in highly self-sufficient local communities are less likely to get involved in large-scale violence than people whose existence depends on worldwide systems of trade. From the point of view of Buddhist economics, therefore, production from local resources for local needs is the most rational way of economic life, while dependence on imports from afar and the consequent need to produce for export to unknown and distant peoples is highly uneconomic and justifiable only in exceptional cases and on a small scale. Just as the modern economist would admit that a high rate of consumption of transport services between a man's home and his place of work signifies a misfortune and not a high standard of life, so the Buddhist economist would hold that to satisfy human wants from faraway sources rather than from sources nearby signifies failure rather than success.

Another striking difference between modern and Buddhist economics arises over the use of natural resources. Bertrand de Jouvenel, the eminent French political philosopher, has characterized "western man" in words which may be taken as a fair description of the modern economist:

> He tends to count nothing as an expenditure, other than human effort; he does not seem to mind how much mineral matter he wastes and, far worse, how much living matter he destroys. He does not seem to realize at all that human life is a dependent part of an ecosystem of many different forms of life. As the world is ruled from towns where men are cut off from any form of life other than human, the feeling of belonging to an ecosystem is not revived. This results in a harsh and improvident treatment of things upon which we ultimately depend, such as water and trees.[5]

The teaching of the Buddha, on the other hand, enjoins a reverent and nonviolent attitude not only to all sentient beings but also, with great emphasis, to trees. Every follower of the Buddha ought to plant a tree every few years and look after it until it is safely established, and the Buddhist economist can demonstrate without difficulty that the universal observation of this rule would result in a high rate of genuine economic development independent of any foreign aid. Much of the economic decay of southeast Asia (as of many other parts of the world) is undoubtedly due to a heedless and shameful neglect of trees.

Modern economics does not distinguish between renewable and nonrenewable materials, as its very method is to equalize and quantify everything by means of a money price. Thus, taking various alternative fuels, like coal, oil, wood, or water-power: the only difference between them recognized by modern economics is relative cost per equivalent unit. The cheapest is automatically the one to be preferred. From a Buddhist point of view, this will not do; the essential difference between nonrenewable fuels like coal and oil on the one hand and renewable fuels like wood and water-power on the other cannot be simply overlooked. Just as a modern European economist would not consider it a great economic achievement if all European art treasures were sold to America at attractive prices, so the Buddhist economist would insist that a population basing its economic life on nonrenewable fuels is living parasitically, on capital instead of income. Such a way of life could have no permanence and could therefore be justified only as a purely temporary expedient.

—1973

Gar Alperovitz
TOWARD A NEW SOCIETY

It is perhaps time that Americans interested in fundamental change begin to define much more precisely what they want. Historically, a major radical starting point has been socialism—conceived as social ownership of the means of production primarily through nationalization. Although the *ideal* of socialism involves the more encompassing values of justice, equality, cooperation, democracy, and freedom, in practice it has often resulted in a dreary, authoritarian political-economy. Could the basic structural concept of common ownership of society's resources for the benefit of all ever be achieved, institutionally, in ways which fostered and sustained—rather than eroded and destroyed—a cooperative, democratic society? My primary concern is with economic and social issues. There must obviously also be discussion of political institutions capable of preserving (and extending) positive elements which, though badly corroded, still inhere in aspects of the Western democratic traditions of freedom. The central question at this point, however, is the structural organization of the economy. Achieve a valid solution, and various political alternatives may be possible (though by no means inevitable); without it, the power thrust of the economic institutions is likely to bypass whatever more narrowly political forms are created.

Some of the critical issues may be posed by reviewing the now familiar critique of state-socialism. A major problem is that the concentration of both economic and political power in a centralized state produces what might be called an "economic-political complex," an institutional configuration not very appealing at a time when there is increasing awareness of, and concern over, the dangers of bureaucratic government. The Soviet and East European experience attest to as much, and the dreary history of British nationalization (to say nothing of America's own recent federal takeover of rail passenger transportation) is fair warning that the structural principle of nationalization is not in itself sufficient.

To the extent decision-making is centralized to achieve the planned allocation of resources, alienation appears to increase. Individuals become ciphers in the calculus of the technocrats; hope of a humanism based on the equality of individuals working together fades. Arbitrary party directives, or (in some cases) the worst forms of market competition, then naturally become dominant modes of administration—for there must be some means of regulating the often inefficient, irrational, and irresponsible practices of bureaucracies set up to achieve "efficient," "rational," and "responsible" control of the economy.

State-socialism largely precludes maintenance of an underlying network of local power groupings rooted in control of independent resources—a political-economic substructure which might sustain a measure of restraint over central authorities. (The destruction of the *soviets* in Russia was a major turning point away from popular, democratic structures.) Effective democracy in most socialist societies is weak, particularly in relationship to economic issues. In instances of error or blatant injustice (as in Poland in late 1970), the citizen's recourse is to violent rebellion—now against precisely those agencies which were supposed to administer resources on the basis of new principles of equity.

For such reasons—and because of restrictions on political freedom, the absence of a sense of equitable community, and the drabness and sheer monotony of most existing socialist societies—it has become extremely difficult to imagine the Old Left objective of nationalization ever alone achieving many ideals—difficult to imagine especially for young radicals who affirm a new vision of personal fulfillment and who urge "let the people decide" in their own local environments. Centralized state-socialism as the center-

piece of radical programs would make a mockery of such principles, especially in continent-spanning America which, by the end
of the century, will encompass 300 million individuals.

In sum, although the concept of socialism involves a broad
humanist vision, it has yet to be demonstrated how in advanced
industrial settings the abstract ideals might be achieved and sustained *in practice*. While some form of social ownership of capital
and the planned use of society's wealth may be necessary to deal
adequately with many economic issues, the question remains precisely *what* form? We return to the basic issue: could society ever
be organized equitably, cooperatively, humanely, so wealth benefited everyone—without generating a highly centralized, authoritarian system?

It is helpful to acknowledge frankly at the very outset that
some traditional conservatives (as opposed to rightist demagogues)
have long been correct to argue that centralization of both economic and political power leaves the citizen virtually defenseless,
without any *institutional* way to control major issues which affect
his life. They have objected to state-socialism on the grounds that it
destroys individual initiative, responsibility, and freedom—and
have urged that privately held property (particularly that of the
farmer or small capitalist entrepreneur) at least offers a man some
independent ground to stand on in the fight against what they term
"statism." Finally, most have held that the competitive market can
work to make capitalists responsible to the needs of the community.

Some conservatives have also stressed the concept of "limits," especially limits to state power, and like some new radicals
have emphasized the importance of voluntary participation and
individual, personal responsibility. Karl Hess, Murray Rothbard,
and Leonard Liggio, among others of the Libertarian Right, have
recently begun to reassert these themes—as against old socialists,
liberals, *and* more modern "statist" conservatives like William
Buckley, Jr. The conservative sociologist, Robert A. Nisbet,
argues additionally that voluntary associations should serve as
intermediate units of community and power between the individual
and the state.[6] Few traditional conservatives or members of the

Libertarian Right, however, have recognized the socialist argument that *private property* (and the competitive market) as sources
of independence, power, and responsibility have led historically to
other horrendous problems, including exploitation, inequality,
ruthless competition, individual alienation, the destruction of
community, expansionism, imperialism, war.

A second alternative—also an attempt to organize economic
power away from the centralized state—is represented by the
Yugoslav argument for workers' self-management. Whereas private property (in principle if not in practice) implies decentralization of economic power to individuals, workers' self-management
involves decentralization to the social and organizational unit of
those who work in a firm. This alternative may even be thought of
as a way to achieve the conservative anti-statist purpose—but to
establish different, socially defined priorities over economic
resources. The Yugoslav model recalls the historic themes of both
guild socialism and syndicalism. It is also closely related to the
"participatory economy" alternative recently offered by Jaroslav
Vanek, and the model of workers' participation proposed by Robert A. Dahl.[7] All alternatives of this kind, unfortunately, suffer
from a major contradiction: It is difficult to see how a political-
economy based primarily on the organization of groups by function
could ever achieve a just society, since the various structural
alternatives seem inherently to tend toward the self-aggrandize-
ment of each functional group—*as against* the rest of the community.

The point may perhaps be most easily understood by imagin-
ing workers' control or ownership of the General Motors Corporation in America—an idea close to Dahl's alternative. It should be
obvious that: (1) There is no reason to expect white male auto
workers easily to admit more blacks, Puerto Ricans, or women into
"their" industry when unemployment prevails; (2) No internal
dynamic is likely to lead workers automatically or willingly to pay
out "their" wages or surpluses to reduce pollution "their" factory
chimney might pour onto the community *as a whole;* (3) Above all,
the logic of the system militates against going out of "their"
business when it becomes clear that the automobile-highway mode
of transportation (rather than, say, mass transit) is destructive of

the community as a whole though perhaps profitable for "their" industry.

While management by the people who work in a firm should be affirmed, the matter of emphasis is of cardinal importance; "workers' control" should be conceived in the broader context of, and subordinate to, the *entire community*. In order to break down divisions, which pose one group against another and to achieve equity, accordingly, the social unit at the heart of any proposed new system should, so far as possible, *be inclusive of all the people*—minorities, the elderly, women, youth—not just the "workers" who have paid "jobs." There are, of course, many issues which cannot be dealt with locally, but at least a social unit based on common location proceeds from the assumption of comprehensiveness, and this implies a decision-making context in which the question "How will a given policy affect *all* the community?" is more easily posed.

When small, territorially-defined communities control capital or land socially (as, for instance, in the Israeli kibbutz or the Chinese commune), unlike either capitalism or socialism, there is no built-in contradiction between the interests of owners or beneficiaries of industry (capitalist *or* local workers) *as against the community as a whole*. The problem of "externalities," moreover, is in part "internalized" by the structure itself: Since the community as a whole controls productive wealth, *it,* for instance, is in a position to decide rationally whether to pay the costs of eliminating the pollution its own industry causes for its own people. The entire community also may decide how to divide work equitably among all its citizens.

Although small scale ownership of capital might resolve some problems it raises others: The likelihood that if workers owned General Motors they might attempt to exploit their position—or oppose changes in the nation's overall transportation system— illuminates a problem which a society based on cooperative communities would also face. So long as the social and economic security of *any* economic unit is not guaranteed, it is likely to function to protect (and, out of insecurity, *extend*) its own special, status quo interests—even when they run counter to the broader interests of the society. The only long-run answer to the basic expansionist tendency of all market systems is to establish some stable larger structural framework to sustain the smaller constituent elements of the political-economy. This poses the issue, of course, of the relative distribution of power between small units and large frameworks, and of precisely which functions can be decentralized and which cannot.

Some of the above questions may perhaps be explored most easily in the context of the alternative to centralization represented by the localized practice of cooperative community socialism in the Israeli kibbutz—an historically agricultural institution which is now rapidly becoming industrialized.[8] The many existing variations of the model suggest numerous alternative ways to make decisions involving not only workers' self-management but community (social) uses of both capital and surpluses. Some approaches have been successful, some obviously mistaken and wasteful.

Within the best communities one major point deserves emphasis: individual responsibility—to act, to take initiative, to build cooperation voluntarily—is a necessary precondition of a community of mutual, reciprocal obligation, and, ultimately, the only real protection against bureaucracy. When the ethic of an equitable, inclusive community is achieved, the efficacy of true "moral incentives" is dramatically revealed: Individuals are neither paid nor valued according to their "product," but simply because of their membership in the community. But there are huge problems even in the best settings, not the least of which is that small communities tend easily to become overbearing and ethnocentric. If they are to break out of conformity they must allow a range of free individual initiative—without waiting for majority approval. And they must find ways to achieve flexibility and openness to prevent provincialism and antagonism against outsiders or (all) "others."

Levels of Community. "The crux of the problem," Kenneth Boulding observed in 1968, "is that we cannot have community unless we have an aggregate of people with some decision-making power . . . It is easier for a relatively small unit to have some sense of community . . ."[9] Although Boulding offered his argument in connection with management of traditional municipal services, in my opinion his point applies in many instances to economic matters as well—but it raises a host of very specific problems:

• Could conflicts of interest within communities, for instance, be more rationally resolved by new cooperative principles of ownership without engendering *local* bureaucracies?

• If each community were restructured so that it might engage its own development more directly, how, more specifically, might it establish a basis for cooperative trade between communities, and for control of larger industry?

• How might large-scale planning, investment, trade, economic balance and ownership/control issues be wisely addressed?

There is no doubt that cooperative development proceeds best in communities sufficiently small so that social needs are self-evident. Voluntarism and self-help can achieve what centralized propaganda cannot—namely, engender group involvement, cooperative enthusiasm, spontaneity. This is a primary reason to emphasize small scale local structures *at the outset*—even if it may entail short-term disadvantages. The hope is that thereafter, with the benefit of a real basis in some cooperative experience, it may be possible to transcend historical starting points in the longer development of a larger framework.

A key question is how to prevent local centralization of power; individuals as well as small groups must obviously retain some power as against the local collectivity as a whole. One answer is self-conscious individual responsibility—and therefore another requirement is the achievement of local practices and relationships which build the experience of responsibility at the same time they constrain bureaucracy. Another answer might be to distribute "vouchers" to individuals so they could freely choose different forms of public services like education and medicine. Such a financial mechanism would permit substantial freedom of operation for a variety of semi-competitive, nonprofit service institutions. ("Socialized surplus," "anarchist administration" . . .[10])

Issues which cannot be resolved alone by one community point up further functions of a larger framework and a larger decision-making body, beyond its function of stabilizing the economic setting. These include managing the ecology of a river system, deciding the location of new cities, establishing transportation between population centers, committing capital in large societal investments, and balancing foreign trade.[11]

Since the socialist argument for a large unit appears to be correct in all these instances, the issues become: How large? And how might it be established without generating a new dynamic towards centralized power? A governing, continental scale "state" would be far too large for any hope of democratic management by localities—and totally unnecessary for technical efficiency save, perhaps, in continental transportation and some forms of power exploitation. (But cooperation *between* areas is feasible, as present international air transport or American tie-ins with Canadian energy sources illustrate.) William Appleman Williams and Robert Lafont have suggested *regional* units organized on the principle of "commonwealth."[12] This is the least developed area of theory; however, some intermediate unit larger than a "community" but smaller than a nation of 300 million people appears to be required. For many economic matters the present states are too small, and most lack a tradition of direct economic responsibility. The unit must be capable of taking over directly (and decentralizing!) capital and productive functions now controlled by, say, the 500 largest economic corporations—without escalating to the scale of the entire social system. In America today, though extremely limited in function, the most obvious suggestive example of a regional unit is the Tennessee Valley Authority,[13] but we should begin to conceive of a system in which this nation, by the end of the century, might be broken into eight or ten confederated regions of 20 to 30 million people, each region made up of confederated communities. Each region might perhaps approximate the scale of the four Scandinavian countries taken together. Part of the answer might also involve regional units of different sizes for different purposes.

Within the larger unit decisions should reflect the needs of real (that is to say, local) communities. But to avoid wastes and inequalities, higher order planning is obviously also necessary. The issues then are: who controls the planners? And how are fundamental planning criteria determined? The thrust of the argument is that controlling criteria should in part be generated out of expressed community needs and experiences, out of specific demands for goods and services—over time, through stages—*and* that these must be bolstered by the development of independent local bases of power. At all levels, the appropriate unit's control of a local market through its direct receipt of some surpluses and its control of some capital, can offer economic leverage, just as its organization principles permit political leverage. The larger unit must have sufficient autonomous power to balance the pressures from the strongest communities—but not so much as to over-whelm them.

In general, the difficult broader principle in a three-level vision of cooperative community, economic region, and confederated nation is to anchor units in new social structures which preserve sufficient independence of decision and power (without which neither freedom nor responsibility is possible), but which are not so powerful as to produce unrestrained competition and deny the possibility of a substantial measure of rational planning. The rule should be to leave as many functions as possible to localities, elevating only what is absolutely essential to the higher unit.

A critical problem is to define *specific* ways in which people living in localities might constrain larger order systems without making it impossible for them to function. Here, some clues are available from modern American experience: In the Tennessee Valley Authority, for instance, local corporation farms (and other private business interests), rather than "communities," to a great extent keep the bureaucrats in line, serving *their* purposes—but T.V.A. authorities still retain sufficient power rationally to control much river development.

What if communities were the power base or building blocks of a new political-economy? They might reduce regional units to more limited roles, largely responsible to (in part "co-opted" by) the interests of the people—organized in new cooperative commu-nity forms. Given the proper social basis, a large unit like a region might be kept in check. Its ultimate role would then be partly simply coordination; its broad policy-making and administrative functions would depend upon the development, and acceptance, of a rationally articulated political program. A two-chamber legislature might perhaps represent the organized communities, on the one hand, and the interests of the people at large, on the other.

In this setting, several other basic questions could be addressed. What, for example, might be the best process for making decisions over such fundamental issues as how population should be dispersed? Whether to make major new society-shaping investments, as in one or another transportation system? How much should be allocated to prevent the destruction of the environment (directly, or indirectly through the greater allocation of time entailed by some—but not all—voluntaristic methods)? How much of society's resources to allocate between consumption and investment (which also entails many ecological considerations, including the question of a zero growth rate)? "Planning" is obviously required here too, but again it is important to recognize that in this sketch of an alternative program, the process of central "planning" would be quite different from that of the rationalized state or the Soviet "command economy." It would be much more organic: social priorities would be developed through local processes in each community, and then "integrated" subsequently through regional and national politics generated out of local experience. Ultimately, the central regional and national bodies would have to resolve conflicting claims about resource allocation through the more broadly representative political processes. "Planning" would likely be an "iterative" phenomenon, involving, first, information, priorities and criteria generated at local levels; next an integration at a higher order "planning stage"; then the implications calculated; a return to smaller units for reconsideration; and finally back up again. (The Chinese call a similar process "two ups and two downs"; and some large U.S. corporations have developed sophisticated linear programming models for their decentralized internal management which are of relevance.)

One must recognize that decentralized, democratic planning inevitably involves inefficiencies and considerably more time; however, if it is successful, the gains in released energies, to say nothing of the quality of life, are likely to more than compensate what is lost.

This returns us to the question of whether the basic social

units in which day-to-day life occurs are, in fact, likely to sustain new, more humane experiences of community. It should again be clear why it is important to place priority on local social structures and processes which have a potential for developing and prefiguring a new ethic of cooperation, even if this may mean local communities initially function to an extent competitively as market operators. Staging is critical: Could social relationships within communities be strengthened so as to alter values and modify external relations *over time*? Could a cooperative development process permit the *subsequent* establishment of the necessary coordinating structures between communities and, in combination with national political efforts, the larger framework for the overall economy?

There are no easy answers to such questions and very little guidance available from foreign experience or past history. Chinese and Israeli developments suggest that communities may be able to sustain and deepen the quality of internal social relations at the same time external relations involve both the limited use of market competition and a larger framework. Marxist theoreticians as different as Charles Bettelheim and Paul Sweezy agree, too, that the use *both* of a limited competitive market *and* planning seem inevitable at certain stages of development under all forms of socialism.[14] Competition can then be viewed not as a method of exploitation, but as a tool of rational administration. One challenge, it accordingly appears, is to be able to recognize the latter and eliminate the former, and—if the social system is to overcome its origins in capitalism—to attempt shrewd trade-offs between competition and cooperation at different stages of development, as a new experimental basis emerges, as mutual needs develop, as larger national political possibilities open up, and as a new vision is created. Indeed, what we are talking about might best be defined not as static goal, but as a stage-by-stage process of increasing mastery of rational and irrational limitations on man's potential.[15] The only alternative to the process of politics is a central decision-making authority which *forces* its program upon all communities. *You simply cannot have it both ways.*

James O'Connor
UTOPIAN ECONOMICS

Today, among those who can afford (emotionally, financially, etc.) to dream about utopia, there is something of a debate in progress— one which hasn't yet reached the pages of the *New York Review* or even the *Guardian,* but one which surfaces frequently when radical economists meet. The debate goes something like this (I have been on both sides, and can do some justice to both sides):

CENTRALIST: There is no such thing as the U.S. economy, rather there is one world capitalist economy. The world capitalist system generates both developed and underdeveloped poles, wealth and poverty. Talk of post-industrial America and post-scarcity is petty bourgeois reactionary bullshit. Socialist America must produce not only for its own people, but also for the people in the underdeveloped world, the Third World people upon whose exploited labor power American property is based. U.S. socialism must radically restructure production in particular, expand the production of capital goods for the Third World, even if this means a decline in living standards at home. This requires overall planning—a central planning board—on which representatives from the Third World must participate. In the absence of such a total "democratization" of the distribution of production (if not a "democratization" of the control over production), a socialist America will only perpetuate existing exploitation and oppression.

DECENTRALIST: Frightening prospect. Planning must be decentralized, to establish maximum democratic control over production. The economy should be organized on a regional or metropolitan-area basis. We want much more than the passive consent of the people to the rulings of a central planning board; we want to maximize the active participation of workers in production. How else can we make the slogan "social control of social production" a reality? When we talk about power to the people—we mean all power, including and especially economic power.

CENTRALIST: Your vision of democracy is unrealistic, and class-bound. We will need strong national and international leaders, leaders of the dictatorship of the proletariat, who are responsive to the needs of the people. The masses of the world aren't interested in this particular variation of bourgeois democracy, as the success of Vietnam, China, and Cuba proves. (The world as one big Cuba, with a great composite picture of Mao Ho Fidel Malcolm John Brown Cleaver in every rocket terminal.)

DECENTRALIST: That's silly. The people in the advanced countries today have different needs and expectations than the people of Cuba or China. One of their needs is self-rule, the extension of democracy into the economic sphere, not the elimination of democracy. After all, it was Lincoln Steffens, not Che Guevara, who said, "The cure for the evils of democracy is more democracy." (To which the centralist retorts, you're a racist-imperialist-chauvinist. You think you're better than Third World people. To which the decentralist weakly replies, not better, but different.)

CENTRALIST: Anyway, if you got your precious democracy, production would fall off, the ability of the economy to satisfy people's needs would be impaired. You would lose economies of large-scale production. You would lose external economies of production. Self-contained production and distribution units on a local scale would mean setting the clock back 200 years.

DECENTRALIST: Not so fast. There are studies that indicate that a unit can capture all the available economies of scale in most industries producing for a market of 10–12 million people disposing of an average income equivalent to per capita income in the U.S. at present. Modern technology frequently requires small-scale decentralized production units. Don't believe the myth that bigness means efficiency.

CENTRALIST: Even if you're right, the fact is that the only reason there is such a wide variety of specialized commodities available today is that there is one great market. In a decentralized economy you might be able to produce a limited supply of goods efficiently, but you could never produce a wide variety of goods.

DECENTRALIST: Yet there is evidence that U.S. metropolitan areas today *are* more economically autonomous. True, the central city becomes more specialized, but the metropolitan area as a whole trades relatively more with itself than with other metropolitan areas.

CENTRALIST: But most large manufacturing plants in most metropolitan areas are branch plants of huge corporations whose parent offices are located on Wall Street or in Detroit. These plants are specialized units, producing not for local markets but for regional markets. To integrate these plants fully into a Bay Area Commune would require dismantling many of them, rebuilding them, making them more flexible, capable of a more diversified output.

DECENTRALIST: That's fine. We want flexible, diversified plants in order to create in every community a wide variety of jobs, so that people can acquire many skills and develop different abilities.

CENTRALIST: Even if you're right, there is still a trade-off between maximum production for the world's peoples and maximum democracy for us.

DECENTRALIST: Not if we define democracy and the good life in part as the need to fulfill our responsibilities to the peoples of the Third World. Hell, I would love to work on an assembly line a certain part of the week if I knew that we were producing use values for China or India. It seems to me that in the last analysis your position is based on a lack of faith in the international class solidarity of the working class in the advanced countries.

(Centralist winces.)

—1972

Notes

Introduction

[1]Edwin P. Reubens, "The Food Shortage Is Not Inevitable," *Challenge,* March/April, 1974, pp. 50–51.

[2]Clark Kerr, John T. Dunlop, Frederick Harbison, and Charles A. Myers, *Industrialism and Industrial Man.* Cambridge, Harvard University Press, 1960. The quoted language is from their "Industrialism and World Society," *Harvard Business Review,* January–February, 1963, pp. 113–126.

[3]"Productivity, Prices, and Incomes", Joint Economic Committee, U.S. Congress, 1967, pp. 83, 84, 16.

[4]"National Economic Conversion Commission," Committee on Commerce, U.S. Senate, 1964, pp. 112, 113.

[5]Emile Benoit and Kenneth E. Boulding, *Disarmament and the Economy,* New York, Harper & Row, 1963.

[6]Simon Kuznets, *Shares of Upper Income Groups in Income and Saving.* New York, National Bureau of Economic Research, 1953.

[7]John Kenneth Galbraith, *The Affluent Society.* Boston, Houghton-Mifflin, 1958, pp. 322–333.

[8]Gabriel Kolko, *Wealth and Power in America.* New York, Praeger, 1962.

[9]*Wall Street Journal,* February 20, 1974.

[10]*New York Times,* December 16, 1974.

[11]S. M. Miller. "The Credentials Trap", Miller and Riessman, *Social Class and Social Policy.* New York, Basic Books, 1968, pp. 69–77. Ivan Illich, *De-schooling Society.* N.Y., Harper and Row, 1971. See also Ivar Berg, *Education and Jobs: the Great Training Robbery,* N.Y., Praeger, 1970.

[12]"Report of the National Advisory Commission on Civil Disorders". New York, Bantam Books, March, 1968, pp. 239–250.

[13]Michael J. Piore, "On-The-Job Training in a Dual Labor Market," Arnold R. Weber et al., eds., *Public-Private Manpower Policies.* Madison, IRRA, 1969.

[14]Gunnar Myrdal, *Economic Theory and Under-Developed Regions.* London, G. Duckworth, 1957.

[15]Edward Steinberg, "Upward Mobility of Low-Income Workers." New York, Institute of Public Administration, 1973.

[16]Sumner M. Rosen, "Merit Systems and Workers," Gartner, Nixon and Riessman, eds., *Public Service Employment.* New York, Praeger, 1973, pp. 143–153.

[17]David Gordon, Richard Edwards, and Michael Reich, eds., *Labor Market Segmentation.* Lexington, Lexington Books, 1975. Katherine Stone's "The

Origins of Job Structures in the Steel Industry," reprinted in that volume, also appeared in *The Review of Radical Political Economics*, Vol. VI, No. 2, Summer, 1974, pp. 113–173.

[18]R. Herding, *Job Control and Union Structure*. Rotterdam, Rotterdam University Press, 1972.

[19]Sumner M. Rosen, "The Unions: Making Out with the Labor Elite," Gartner, Greer and Riessman, eds., *What Nixon is Doing to Us*. N.Y., Harper and Row, 1973, pp. 124–138.

[20]Stephen K. Bailey, *Congress Makes a Law: The Story Behind the Employment Act of 1946*. New York, Columbia, 1950.

[21]"Unemployment in the United States and eight foreign countries", *Monthly Labor Review*, U.S. Department of Labor, January, 1974, plus supplements. The table omits Australia and Sweden.

[22]A. W. Phillips, "The Relation Between Unemployment and the Rate of Change in Money Wages in the United Kingdom, 1861–1957", *Economica*, November, 1958.

[23]James O'Connor, "The Fiscal Crisis of the State," *The Corporations and the State*. New York, Harper & Row, 1974, p. 136.

[24]Philip Stern, *The Great Treasury Raid*, New York, Random House, 1964. O'Connor, *op. cit.*, p. 141.

[25]*The Affluent Society, loc. cit.* Colin Greer, *The Great School Legend*. N.Y., Viking, 1973.

[26]O'Connor, *op. cit.*, pp. 121–123.

[27]Testimony of Reginald H. Jones, Chairman of the Board, General Electric Company. Joint Economic Committee, U.S. Congress, May 8, 1974.

[28]New York, Pantheon, 1971.

[29]"Black Americans—A Chartbook." Bureau of Labor Statistics, U.S. Department of Labor, 1971, p. 43.

[30]"Income Transfer Programs: How They Tax the Poor," *Studies in Public Welfare, Paper No. 66*. Joint Economic Committee, U.S. Congress, 1972.

[31]Lester C. Thurow and Robert G. B. Lucas, "The American Distribution of Income: A Structural Problem," Joint Economic Committee, U.S. Congress, 1972.

[32]*Griggs v. Duke Power Company* (401 U.S. 433).

[33]Lloyd Ulman, *The Rise of the National Union*, Cambridge, Harvard University Press, 1955. Charles Levinson, *Capital, Inflation and the Multinationals*, New York, Macmillan, 1972.

[34]Irving Louis Horowitz, "Capitalism, Communism and Multinationalism," *Society*, vol. 11 no. 2, January–February, 1974, pp. 32–43.

The End of the Keynesian Era?

[1]Quoted by Hobart Rowen, *Washington Post*, May 12, 1974.

[2]Samuelson is quoted in Herbert Stein's "Tax Cut in Camelot," *Transaction*, March, 1969.

[3]"Full Employment and the New Economics," *The Scottish Journal of Political Economy*, February, 1969, pp. 1–19.

[4]Alvin H. Hansen, "Inflation and the New Economics," *Challenge*, vol. 15 no. 2, November–December, 1966. p. 41.

[5]John Kenneth Galbraith, "Interview: The Public Sector is Still Starved," *Challenge*, January–February 1967, p. 19.

[6]"The Economics of Restraint," *Social Policy*, November–December, 1974, pp. 4–7.

[7]*Social Policy*, November–December, 1973, pp. 56–57.

[8]Thomas Balogh, "Inflation and the New Economy," *Challenge*, November–December, 1973.

[9]"The Politics of Full Employment," *Trans-action*, May, 1969, p. 45.

[10]Robert Lekachman, in *Social Policy*, September–October, 1974, p. 11.

[11]*New Republic*, May 5, 1973; see also his "The Economics of Full Employment," *Social Policy*, November–December, 1973, and "Mr. Nixon and the Market's Last Stand," *Challenge*, November–December, 1973.

[12]Senate Subcommittee on Employment, Manpower and Poverty, April 26, 1972.

[13]"A Full Employment Policy for America," A Symposium at UCLA, October 13, 1973, p. 57; data developed by Peter Henle, cited by Bennett Harrison.

[14]The War Contracts Subcommittee of the Senate Military Affairs Committee.

[15]Arthur S. Miller, "Legal Foundations of the Corporate State," *Journal of Economic Issues*, March 1972, p. 68.

[16]J. M. Keynes, *The General Theory of Employment, Interest and Money*. New York, Harcourt, 1936, p. 378.

[17]The leading case is *Wyman v. James* which affirmed the constitutional authority of New York City welfare authorities to condition continued benefits for Mrs. James upon her agreement to accept mandatory home visits by her caseworker. Writing for the majority, Mr. Justice Blackmun asserted, in the course of denying Mrs. James's claim that the Fourth Amendment protected her privacy against invasions by public authority, that "one who dispenses purely private charity naturally has an interest in and expects to know how his charitable funds are utilized and put to work. The public, when it is the provider, rightly expects the same."

[18]As of mid-1974, the income median was approximately $12,700.

[19]On this, see "The Long-Run Decline in Liquidity," *Monthly Review*, September 1970; reprinted in Paul M. Sweezy and Harry Magdoff, *The Dynamics of U.S. Capitalism*, Monthly Review Press, 1972, pp. 180–196.

[20]This title is derived from Robert A. Brady's *The Spirit and Structure of German Fascism* (New York, 1937). Chapter 11, "Science, Handmaiden of Inspired Truth," describes the accommodation of German scientists to the social philosophy of Nazi state power.

[21]"New economists" ordinarily refers to those using the analytical tools derived from Keynes and concerned with his problems and methods.

[22]*Newsweek*, Nov. 4, 1968.

[23]Quoted in Hobart Rowen, *The Free Enterprisers, Kennedy, Johnson and the Business Establishment* (New York, 1964), p. 162 (emphasis added).

[24]Walter Heller, *New Dimensions of Political Economy*. Cambridge, Mass., 1967, p. 12.

[25]Arthur Okun, *The Political Economy of Prosperity* (New York, 1970), p. 9.

[26]The investment incentive proposal of April 1961 was conceived by E. Cary Brown of MIT and Joseph A. Pechman of the Brookings Institution. The latter has been closely associated with the "new economics" and the Democratic Party.

[27]One of the few attempts by an economist to evaluate the progressivity of these tax cuts (S.O. Hermansen, "An Analysis of the Recent Tax Cut," *National Tax Journal*, Dec., 1965) concluded that the income tax reductions by themselves were probably regressive; when the business investment credits and the hikes in social security taxes were also taken into account, "changes in federal revenue laws since January 1, 1963, by 1968 will have overwhelmingly benefited the higher income groups in relation to the lower income groups."

[28]James Tobin, *National Economic Policy*. New Haven, 1966, p. 20.

[29]John Kenneth Galbraith, *The Affluent Society*. Boston, Houghton-Mifflin, 1958, chapt. 12, "The Illusion of National Security," and p. 352.

[30]*National Economic Policy*, p. 59.

[31]Quoted by James L. Sundquist, *Politics and Policy: The Eisenhower, Kennedy, and Johnson Years*. Washington, 1968, pp. 37–38.

[32]W. W. Rostow, "The Problem of Achieving and Maintaining a High Rate of Economic Growth," *American Economic Review*, May, 1960, pp. 112–113. Tobin was also pointing to American consumption propensities as the Communists' "advantage" in the Cold War struggle; see "Growth Through Taxation," *New Republic*, July 25, 1960.

[33]See Ralph Lapp, *The Weapons Culture* (New York, 1968), chapt. 2; and two articles by I. F. Stone in the *New York Review of Books:* "McNamara and the Militarists," November 7, 1968, and "Theatre of Delusion," April 23, 1970—both reprinted in Stone's *Polemics and Prophecies 1967–1970*. New York, Random House, 1970.

[34]Edward S. Flash, Jr., *Economic Advice and Presidential Leadership: The Council of Economic Advisers*. New York, 1965, p. 185. Flash attributes this information to Tobin, then a CEA member.

[35]Seymour Harris, *Economics of The Kennedy Years*. New York, Harper & Row, p. 197.

[36]Paul A. Samuelson, *Economics*, 8th ed. (1970), pp. 803–4, and 6th ed. (1964), p. 785.

[37]CEA *Annual Report*, 1966, p. 59.

[38]In Walter Heller, ed., *Perspectives on Economic Growth*. New York, 1968, p. 13.

[39]Quoted in *Time*, December 31, 1965, p. 67B. As for what he was really observing, see his *Political Economy*, pp. 66–73.

[40]CEA *Annual Report*, 1966, p. 31, Despite his co-authorship of this *Report*, Eckstein later claimed that "taxes were not increased [in early 1966] because the President could not get the American people to pay for the war." *The Public Interest*, Spring 1970, p. 90.

[41]The "Statement" and list of signers are found in *President's 1967 Tax Proposals*, Part 2, pp. 631–636.

[42]*Ibid.*, pp. 518, 520–1.

[43]Eisner, "War and Taxes: The Role of the Economist," *Bulletin of the Atomic Scientists*, June, 1968, pp. 16–17.

[44]*Business Week*, January 6, 1968, p. 60.

[45]Comment in *American Economic Review*, May 1962, pp. 351–2.

[46]*New Republic*, March 7, 1964. Reprinted in Arthur Okun, ed., *The Battle Against Unemployment*. New York, 1965, p. 155.

[47]For an account of the profit-maximizing activities of some of the New Economists, see "Economists Go for the Money—And Get It," *Business Week*, Jan. 29, 1972, pp. 60–2. "Today's superstars," this article points out, "are rich."

Oil

[1]Christopher T. Rand, "After the Oil Embargo," *New York Times,* March 27, 1974.

[2]The oil multinationals have a disconcerting habit of changing names. Thus Exxon was formerly known as Esso or Standard Oil Co. of New Jersey. Mobil as Socony or Standard Oil Co. of New York, and British Petroleum as the Anglo-Iranian Oil Co. Similarly the Standard Oil Co. of California is also known as Stancal, Calso, or Chevron. In the present essay they will all be referred to by their official names as of early 1974.

The End of Imperialism?

[1]Karl Marx, "The British Rule of India," *New York Daily Tribune,* June 25, 1853; quoted in Shlomo Arineri, *Karl Marx on Colonialism and Modernization,* New York, Doubleday, 1969.

Corporate Dominance

[1]"Employment, Growth and Price Levels." part 7, "The Effects of Monopolistic and Quasi-Monopolistic Practices." Hearings before the Joint Economic Committee, U.S. Congress, September, 1959.

[2]Manuscript courtesy of the author; the reader is referred to his forthcoming book, *Scarcity,* to be published by Quadrangle.

[3]"Investigation of Conglomerate Corporations," A Report by the Staff of the Antitrust Committee, Committee on the Judiciary, June 1, 1971, p. 42.

[4]Staff Report for the Subcommittee on Domestic Finance of the Committee on Banking and Currency, House of Representatives, Ninetieth Congress, Second Session, *Commercial Banks and Their Trust Activities: Emerging Influence on the American Economy,* Vol. I, July 8, 1968, p. 18.

[5]"Disclosure of Corporate Ownership," prepared by the Subcommittees on Intergovernmental Relations, and Budgeting, Management, and Expenditures, Committee on Government Operations, U.S. Senate, March 4, 1974.

[6]*Ibid.* Details are provided on pp. 345–372.

[7]In recent anti-trust cases the Supreme Court has given some indication that it will look not only at market shares but at broader effects of corporate acquisitions in judging whether competition is reduced, but the court remains divided and the trend is not yet established. Cf. Betty Bock, "Rediscovering Economic Realism in Defining Competition," Conference Board Record, June, 1974, pp. 6–12.

[8]"Economic Concentration, part 3: Concentration, Invention and Innovation," Hearings Before The Subcommittee on Antitrust and Monopoly of The Committee on The Judiciary, U.S. Senate, 1965, p. 1133.

[9]William Appleman Williams, *The Roots of Modern American Empire.* New York, Random House, 1969.

[10]Ben Seligman, *Economics of Dissent.* Chicago, Quadrangle, 1968.

Multinationals

[1]Richard J. Barnet and Ronald E. Müller, *Global Reach.* New York, Simon and Schuster, 1974.

[2]Peter Dooley, "The Interlocking Directorate," *American Economic Review,* 1969.

[3]Raymond Vernon, *Sovereignty at Bay: The Multinational Spread of U.S. Enterprises.* New York, Basic Books, 1971.

The Military Economy

[1]Sumner Rosen, "New Approaches to Conversion," *New Priorities.* Fall, 1971.

[2]This article is based on extensive interviews with Washington representatives of ranking defense firms, and has since been published in somewhat different form in *The Pentagon Watchers: Students Report on the National State,* Leonard S. Rodberg and Derek Shearer, Eds. New York, Doubleday, 1970.

Unequal Shares, Unfair Taxes

[1]Monthly Economic Letter, April, 1972.

[2]"The Truth about Income Inequality in the U.S.," *Fortune,* December, 1972.

[3]"Taxes, Poverty, and Equality," *Public Interest,* Fall, 1974.

[4]S. M. Miller and Paolo Roberti, "Taxes People Pay: An Eleven Country Comparison," *Challenge,* January–February, 1974.

[5]R. Heriot and H. Miller, *Who Paid Taxes in 1968.* New York, National Industrial Conference Board, table 3.

[6]Joseph A. Pechman and Benjamin A. Okner, *Who Bears the Tax Burden?* Washington, Brookings, 1974.

[7]Ibid.

Losers

[1]National Urban Coalition, *Counterbudget: A Blueprint for Changing National Priorities.* New York, Praeger, 1971.

[2]"A Freedom Budget for All Americans," a pamphlet published by the A. Philip Randolph Institute, 1967.

[3]Committee for Economic Development, *A Fiscal Program for a Balanced Federalism.* New York, 1967: L. Laszlo Ecker-Racz, "Going Broke on a $600 Billion National Income", speech before the U.S. Conference of Mayors, June 14, 1966, reprinted in "Revenue Sharing and its Alternatives: What Future for Fiscal Federalism?", U.S. Congress, Joint Economic Committee, July, 1967. "Federal Revenue Sharing: Concept and the Proposals", Municipal Finance Officers Association of the United States and Canada, Chicago, 1970.

[4]Edward R. Fried, Alice M. Rivlin, Charles L. Schultze, Nancy H. Teeters, *Setting National Priorities—The 1974 Budget,* Washington (Brookings), 1973, pp. 26–28.

[5]Arthur Pearl and Frank Riessman, *New Careers for the Poor,* Free Press (Glencoe 1969).

[6]"Upgrading Nurse's Aides to LPNs Through a Work-Study Program: toward a career ladder in nursing", U.S. Department of Labor, Manpower Administration, 1971.

[7]"Comfortable Coexistence," *Social Policy,* May/June 1974.

[8]Herbert G. Birch, "Health and the Education of Socially Disadvantaged Children," *Developmental Medicine and Child Neurology*, 10:580–99, 1968.

[9]*Report of the Farmworkers Task Force*, U.S. Department of Labor, September, 1973, p. 4.

[10]*The Farm Index*, May, 1973, p. 15.

[11]*Report of the Farmworkers Task Force*, p. 9.

[12]Ibid., p. 15.

[13]*Grim Facts*, Housing Assistance Council, 1973.

[14]Early in 1974 President Nixon signed a minimum wage bill he vetoed in 1973. It will increase farmworker wages to $2.30 an hour by 1978.

[15]*Report of the Farmworkers Task Force*, pp. 12–13.

[16]Ibid., p. 16.

[17]Ibid., p. 17.

[18]John Donahue O'Shire, *Boycott*, Archdiocese of Hartford, Connecticut.

[19]Ira E. Harrison, "Migrant Papers," *Behavioral Science Working Paper 72–3*, Pennsylvania Department of Health, February, 1972, pp. 58–59.

[20]Ibid.

[21]*The Hired Farm Working Force of 1973*, statistical report of USDA Economic Research Service.

Our Long-Run Fate: What Choices? Who Chooses?

[1]"Environmental Imperative—Economic Implications of Environmental Crisis," *Society*, November–December, 1973 pp. 13–20. Henry C. Wallich argued the contrary in "How to Live with Economic Growth," *Fortune*, October, 1972.

[2]Economic and Social Board, Government of the Union of Burma, *The New Burma* (1954).

[3] Ananda K. Coomaraswamy, *Art and Swadeshi*. Madras, India, Ganesh & Co.

[4]J. C. Kumarappa, *Economy of Permanence*, 4th ed. Raighat, Kashi, Sarva-Seva Sangh Publication, 1958.

[5]Richard B. Gregg, *A Philosophy of Indian Economic Development*. Ahmedabad, India, Navajivan Publishing House, 1958.

[6]See especially Nisbet's *Community and Power* (original title, *Quest for Community*, 1953) (Oxford University Press, 1962).

[7]See, for instance: Vanek, Jaroslav, *The Participatory Economy* (Cornell University Press, 1971); *The General Theory of Labor-Managed Economies* (Cornell University Press, 1970); Dahl, Robert A., *After the Revolution?* (Yale University Press, New Haven & London, 1970); Coates, Kenneth, and Topham, Anthony, *Industrial Democracy in Great Britain* (MacGibbon & Kee, Great Britain, 1968).

[8]The kibbutzim demonstrate, incidentally, that small industrial units can be highly efficient—contrary to theorists who claim large scale is a technical necessity. The kibbutz movement has continued to grow in Israel, although the proportionate role of this section has diminished as huge migrations have swelled the capitalist economy since 1948.

[9]Boulding, Kenneth E., "The City as an Element in the International System," *Daedalus*, Fall, 1968, p. 1118.

[10]This approach is already in use, obviously, in Medicare payments and in some transferable higher education scholarships. It will surely be extended for

health care. "Tuition vouchers" for elementary education have been proposed by a diverse group ranging from Paul Goodman to Milton Friedman and Christopher Jencks. Housing "vouchers" are also now being tested. The "voucher" approach may perhaps be best understood as a "transition mechanism"—(to facilitate the establishement of a variety of voluntary and community controlled institutions), rather than as a final solution to the problems of public bureaucracy.

[11]And, of course, unless such a larger framework is established, it is hard to see how the insecure conditions out of which international expansionism and imperalism grow can be eliminated.

[12]See Williams, William Appleman, *The Great Evasion* (Quadrangle Books, Chicago, 1964); Lafont, Robert, *La Revolution Regionaliste* (Editions Gallimard, France, 1967). For the idea of regionalism, also see the writings of the American anarchist Alexander Berkman.

[13]The T.V.A., of course, is not offered as a "model"—as its failure to resolve many issues (from participation to ecology) warns.

[14]See, for instance, their exchange in *Monthly Review*, Vol. 22, No. 7 (December, 1970), pp. 1–21. For an introduction to Chinese practices, see Gurley, John G., "Capitalist and Maoist Economic Development," *Monthly Review*, Vol. 22, No. 9 (February, 1971).

[15]Because of limited space, Alperovitz' important exploration of equality and its process could not be included. Readers are referred to his forthcoming *A Long Revolution.—Ed.*

Suggested Readings

Walter Adams and Horace M. Gray, *Monopoly in America: The Government as Promoter*, Macmillan, 1955.

Irma Adelman and Cynthia Taft Morris, *Economic Growth and Social Equity in Developing Countries*, Stanford, 1973.

Richard T. Barnet, *Economy of Death*, Atheneum, 1969.

John M. Blair, *Economic Concentration: Structure, Behavior and Public Policy*, Harcourt Brace Jovanovich, 1972.

Barry M. Blechman *et al.*, *Setting National Priorities: The 1975 Budget*, Brookings, 1974.

Kenneth Boulding, "The Great Society in a Small World: Dampening Reflections from the Dismal Science," in Bertram M. Gross, ed., *Great Society*, Basic Books, 1968.

Harry Braverman, *Labor and Monopoly Capital*, Monthly Review, 1974.

Barry Commoner, *The Closing Circle*, Bantam, 1972.

Edward F. Cox, Robert C. Fellmeth, and John E. Shulz, *The Nader Report on the Federal Trade Commission*, R. W. Baron, 1969.

G. William Domhoff, *Who Rules America?*, Prentice-Hall, 1967.

Richard C. Edwards, Michael Reich, Thomas E. Weisskopf, *The Capitalist System: A Radical Analysis of American Society*, Prentice-Hall, 1972.

Robert C. Fellmeth, *The Interstate Commerce Omission: The Report on the Interstate Commerce Commission and Transportation*, Grossman, 1970.

Daniel R. Fusfeld, *The Basic Economics of the Urban Racial Crisis*, Holt, 1973.

John K. Galbraith, *Economics and the Public Purpose*, New American Library, 1975.

Herbert J. Gans, *More Equality*, Pantheon, 1973.

Mark J. Greene *et al.*, *The Closed Enterprise System: Ralph Nader's Study Group Report on Antitrust Enforcement*, Viking Press, 1974.

Andrew Hacker, *The End of the American Era*, Atheneum, 1971.

David Hapgood, *The Screwing of the Average Man*, Doubleday, 1974.

Bennett Harrison, *Urban Economic Development*, Urban Institute, 1974.

Robert L. Heilbroner, *An Inquiry into the Human Prospect*, Norton, 1974.

————, *The Limits of American Capitalism*, Harper & Row, 1965.

Jane Jacobs, *The Economy of Cities*, Vintage, 1969.

L. William Kapp, *The Social Costs of Private Enterprise*, Schocken, 1971.

Gabriel Kolko, *The Triumph of Conservatism*, Quadrangle, 1964.

Juanita Kreps, *Sex in the Marketplace: American Women at Work*, Johns Hopkins, 1971.

Robert J. Lampman, *The Share of Top Wealth-Holders in National Wealth, 1922–1956*, National Bureau of Economic Research, Princeton University Press, 1962.

———"Transfer and Redistribution as Social Process" Institute of Research on Poverty, University of Wisconsin, reprint No. 49.

Robert Lekachman, *Inflation: The Permanent Problem of Boom and Bust*, Vintage, 1973.

Sar A. Levitan, *The Great Society's Poor Law*, Johns Hopkins, 1969.

Harry Magdoff, *Age of Imperialism*, Monthly Review, 1969.

Dennis Meadows *et al.*, *Dynamics of Growth in a Finite World*, Wright-Allen, 1974.

Gardiner C. Means, *The Corporate Revolution in America*, Collier, 1964.

E. J. Mishan, *The Costs of Economic Growth*, Praeger, 1967.

Ralph Nader and Mark Green, *Corporate Power in America*, Grossman, 1973.

Joan Robinson, *Freedom and Necessity*, Vintage, 1971.

Alvin L. Schorr, *Explorations in Social Policy*, Basic Books, 1968.

Joseph Schumpeter, *Capitalism Socialism and Democracy* (3rd Edition), Harper & Row, 1950.

William Shepherd, *Market Power and Economic Welfare*, Random House, 1970.

Study Paper No. 2, "Industrial Structure and Competition Policy," Studies by the Staff of the Cabinet Committee on Price Stability, January, 1969.

Richard Titmuss, *The Gift Relationship*, Vintage, 1972.

James S. Turner, *The Chemical Feast: Report on the Food and Drug Administration*, Grossman, 1970.

U.S. Senate, Committee on the Judiciary, Subcommittee on Antitrust and Monopoly, *Administered Prices: A Compendium on Public Policy*, 1963.

Benjamin A. Ward, *What's Wrong with Economics?* Basic Books, 1972.

James Weinstein, *The Corporate Ideal and the Liberal State, 1900–1918*, Beacon, 1968.

Harrison Wellford, *Sowing the Wind: The Report on the Politics of Food Safety*, Grossman, 1972.

Lawrence White, *The Automobile Industry Since 1945*, Harvard University Press, 1971.

William Appleman Williams, *The Roots of the Modern American Empire*, Random House, 1969.

Index

About the Editor

Sumner M. Rosen has written extensively in the areas of manpower, social policy, health, and trade unions. He directed an innovative manpower program for the U.S. Department of Labor, taught full-time at Simmons College and Northeastern University and part-time at other universities. He serves as mediator and arbitrator in the public and private sector. In 1974, he was elected chairman of the Academic Freedom Committee of the American Civil Liberties Union.

About the Contributors

Gar Alperovitz is a co-founder of the Cambridge Institute and is co-director of Exploratory Projects for Economic Alternatives.

Leonall C. Andersen is a senior vice-president of the Federal Reserve Bank of St. Louis.

Stanley Aronowitz teaches at the New School for Social Research and the experimental college of Staten Island Community College, CUNY.

Russell Baker is a columnist for *The New York Times.*

Peter F. Bell is an associate professor of economics at the State University of New York, at Purchase.

Thomas Bethell is director of research for the *United Mine Workers Journal.*

Lester R. Brown is a senior fellow of the Overseas Development Council.

Arthur F. Burns is chairman of the Board of Governors of the Federal Reserve System.

Arnold Cantor is assistant director of the AFL-CIO department of research.

Alexander Cockburn writes for *The Village Voice* and other journals.

Henry Steele Commager is John W. Simpson Lecturer at Amherst College.

Barry Commoner is chairman of the Scientists' Institute for Public Information and director of the Center for the Biology of Natural Systems.

Richard B. Duboff is an associate professor of economics at Bryn Mawr College.

John Emshwiller is a staff reporter for *The Wall Street Journal.*

Lewis A. Engman is chairman of the Federal Trade Commission

Nat Goldfinger is director of the AFL-CIO department of research

Bertram M. Gross is Distinguished Professor of Planning and Urban Affairs at Hunter College, CUNY.

Bennett Harrison is an associate professor of economics and urban studies at M.I.T.

Jules Henry was the author of *Culture Against Man* and, until his death, taught anthropology and sociology at Washington University, St. Louis.

Edward S. Herman is a professor of finance at the Wharton School, University of Pennsylvania.

Mary Kaldor is a senior research fellow at the Institute for the Study of International Organizations, at the University of Sussex.

Albert Karr is a staff reporter for *The Wall Street Journal*.

Michael T. Klare is research director of North American Congress on Latin America.

Robert Lekachman is Distinguished Professor of Economics at Herbert H. Lehman College, CUNY.

William N. Leonard is professor of economics and chairman of the department at Herbert H. Lehman College, CUNY.

Harry Magdoff is an editor of *Monthly Review*.

Seymour Melman is a professor of industrial engineering at Columbia University.

Stanley Moses is an assistant professor in the department of urban affairs, at Hunter College, CUNY.

Ralph Nader is the founder of the Center for Responsive Law, Public Interest Research Group, Center for Auto Safety, and the Project for Corporate Responsibility.

James O'Connor teaches economics at San Jose State University.

James M. Pierce is the executive director of the National Sharecroppers Fund and the Rural Advancement Fund.

Stephen A. Resnick is a professor of economics at the University of Massachusetts.

E. F. Schumacher is the founder and chairman of the Intermediate Technology Development Group in London, England.

William Spring is director of the regional institute on employment, training and labor market policy at Boston University.

Philip M. Stern writes for *The Washington Post* and is author of *The Great Treasury Raid* and *The Rape of the Taxpayer*.

Paul M. Sweezy is an editor of *Monthly Review*.

Thomas Vietorisz is a professor of economics at the New School for Social Research.

Robert Zevin is an investment counselor in Cambridge, Massachusetts.